MERRY MARINER

MERRY MARINER

And His Rudderless Boat

A. K. Girisam

PARTRIDGE

ISBN:	Hardcover	978-1-4828-7524-9
	Softcover	978-1-4828-7523-2
	eBook	978-1-4828-7522-5

To order additional copies of this book, contact
Partridge India
000 800 10062 62
orders.india@partridgepublishing.com

www.partridgepublishing.com/india

CONTENTS

PART 3: <u>CLOSE ENCOUNTERS</u>

PART 4: <u>FEATHERS IN THE CAP</u>

PART 5: <u>MY FAMILY AND I</u>

PART 6: <u>POTPOURRI</u>

DEDICATION

In 19th century, there was an evil custom in certain parts of southern India wherein young, pre teen girls were married off to rich, old men and the young girl would become a widow even before she crossed her teens. My great grandfather, Sri Gurajada Appa Rao, a great social reformer and an eminent scholar, eradicated the evil custom, with an actual stroke of his pen. His famous play *'Kanya sulkam'*, not only uprooted the custom and inspired many young men to marry young widows but also transformed Telugu literature. He is renowned as the father of modern Telugu literature.

I dedicate my book to Sri Gurajada Appa Rao, and I chose 'Girisam' as my pen name, as a mark of respect to him and the famous character he has created in *'Kanya Sulkam'*.

Acknowledgement

I am grateful to so many wonderful people that if I list out, it would be as voluminous as this book.

If my wife hadn't volunteered to make many sacrifices and be a single parent for most of the time (in fact, when I am at home, her workload increases), this book would not have come into being. I am indebted to her, my kids, my parents and all family members, and every single member of the crew and the officers that I have sailed with, and my employers.

Though, most of the experiences are my own, I borrowed few from others, and a few are imaginary. Hence, any resemblance to any person is purely coincidental and not intentional.

Mrs Indira Gandhi (former prime minister of India) was a great fan of the 'Yes, Minister' TV series from the UK. She asked 'Door Darshan' (state sponsored TV channel) to make a similar one in an Indian context. There was such uproar and protest from politicians that they were insulted and humiliated that the show was withdrawn after a few episodes. Humor is the best medicine and should be taken in large doses, even if, and, especially, if the jokes are on one's self.

Most of the stories and incidents narrated in this book are intended to make the readers laugh, and enjoy the book, and most stories are directed at me. Any funny references to people, places, languages or regions, are just that, and I hope same will be taken in lighter vein and proper spirit.

PROLOGUE

I have been sailing for more than three decades. Most of those thirty years, in the capacity of a chief engineer. There are not many books that depict the excitement, challenges, and adventures of sailing on the high seas.

Anyone with over a decade of sailing experience would have accumulated enough adventures, anecdotes, and strange experiences (funny, exciting, or interesting) to fill a book. I am no exception. Once when I was narrating a particular near-miss incident to my relieving chief engineer, the captain, who was also present, was incredulous.

'What, Chief,' he admonished me, 'you are telling the story as if you are narrating what you had for breakfast. This story is studded with elements of suspense, thrill, excitement, and courage, in fact, everything except sex. I will show you how it should be told.'

Then he narrated the same story with such passion and intensity that the relieving chief engineer was floored.

I realized that one thing that I begrudgingly conceded to is that navigating officers have a flair for eloquence and the gift of gab, which they develop because of the nature of their duty, i.e. the unavoidable necessity of conversing with and entertaining pilots, agents, surveyors, port authorities, cargo foremen and others.

In sharp contrast, engineers are always drowned in the engine room noise and communicate only when necessary. They have no need to entertain strangers and rarely blossom into good conversationalists.

When my nephews and nieces ask me to relate my adventures, my inability to narrate stories in an exciting and gripping manner forced me to evade them.

Recently my daughter unearthed a folder from my father's shelves. It contained short stories that I had written in my school and college days.

I suddenly realized that I need not narrate my experiences verbally.

The written-format option appealed to me immediately, hence this attempt.

I had several pleasant and memorable experiences while sailing.

We had joy, fun, parties, and laughter along with tensions, anxiety, and worries.

My family and I thoroughly enjoyed our sailing and stay on board the ships. My elder daughter feels she had the best childhood a child can hope for. She has seen the pyramids in Egypt, the Leaning Tower of Pisa, Tokyo Disneyland, the USA, Vietnam, Poland, and several countries. She was pampered by everyone on board.

In those days at least two to three families with kids sailed on a ship. We would get long port stays. Life was one long party.

These stories are not just monotonous recitals of events; they are interspersed with events in social life also.

Golden College Days contains some funny incidents of my college days.

Golden Days as a Junior Engineer has some hilarious episodes in my first ship.

Close Encounters has stories about my adventures, near-miss incidents, and some heart-stopping events.

Feathers in the Cap, as the name suggests, is about pats on the back from me to myself (After all, it is my book and I can afford to do so. Besides, who else will do that?).

My Family and I is self-explanatory.

Potpourri is a collection of assorted thoughts on various themes.

I am a great fan of Jerome K. Jerome, author of *Three Men in a Boat* and other books. You can open his books at random and read any chapter and you will find it quite enjoyable since all chapters are independent, and it is not necessary to have read previous chapters to understand, unlike, in the case of Novels. I have read his books many times and enjoyed them immensely, each time, whereas many suspense thrillers lose novelty after you read them the first time.

Merry Mariner, I hope, will also enthral readers.

GOLDEN
COLLEGE DAYS

Joining college

(I think parental guidance may be required, not because of any adult content but because our approach to exams and education is certainly not a role model for kids.)

I would not have written this article, at least, until my daughters were grown up, married and settled. While describing all the fun we had in college, I would have to reveal that we bunked (absconded) classes, did nights out before exams to complete reading piled-up portions and went to late night-show movies even when we had a very tough exam on the next morning. We did all the wrong things that we preach and lecture our kids not to do.

I went a step further. I told my kids that I was a model student, son, and brother. I never bunked classes (which was partially true, in school my attendance was always above 90 per cent), I studied hard (again partially true), and I regularly exercised and cycled more than twelve kilometres a day and played cricket. I told them that my college was on a hill and I had to push the bicycle for one stretch of the road (I avoided telling them that scooters were a luxury then and next option was to travel in crowded buses).

Recently my wife and kids attended the marriage function of the daughter of my 'Wild Bunch" friend. In college our seniors nicknamed our friends' group Wild Bunch since we were unruly, boisterous and reminded them of characters of a hit movie of that name. We were six in the group. Five were from the same city. Eashwar was from a different town, and he was admitted into the bunch after many heated discussions, deliberations, and almost fist fights (since we wanted Wild Bunch to be exclusive for friends from our city).

My elder daughter innocently asked my other Wild Bunch friends how they were all so well behaved, never bunking classes and preparing well for exams without necessity of nights out, and like that, the cat was out of the bag.

Dinesh stared at her and asked, 'Who told you that we didn't bunk classes?'

My daughter was surprised. 'You bunked? My dad said you were all very punctual, never bunked, studied hard... and that he was a live wire...'

They laughed and laughed so much that Anil, the bride's dad, came over to ask what the joke was.

'Listen, she says Girisam told her that he was a live wire. You remember how lazy he was? We had to drag him from bed,' said Eashwar, between peals of laughter.

'And he told her he never bunked classes. Do you remember, our address used to be Regal and Select theatres in the afternoon?' Balu cut in.

But Anil was reasonable.

'I used to drag you all to movies. It was not entirely Girisam's fault.' He said, as he tried to defend me.

Then they regaled my family with all our college stories. So, when I went home on leave, my daughters told me that bunking, nights out, were a hereditary trait and they were not at fault.

Hence there is no need to wait to write this chapter.

Timely advice can make or break a career. If person giving advice and the one receiving are of the same wavelength or frequency, the recipient's life can transform for good, or bad.

When I was a chief engineer in one Indian ship, I had one motorman, Nair. He was in his forties, spoke fluent English, and had good knowledge. Not many crew members can read and understand technical books. I was impressed.

I asked him one day, 'Why don't you prepare and appear for second engineer's exam?'

He laughed and said, 'Are you joking, sir? At my age, how can I read and pass such tough exam? People will laugh and ridicule me.'

I told him 'I know you have potential, otherwise I wouldn't have told you. This time when you go on leave, just give it a thought. Don't worry about what people say or think. It is your life. You have every right to take decisions that benefit you.'

I met him after nearly fifteen years, when I went for my revalidation course. There he was, now a chief engineer.

Similarly, if my second brother didn't guide me, I probably would not have become an engineer.

In my teens, I was fascinated by my cousin, who could not clear a B.A or B.Sc degree (I forget which one) even after several attempts. But he was jovial, always joking and pulling pranks. He was a very good mimicry artist and he would have us all in splits, by imitating his lecturers. His college was a coeducational one and he had lot of fun and enjoyed college life to the hilt. It was at that time that I read and enjoyed stories and novels where the authors describe hilarious college life.

I thought, '*This is life.*'

In contrast, my second brother, who was studying engineering, would always work hard and didn't have much fun. In those days, there was hardly any "colour" (girls) in engineering colleges.

One day I asked my brother, 'Don't you miss all the fun that our cousin had in college? I think I will also go to such college and have fun.'

My brother's advice had only one sentence: 'You have to decide if you want to work hard for few years and enjoy rest of your life or if you want to enjoy life for few years and struggle for rest of your life.'

I thought it over and opted for the first choice.

I was an average student, middle class in academics, neither a frontbencher nor a backbencher. I managed 78 per cent in high school and got admission to civil engineering in one college and to mechanical engineering in another college.

My eldest brother was employed in the city where I got admission in civil engineering, so it was obviously preferable but I was not too keen on civil engineering. I was told that I could get transferred to that college later since both colleges were in the same university.

So I joined civil engineering and I stayed at my aunt's house.

In those days there were no anti-ragging laws. It was a daily nightmare to go to college and return unscathed. Though my cousin was in fourth year in the same college, he told me to tough it out. He said he would save me if he was around but he would not go out of his way to protect me. He named one cat Koteswara after a professor who tormented him. One day Koteswara stealthily approached an unsuspecting pigeon, jumped, and grabbed its throat. My cousin ran after Koteswara, shouting, 'Koteswara, leave that pigeon,' but could not save the pigeon. He felt very sad for several days.

In our locality, there were three more first-year students. One of them was very smart; he knew all the lanes and by-ways and would take us to college through some narrow, unused paths where wild grass and thorny bushes grew abundantly and shielded us from predatory seniors.

Only once I was captured by a senior, and his ragging session continued till late evening. He was a tall, lanky guy with thick spectacles. He and his friends took a room in town on rent and he took me there. He reluctantly let me go when his friends told him firmly it was enough for a day.

For several days I used to daydream of various scenarios where I would exact sweet revenge.

In one dream, I would be a CEO and he would apply for a small job. I'd see his photo and recognize him. I'd call him in and rag him till he weeps. Then I'd magnanimously give him a job and lecture and finally reveal to him my identity. He'd weep louder uncontrollably and thank me for my generosity.

In another scenario I'd marry his sister and make his life miserable with unreasonable demands during the marriage ceremony and make him cry and beg me for mercy. (It was common in those days for a bridegroom's side to rag and harass the bride's side. In my sister's marriage, one boy—later, I'd called him Thos, after a P.G.Wodehouse character—asked me to make holes on a Pond's face powder tin. How could I find a nail and a hammer at 2 a.m. in a marriage hall?)

Here I have to deviate to write an interesting incident.

A few years back, I was waiting for a flight in Dubai. I was returning home from Italy. One gentleman sat opposite me in a restaurant. His surname was on his card which he placed on his briefcase. I have many relatives with that surname.

So, I overcame my reluctance to prod strangers and asked him if he knew so-and-so.

He was quite affable and friendly. After chatting for a while, I asked him where he graduated from. He told me name of an engineering college and the year of passing out. We graduated in the same year.

I told him about my short stint in that college before getting transferred to another college and how we hoodwinked seniors and escaped ragging. He suddenly froze and stared at me, wide-eyed.

He shouted, 'And yours truly was the friend who guided you.'

It was my turn to stare at him. We laughed and hugged. Years rolled back and we were no longer two middle-aged men but two teenagers, giggling and recalling our escapades.

Time rolled fast and it was time to board our flights. He had a son settled in the US and he was looking for suitable girls and enquired about my daughter. As I was telling him, an announcement was made that his gate was changed.

He had to rush. We didn't exchange phone numbers or contact details. We couldn't find our misplaced pens. He hurriedly told me one email ID and password and told me that he was hardly using it, but it had contact details of other friends of our group. He told me to send an email and hoped our kids would bring us even closer. He waved and rushed to board his flight.

I found my pen and jotted down his ID. I am still in touch with him. But my mom passed away soon after and the alliance didn't materialize.

After about a month, I shifted to mechanical section to my brother's city in an exchange program.

My eldest brother stayed in a house opposite one movie theatre. I stayed with him and sister-in-law for two years, until he left for another city in north India. My uncle was working in our college office and tried to coax me into joining the electrical stream.

He was staying in the next building. I completed all formalities one day before and was nervously waiting to go to college. Luckily for me, the initial heat of ragging was spent, since the classes started a month earlier.

But still, some sadistic seniors might be on the hunt, looking for faces that had managed to slip through the net. My uncle told me that for a few days, I could accompany him on the college bus, which would drop me at the college entrance.

I liked that bus. It had a snout like a hippopotamus where the engine was fitted. You only see such buses in World War II movies. My uncle told me to be at his home by 8 a.m.

I went to one Chadagas Hotel across the street for breakfast.

'Hello, how are you?' someone asked me.

I looked up. It was another student I had seen in the college office yesterday while completing formalities.

We started talking. His brother-in-law had a medical shop just round the corner. He was staying with them. He took admission in civil engineering.

'I also joined late. Do you think ragging has ended?' He asked the question that was bothering me also.

'I hope so. Even if it hasn't, we joined almost at the end of it.' I tried to sound optimistic.

'Was your schooling in English medium?' he asked.

When I said no, his face lit up.

'I also studied in Telugu medium. Do you think we can cope?' he asked.

I assured him that I was told that studying in English would be far easier.

It is true. For 'Total refraction' our Telugu text book term was "*Sampoornnantara Paravartanamu*" and for "Involuntary reaction" it was "*Asankalpita Pratikara charya*".

'Let us stick together and go to college together until this ragging is over. I will wait for you at medical shop,' he said and showed me the medical shop through the hotel window.

I said OK. I didn't have the heart to tell him that I was going to college in the college bus with my uncle. When I was boarding the bus, I squashed an uneasy thought that maybe I should have told him not to wait for me.

As the huge majestic college building loomed into view from the bus window, my heartbeat increased to the speed of racehorse hoof beats. I thanked my uncle and got down the bus at portico.

'*For the next five years, this place will be a second home,*' I thought grimly as I entered college.

WILD BUNCH

I arrived safely into the first year engineering classroom. There was pandemonium as there were more than a hundred students in the classroom.

All subjects were common for all departments in I year, so civil, mechanical, electrical, and electronics students were in the same room.

A few people looked at me curiously. Other than that, I was ignored. I sat in the last bench, introduced myself to the people adjacent to me, and enquired about them. Then I asked the obvious question; 'were there any students from my city?'

It is the most natural reaction. If you keep a hundred people in a room, you will find groups forming on regional basis.

They showed me three teenagers sitting a few rows away. I got up, pulled a chair close to them, and said hello and that was the beginning of a friendship that is still going strong. I will refer to them as Anil, Balu, Chandu, Dinesh, and Eashwar to avoid inadvertent embarrassment to them. Later we were nicknamed 'Wild Bunch' by our seniors.

Anil and Balu were from the same school, Anil was in the mech marine section and Balu was in civil. Chandu was in electrical. I was in the mechanical section. So we completed the spectrum.

The lecturer entered and slowly pandemonium levels dropped. I whispered to Anil if ragging was still in full swing.

He smiled. 'Don't worry, it is almost over.' I heaved a sigh of relief.

Here, I have to introduce my friends. All of them have become big shots but I will desist from writing about their present status. We were all young, brash teenagers and I have to record that status (I have to be careful though; one friend who is featured in some stories already warned me that he would haul me over the coals. He might apply an ointment later, if I write a few nice things about him).

ANIL, THE WOODPECKER

A nil is dynamic, active, energetic, and smart. He belongs to the millionaire club, grades wise. His scorecard looks like Sachin's, all 'A's, I don't think he had more than couple of 'B's in the entire five-year course.

But he has the skill to run with hares and hunt with wolves, without offending either. He would bunk classes, go to movies with us. In fact, he is a movie addict, even now. He goes to second-show movies and sleeps; those days he would drag us. He has great persuasive powers; if he wants you to go to the movies with him, you will go. He will wear down your resistance, like a woodpecker. He has all the fun, defying the logic that only bookworms get the grades.

And he did score 'A's. When and how he studied remains a mystery. He was never high browed or supercilious.

He stayed with his brother, a bank officer, and his mother. I think God gets bored when making millions of humans, and to have some fun, he gives different shades to siblings. My dad was very fair and his younger brother was very dark and I have seen same in many families, including mine. And that is to say that Anil is dark while his brother is very fair.

Another interesting feature was he kept accounts scrupulously. After we returned from movies or outing, he would inform each one who owed whom, to the nearest paisa. He had a high-pitched voice and would enthral us with his 'opera' singing and Barbara Streisand songs.

Balu, the Black sheep

B alu and rest of us were middle-class citizens, happy with our 'B's and 'C's and occasional 'A's. He was well behaved, non-controversial, and always laughing.

True to our name Wild Bunch, we would quarrel with each other, and patch up after a few days or weeks. Some times for very silly reasons. Once, one friend was miffed with another and stopped talking for several months since his friend called him an idiot and fool when they were surrounded by several beautiful girls in a movie theatre. There was never a dull moment. The only exception was Balu. He was the Black sheep of our Wild bunch. He was like Switzerland, friends with every one, all the time.

The rest of us were truly the Wild Bunch gang. Anil would fight with Chandu, Dinesh with Eashwar, and all of them with me, when I tried to broker peace. We had fights in all permutations and combinations, except with Balu. In fact, when we left college, a few of us were not even on talking terms. I really liked the movie *Dil Chahta Hai*. It very accurately portrayed the fun, frolic, and fights among friends.

Another typical admirable trait in Balu was he never meddled in others' affairs, even if invited, nor allowed others into his.

In sharp contrast, I was an enthusiastic mediator between an often-quarrelling friend and his girlfriend. They split and patched up more times than Elizabeth Taylor and Richard Burton. For every and any silly reason, one of them would get angry and the other party requested me to mediate. When I

13

went to meet him, she (she was his neighbour) would ask me to meet her at temple and pour out her woes. For example, there were times when he didn't respond to her letters. When I asked him, he said she didn't smile at him. Or he would plead with me to convince her to talk to him.

I sincerely tried to keep patching them up until I realized that both of them were not serious but were playing this charade to boost their ego and just to pass time.

Balu was my neighbour when I was a day scholar. He stayed with his parents. Together, we shifted to hostel in third year.

CHANDU, THE CHOCOLATE HERO

Chandu was quite handsome. Anil would call him lady-killer. Unfortunately, there were no ladies to kill in our campus. The only lady was our batch-mate in electronics and communication. As I mentioned elsewhere, she was not what you would call a traffic stopper. If he killed any ladies outside, he did it silently and we were not aware.

He was always laughing, joking, and happy-go-lucky. In our Wild Bunch, he was the only one from his department, electrical. It affected his academics. One of us would drag, pull, and help others and we would trudge through numerous exams. But he had no one to do that or push him.

The math professor was his uncle and his uncle had a beautiful daughter. Chandu warned us all not to fall in love with his cousin, as it could be injurious to our academic health, as her dad would ensure we never left college. We respected his advice but I suspect she may have fallen in love with someone (this is just my presumption) and her dad presumed Chandu was the culprit and harassed him severely, more than any other lecturer or all other lecturers combined.

I met Chandu's dad a few times. He was a freedom fighter and donated all his lands to Vinoba Bhave when he visited his village. He was so kind-hearted he would give his footwear or apparel if he came across needy people.

What our scriptures say is true. Your good deeds will reward you or your successors manifold. I recently met all his brothers and sisters. All of them have reached top positions, with their children settled abroad, and all of them were affluent.

Chandu's eldest brother told me that their father's generosity and sacrifices were the root cause of their success. Theirs is a large family, four brothers and four sisters. Only one child is in India. The rest of their kids are settled abroad.

Coming back to the story, at short interval after two periods, I saw the friend whom I met at Chadagas Hotel in the morning, walking towards me. I could not duck or hide. I was frantically trying to think of some excuse for my inability to meet him before coming to college.

Should I tell him my uncle volunteered to drop me? Or my brother's friend gave a lift? Alternatively, should I tell the truth?

My jaw dropped when he said in an apologetic tone, as if he was the perpetrator and I was the aggrieved party, 'I waited for one hour. When you didn't turn up, I came.'

I immediately liked him. I suffer from a malady. Apart from laziness, five minutes more sleep and amnesia; it is called *mohamaatam*. (I am unable to find a suitable English word.) He seemed to suffer from *mohamaatam* to a far more advanced and chronic stage than I. I would not have waited for more than five minutes for a chap I met five minutes back and would pounce and demand an explanation from him for not turning up when I met him next.

Here he was, actually apologizing for not waiting longer.

I almost hugged him. He was Dinesh, fifth member of Wild Bunch. I introduced him to the others.

Now, I will introduce Dinesh.

DINESH, THE DIFFIDENT

Dinesh can be termed as a universally liked person. He is extremely shy. When introduced, he floors other persons with his innocence, good nature, and charm, not intentionally, of course. A person may feel his life is wasted if somehow he misses a chance to extend help or assistance to Dinesh.

It is very simple, really. If you see the villains Voldemort or the Joker, you want to bash them up and strangle them to stop their loud, evil laughter. If you come across some innocent, adorable child, you ruffle its hair and give a chocolate or candy.

People didn't actually ruffle his hair but would plead with him to honour them by giving them a chance to help him.

His is a story of unbelievable twists and swings. He lost his parents early and was the last child of a huge family (three brothers and five sisters). He completed his schooling staying with one sister. He passed with very good marks but none of his siblings came forward to support his education. So he took up a job in a movie film processing colour lab in Mumbai and was staying with sister's family. He would proudly tell us that he did the processing of *Haathi Mere Saathi* and a few hit movies of that era. We were jealous when he told us he had the privilege to see uncensored versions.

His brother and was transferred to Punjab. Before he left, he put in Dinesh's application to engineering college. Dinesh was selected and his brother-in-law and sister volunteered to assist him.

His life took a sharp U-turn and a road to success.

He was scared. He left school long back and he almost forgot everything. Math gave him nightmares; he told me recently that even now, he has nightmares about math exams and wakes up in cold sweat. But he struggled and succeeded.

The next day, our lecturer Venugopala (we later nicknamed him 'elephant milk won't come', deforming his name to *enugu palu ravu* in Telugu) told us that a seminar would be conducted in the auditorium.

We all assembled and he told us that they thought of a revolutionary concept, internal assessment. Our seniors had their papers corrected by other colleges and there was always a problem of questions appearing out of syllabus or from chapters not taught and dissatisfaction with marks awarded.

So our college wanted to experiment with our batch with this new concept. In this, our lecturers would teach, conduct exams, and correct papers. So there was no possibility of questions being asked out of syllabus or portions not taught.

In addition, there were no marks, only grades. Suppose paper was very tough and the highest mark scored was 35 per cent, then the person scoring 35 per cent would get an 'A' grade and likewise grades would be awarded.

I think I was far wiser than all those professors, even at that young age; maybe my stint under the bodhi tree helped. I knew it would never work. Rich would become richer, poor would become poorer. Some people are born or gifted with mercurial brains, which can assimilate like a computer. They can very easily learn faster and would always be in the front. Lesser mortals can never compete with them, irrespective of any amount of hard work they put in. Our professors were under the misguided delusion that with sheer hard work, a backbencher could bag 'A's.

This is not to demean the lesser mortals. We, some of the lesser mortals, have succeeded far beyond our expectations and even those of 'A' graders.

So those who get 'A' grades would always get 'A's. Since I had that realization and illumination, I was happy and never cried about sour grapes or grades.

I used to pity those chaps who would study day and night to beat those frontbenchers and end up behind us, though we would go to movies and study a day before exams. Momentarily, the greed would tempt us after each exam that with a little more effort maybe we could get 'A' grades but wiser counsel prevailed and saved us from making that stupid mistake of falling into a rat trap.

After the meeting was over, I don't remember why I stayed back; maybe I was waiting for Balu. I met Eashwar, our sixth member. The hall was empty; only he and I were there. He was waiting for Chandu, who was his neighbour and friend.

I said hello and we became friends.

EASHWAR, THE ENIGMATIC

He reminds you of a coiled spring; you never know which direction it will take off once you release it... or like the toys of that era when you would wind a spring and the toy keeps jumping until the energy is spent.

Only he had inexhaustible energy; he could never stay still for a second. He would be joking, singing songs, murdering them at will. He has a ready and sharp wit and humour. He had high intelligence but zero or negative industry. He neither craved nor bothered about grades. He was like an impatient butterfly; had he concentrated and stayed on one flower (subject) for a few minutes, he would have bagged 'A's. But he would stay on the flower only for the required duration for him to get 'B' or 'C' and sometimes 'D'.

He stayed with his parents in what Anil called *sambarala rambabu* house. Those days, the movie of that name was a big hit; hero stays in a house which has many portions and many families. Like me, he also had three brothers and one sister.

His mother used to make and send the yummiest food. Like Mumbai *dabbawallahs*, some ladies would bring us Tiffin carriers from home. At lunch time, we would share all the items. Poor Eashwar, we would snatch his dishes and tell him curtly that he could enjoy his mom's cooking anytime and dump on him some of the unappetizing items from our Tiffin carriers.

Some of his memorable repartees or spontaneous jokes always make us smile when we think of them.

Once he was describing a card game. Anil interrupted him, saying that he knew a thousand games and Eashwar need not tell him. Without breaking stride, Eashwar told him this is thousand and first game so Anil should shut up and listen.

On another occasion, I was describing to my friends how I attained enlightenment when I sat under a bodhi tree in my schooldays and became a good boy overnight, Eashwar expressed shock.

'What? You never sat under a bodhi tree till schooldays? My mom told me that I used to crawl, go out of the house, and play under a bodhi tree and would kick up a racket if I was restrained. I used to spend most of my waking time and sleep time under bodhi tree in my infancy. That is why I am so wise and mature compared to you ignorant idiots,' he told me with a straight face.

One evening we were all going for tea to Apparao's roadside tea shop (We liked his one-metre tea; Apparao had a technique of pouring tea quite fast from one container to another, increasing the distance between containers to more than a meter). It was about half a kilometer from our hostel, so we didn't bother to change up and were clad in lungis and shirts.

Those days, lungis came in different virant colours and designs. We saw Eashwar going towards hostel on his bicycle. We shouted and whistled.

He saw us, came over, got down from the bicycle, and stared at us from head to toe and asked, '*Lungilu langalla kattukuni ekkadikira veltunnaru?*' (Where are you going wearing those lungis like petticoats?)

About Grades and Snakes

Our Wild Bunch members' intelligence, industry, and grades were like this:

Anil—intelligence 60 per cent, industry 40 per cent, grades 'A'

Balu, Chandu, Girisam., Dinesh—intelligence 30 per cent, industry 30 per cent, grades 'B' and 'C' with occasional 'A' and 'D'

Eashwar—intelligence 80 per cent, industry -20 per cent, grades 'B' and 'C' with occasional 'A' and 'D'.

Eashwar managed to squeeze through and make it to first class. His final percentage read 59.99 per cent. It was like a last ball six to win the match and the last exam of our course was viva voce about our project work (design and construction of marine propeller) conducted by a professor of another college. Eashwar had to score an 'A' to get first class. And he scored (his first and last 'A').

I will relate incidents, as I remember them, not necessarily in any particular chronological order.

I was not meant to be an academician. I would have happily been a farmer if my dad had paddy fields. It would be heavenly, lazing under the cool shade of trees and enjoying fresh, clean air in a hammock tied between two coconut trees. Or looking after business if he had one.

For me, textbooks served few purposes other than intended. During combined studies when many friends swarmed into our room and we ran short of pillows, these thick books would serve as pillows (*Electrical Technology* by Theraja, *Theory of*

Machines, math book by Kreyszig and other thick books).
There was also a desperate theory that even if you didn't read,
if you go to sleep with the textbook of that subject under your
head as a pillow, the required knowledge for that exam would
seep into the brain.

Second purpose is, it is an excellent remedy for insomnia.
But for my laziness, I would have patented my theory and saved
many from that affliction. Drug manufacturing companies are
lucky that I didn't propound my theory.

Next time when you are unable to fall asleep, try this.
Pick up a most boring subject textbook of your student days
and start reading it. I guarantee that you would fall asleep
before you complete reading two pages. I tried this successfully
when it would be humanly impossible to expect to sleep after
sleeping soundly for fourteen hours or more and then you
wanted to sleep further.

Third advantage of those voluminous books is that you
might score a few points with beautiful girls; they might think
you are an Einstein in the offing. But when I saw slender
girls carrying many such books in the university library, I
gave up. Those days, like doctors' trademark is a white coat,
an engineering student's trademark was a T-square. It is just
a piece of wood shaped like a T. It is used for engineering
drawing.

In one hit Telugu movie of that era, Kanchana sang,
'Hello…Engineer… come near… don't fear …oh dear' and
chased ANR, who keeps running away carrying a T-square.
Our hopes of thwarting beautiful girls chasing us when we
carried those ungainly T-squares were dashed, since doctors
with their spotless white coats were more attractive and
most probably girls were put off since we reminded them of
condemned men of the Roman era who carried crosses on
which they were crucified.

But people do exist in this world who absolutely relish
reading textbooks, like others enjoy reading Robert Ludlum,

Wilbur Smith, or James Hadley Chase (in our college days) or Harry Potter (present generation). They couldn't put down the book and simply couldn't wait to go to the next chapter, where cam profile design or foundry techniques are discussed about manufacturing a crankshaft.

They are not freaks. They are different.

Once, Eashwar wondered about one Swami, our classmate, a textbook worm who was reading *Theory of Machines* with rapt attention.

'What is so exciting about textbooks? See that expression on his face. It is as if he is reading a chapter where heroine is turning the key to the lock, unaware that a villain is waiting in the room to kill her,' he said, baffled.

I also found it strange; a crankshaft or a cam can neither kill or get killed.

I looked and agreed. 'Yes, the way his eyes are wide like saucers and the way he is almost drooling and biting fingernail. Either he is reading a suspense thriller or *Playboy* or *Penthouse* ... hiding it in that textbook,' I told Eashwar.

Eashwar said he could not wait any longer and sneaked behind him and peeped over his shoulder.

Eashwar's face was blank with astonishment when he came back and told me, 'He is indeed reading textbook.'

Even hard-core bookworms would take it easy for the first few days after beginning of a new semester (of course, we would take it easy until a few days before exams). Swami would wake up at 3 a.m. on the first day itself and start mugging up.

Such persons were referred to as *paamulu* (snakes). I didn't coin that word; it was handed down from several batches, maybe generations. No one knew why they were called *paamulu*.

It is like that story on management. A few monkeys were put in a cage and bananas were hung from the ceiling. A ladder was kept there to reach them. Every time a monkey tried to climb the ladder, a powerful water jet would drench all of them. So the monkeys learnt not to get tempted. They took out two or three monkeys and put new monkeys. Old monkeys would bash up new monkeys if they tried to climb the ladder. Finally, even when all monkeys were new and water jet was discontinued, none of them would climb the ladder and none of them knew why they should not climb the ladder for those bananas.

Similarly, the real reason behind nicknaming them as snakes is lost to the mankind. But I tried to investigate why they were called snakes and came up with few probable answers.

Our college emblem had two intertwined serpents. Maybe such dedicated students were compared to the snakes in the emblem, proudly upholding traditions. But it was far-fetched; teenagers hardly have such lofty notions while tagging nicknames.

Snakes can gobble up huge animals stretching their mouths to impossible limits and then digest too. These 'snakes' can gulp huge textbooks and keep asking for more.

Snakes can pass through very narrow apertures; these 'snakes' can squeeze reading many subjects irrespective of time constraints. Snakes discard the skins effortlessly; our snakes shed remembrances of the previous semester subjects' horrors and take on new semester subjects. For the rest of us, the relief of getting rid of last semester's nightmare subjects would be so overwhelming, we would wake up to the new horrors rather late.

Snakes come in different sizes and shapes. Guys like Swami were like anacondas. Then there were all types and varieties, depending on their levels of commitment. Some were like the characters in the movie *Nagin*, humans for most of the time, turning into snakes for the duration of exams. Some subjects never stop haunting.

I have very fond memories of our math classes of first year.

Professor Shyam (father of Chandu's beautiful cousin) would arrive in a crisp black coat and spotless white trousers and take attendance. It would take quite some time since there were around 100 students.

The blackboard was quite long, maybe twelve feet. He would start writing on the board and soon he would be lost. When he started solving a problem, you had the feeling that he was entering a quicksand pool. Within no time the entire blackboard would be full and he would still be puzzled. The more he thrashed, more he would be sucked into the intricate, puzzling problem. He would be pulling his nose, rubbing his cheeks, and then clasp a hand to the brow, saying, 'Oh, how did I miss that one?'

Then he would wipe a small area, about six inches, and scribble something. He fought his own battles daily, never bothering us. He never asked us questions or embarrassed us to confess about our ignorance. In fact, we used to sneak out to canteen and came back a few minutes before end of class. We were very honest, unlike some people who went to hostel to sleep after giving attendance. He never noticed why the class which was full at the beginning of period was half full when he left.

We used to call him 'Devudu' (God) for his benevolence. On a few occasions, he would solve a problem and would be triumphant. But invariably, when he left class, his black coat would become white with chalk powder dust and his entire face and hair (except glasses) would be covered in streaks of chalk powder.

In those days we considered him an absent-minded genius. Now, I am not sure. Day after day, year after year, he was teaching math; it beats me how he managed to get himself tied up in knots every day. He should have been solving those problems in a jiffy. He followed one textbook by Kreyszig.

There were only two books in university library and none available in the market. New stock was expected after a few weeks. So, after Professor lost himself in a quagmire and to the world, it was time for sojourn to the canteen. We told Balu to rush to university library and grab the Kreyszig textbook.

Balu pedaled his bicycle like a champion and reached the library in record time. He laid his hands on the book triumphantly. He was waiting at the counter in the queue when a voice said, 'Excuse me.'

He turned and saw it was our *aadabaduchu* (sister), our classmate, lone lady in our college.

'Please give me that book, I will make notes and return in two days,' she requested him.

Balu gulped and handed over the book and faced a barrage of ridicule and jibes from us later.

He protested feebly, 'How you can you say "no" bluntly to the only girl in our college?' He was being chivalrous.

Art of Bunking

U nfortunately, my friends gave the impression to my family that we bunked so many classes so extensively that our attendance was negligible.

It is not true. We were not hard-core, compulsive, or addictive bunkers (those who bunk or abscond classes). Every time we bunked, our hearts suffered pangs due to pricks of conscience. Our parents and guardians sent hard-earned money for our education, pocket money, and hostel expenses. They expected us to struggle, succeed, and prosper in life.

But minds overruled our hearts. We were helpless. But there was a method to our madness.

At the beginning of each semester, we calculated the number of working days, take 25 per cent and arrive at a figure of 'safe' *bunkable* days, and work towards fulfilling that quota.

In spite of our best efforts, we always exceeded the limit and pleaded with lecturers to give us one more chance, received a proper dressing-down and a lecture about preciousness of time and perils of irresponsibility and a 'final warning', thanked them, and came out and the process was repeated.

If our quota exceeded it was not entirely due to our fault. Three or four new movies being released in a short span of time or incessant rains (we didn't mind getting wet, but would not miss the beautiful view from hostel window, the hills and clouds for some frivolous attendance statistics) were few excuses. We would bunk for the inter-university women's volleyball championships or women's tennis events conducted on our campus, and a few more such instances were beyond our control.

I almost fell in love with a beautiful volleyball player from another state. She played so brilliantly and heroically and won the match for her team single-handedly. I was bowled over. Dinesh and I went to meet her after the match to congratulate her.

When we complimented her, she blushed, panicked, and hid behind her coach. She told something to her coach in a Sivaji-Ganesan-trademark long, agitated monologue in her language (Sivaji Ganesan was famous for his kilometre-long dialogues which he would deliver in one shot and one take). She must have thought we were rowdy elements. Coach told us in broken English that she could not speak English but only her state language and threw a spanner into the works. As I picked up broken pieces of my heart, and we were coming out, I told Dinesh that I would go back and get her autograph, at least I could look at the full moon and at that autograph and sing sad songs of Hemanth Kumar (*Tum pukar lo*).

There was not a piece of paper in any of our pockets, not even a bus ticket. I fired Dinesh for his stupidity. Why couldn't he keep a small receipt or paper of any kind? Would it weigh a ton? He snarled at me, why was I not smart enough to keep a few papers handy?

The girls were getting into a bus, and I located a one-rupee note in his purse. I grabbed it, ran to that girl, and asked her to give me her autograph. Again she panicked and gave another long hysterical monologue to coach in her language; coach convinced her that there was no harm.

She signed her name (L. Kumari) and I thanked her and waved as the bus vanished into the horizon. I gave Dinesh his rupee back and told him not to spend it. I would give him a rupee and take the autographed one.

Before I rushed and brought the rupee, he spent it; he told me he had to urgently post a letter to his girlfriend and he had to buy stamps. We had a heated argument; I accused him of treachery.

He told me not to be an idiot and asked me to wake up to realities of life.

He told me, 'She might relish fish and non-veg. Fish fried in coconut oil would emit such aroma to make seasoned people rush outside gasping for fresh air.'

I asked him, 'Are you living in Middle Ages? Don't you read novels and watch movies? She will gladly give up everything for love.'

He laughed sardonically and said, 'Can you bathe, eat, drink, and sleep in coconut oil the rest of your life? Half of your salary would go towards buying barrels of coconut oil every month. You and your life will reek of coconut oil.'

We shouted at each other for a while. Time healed the wounds. But I never forgave him for spending that rupee.

Major share of blame for our bunking should go to Anil. He is a movie addict. Those days, money was sent from home by way of money orders. Our money would last a maximum of two weeks.

Movie theatres had poor, middle-class, upper middle-class, and rich (balcony) sections. We would go to the rich section with heads held high for the first few days. Then as our finances dropped, our swagger dropped and we came down the ladder, and by middle of the month, we would be at middle-class, trying to sink lower in seats and to avoid looking back (our friends might be sitting in back rows).

When our finances reached rock bottom, Anil would try to incite us to watch movies sitting in poor section. We refused point-blank.

'How will you know what it feels like to watch a movie from close quarters? We should try everything once.' He tried to brainwash us. I am not very sure if he succeeded in that.

I don't recollect watching a movie sitting in the 'poor' section but I remember our lecturer Polonkov and his wife sitting in the 'poor' section a few rows ahead of us when we were in middle-class section.

Everyone forgot Polonkov's original name. It was some Swami or Murthy. Eashwar was notorious for his language; every second word in a sentence had to be in parliamentary language (In my youth, such words were referred to as 'un-parliamentary language'). He had ready wit and spontaneous repartee.

One day when we were having tea in the canteen, I asked Eashwar what was the next period, with intention to bunk and go to a matinee show. He said, 'Production technology. That *Potti Lan— Koduku's* [short bas—d's] class.'

Eashwar is also short, but kettle never thinks about self while ridiculing pot.

Then I added all first syllables, and his nickname Polonkov was born. It became so famous and stuck like glue. I met a junior of several years some time later and when we were discussing about lecturers, his name cropped up. My junior did not know how the name originated, and its full form; he said that lecturer was referred to by only that name by everyone.

Polonkov used to bring all Russian books and beat us to death with his gruff, nasal, monotonous whining voice. And the sound of his grating voice was like scraping of a sharp metal object on an iron sheet. One hour of his lecture used to bring stout-hearted heroes, who stared fearlessly into the opponent's face in boxing matches, to their knees and to the verge of tears. Our thoughts used to wander on melancholic topics like life after death, at the end of his class.

We were shocked to see Polonkov and his wife sitting in the poor section. He was not trying to hide; he was talking and joking with his wife normally. He had graduated from a Moscow university, so those communist ideas of equality and classless society must have been ingrained in his soul.

Later, Anil took us all to the cleaners; he said we should be ashamed of our hypocrisy, pseudo prestige, and snobbishness.

We should learn simplicity from Polonkov and happily watch movies while seated in poor section. Though, I remember feeling ashamed about being a hypocrite, I have no recollection of watching movies while seated in the poor section. I think Anil's persuasive powers had fallen short.

The decision to bunk was normally taken in a democratic manner in the canteen. A few reluctant people would be convinced by our woodpecker Anil.

My mind troubled me. I wanted to bunk class but a feeling of guilt would gnaw at my heart. So, I used to suggest that we toss a coin. They reluctantly agree.

Then I would toss a coin; heads we go to class, tails we go to a movie. The coin spins, lands and passes judgement that we should go to class.

There would be a reluctant silence. Then someone suggests that it should be best of three.

This time another friend takes over, declaring mine was an unlucky hand. Best of three also goes in favour of attending class. When best of five, and best of seven, also insist, we go to class; everyone is agitated, angry, and upset with each other as if it is the fault of the guy who is tossing the coin.

'That idiot doesn't know how to toss' is the general feeling. Someone suggests checking the coin, if it doesn't have both sides heads like in *Sholay*. In the movie, the hero has a special coin that has 'heads' on both sides. He tricks his friend to have his own way, every time they disagree. Hero's friend discovers this, only after the hero dies.

We check and see it has a tails also. Eashwar suspects the integrity of the coin; maybe it is a stooge of lecturers.

Then we start afresh with a different coin borrowed from the cash counter.

When it lands and permits us to go to movie, we immediately hurry up before anyone suggests best of three, not that anyone would have.

Dinesh was fed up with this charade. He asked why we should make a hue and cry; if we wanted to bunk class, then bunk we should. When we have no intention of honouring the verdict of the coin, why take the trouble of tossing? He didn't understand; it was just to assuage our troubled minds, reassuring us that we had given a fair chance to the lecturers and the college to force us to attend classes.

We didn't bunk just to go to movies; once we bunked to go on a trekking adventure. Behind our college, was a huge, majestic mountain stretching from our college to the railway station. I always wanted to climb the mountain and enjoy a picturesque view and feel my head in the clouds.

I learnt a few wood-pecking techniques from Anil and brainwashed all my friends to undertake trekking. Anil, Balu, Chandu, Eashwar, myself, and three other friends (Bikki Mubber, Jeella Babu, and one junior) started one day at 7 a.m. Only Dinesh refused to be a part of this foolishness; he said he would wash clothes and enjoy a nap.

This Bikki Mubber was gentle, shy, and a regular member of our combined studies. He had a habit of saying that he is a poor Brahmin, so he should be left alone (*Bikki brahmannira, vadileyyandi*) when we insisted he accompany us to movies or outings. We used the term *mabbu* (cloud) when referring to a chap who is slow on the uptake and slow to grasp (like 'tube light', used by the next generation). So his name became Bikki Mubber (He is anything but a *bikki* or *mabbu*; he is now a very top official in Central Government enterprise).

Jeella Babu was nicknamed because of his excess and unnecessary zeal. He was also called Z and N (*Zaddi, Nangiri*). *Jeellu* is plural for *Jeedi*, a village sweet which is famous for it's elastic property. A very lengthy movie or a TV serial which stretches on and on is often compared to *Jeella paakam* (Elastic paste like material in the process stage of *Jeedi* preparation which will stretch to a long distance without breaking when pulled).

We had a small test on Tumburudu's subject, which we decided to skip (That lecturer was nicknamed thus because he used to scratch his tummy, reminding one of Tumbur's strumming his veena).

To reach the base of the mountain, we had to pass through many lanes and houses. When we heard someone shouting and calling us, we turned and were rooted to the spot.

It was Tumburudu, clad in a banian and a lungi standing in front of his house. We had no option but to approach him and greet him.

'There are no movie theatres in this direction, only that hill is there. It is also too early for a movie. So what is your excuse now for skipping exam in my subject?' he asked point-blank.

We were nonplussed.

Anil flashed his magnetic smile and said, 'Sir, we deserve some fun and adventure also along with studies. Girisam had been pestering us for trekking expedition for a long time. Today we spontaneously decided to climb that mountain. Even if we miss this test, we will answer the next two and since you will consider best of three, we will take our chance.'

If Anil were not there, we (Wild Bunch gang) would have stood with bowed heads, listened to Tumburudu's scathing attack, brushed it off, and continued with our expedition. Bikki Mubber and Jeella Babu would have apologized, gone back to college to write the exam, if not for Anil.

Tumburudu stared at the hill, its height and length, and looked at me with suspicious admiration; somehow he seemed to feel that I could not have been enthusiastic about this sheer hard work. It was more likely, he felt, that I was pulled and dragged by others.

He sadly looked at his paunch and, while scratching, must have rued why he didn't scale that mountain when he was fit and agile.

Then he smiled ear to ear.

'Great. For once, I appreciate your reason for bunking. You are going to climb and come back?' he asked.

'No, sir, we are going to climb, walk the entire length, and get down at that other end,' I told him.

He was shocked. 'Oh, I see. Then don't waste any time. You have to get down before it is dark. I see you are carrying a camera, show me photographs later.' he told us and went back into the house.

As we were standing at the foot of the hill and looking up, I think everyone was scared. Recklessness is a by-product of youth. We started before anyone developed cold feet.

We carried water and food in *jhoola* bags, which, seemed to get heavier with each step. We did not take any breaks, and by the time we reached the top, we were gasping for breath, sweat streaming down and drenching us.

It is an exhilarating feeling. We knew exactly how Edmund Hillary felt when he conquered Mount Everest. We were all dancing, laughing, and jumping when Bikki Mubber suddenly stopped and said, 'Okay, Okay, don't overdo it.'

We wondered what bit him and looked in the direction of his gaze.

A six-year-old boy, who was resting his chin on a stick with which he controlled his goats, was staring at us wide eyed. His flock of goats was grazing.

We all hated him for spoiling our sense of achievement. I think all of us wanted to scold him for treating his animals cruelly, as if grass was not available at foot of the hill.

The view was magnificent and cool winter sun and wind soothed us and we recovered our composure.

Eashwar tried to comment that maybe we were the first adults in our city to scale this mountain but stopped midway when he met our stony and angry gazes. We were trying to forget about the boy.

We had our food, played some games, and slowly walked the length of the mountain. By the time we touched ground zero, it was beginning to get dark.

We went to see a lighthouse and few other interesting places when we were bunking classes. I am not sure if we bunked and went to Araku picnic or it was during the holidays. It is unlikely we would have wasted precious holidays when we could afford to bunk.

The only movie that Anil agreed to abandon and come out midway was a Dev Anand, Hema Malini starrer. We felt Polonkov's class was much more entertaining and relaxing and that we didn't deserve our self-inflicted punishment or rather any punishment meted out by Anil.

When our funds reached rock bottom and we didn't have money for 'poor' tickets also, we used to play textbook cricket in class.

One chap opens a book at random; if the last digit of page number is 0, he is out. Next batsman would come to bat. Numbers 1,2,3, 4(boundary), and 6(sixer) were runs. The rest of the numbers were dot balls.

About Grades,
Nights Out, and
Combined Studies

G RADES
   One misconception that has been engraved into our souls ever since Adam and Eve began sending their children to school is that frontbenchers are always 'A' graders and backbenchers are all washouts.

I dare not say that it is farthest from truth but I would definitely say that 'A' graders need not be frontbenchers and frontbenchers need not be 'A' graders.

For instance, in my schooldays the first two rows of Physics Sastry sir's class were always unoccupied (We had two Sastry sirs: one taught us physics and another, chemistry). Physics Sastry was quite fond of chewing paan and whenever he spoke, he would spray on the unfortunate person stationed opposite him, a fine colourful drizzle. So, no one dared to sit in the front two rows. He would force backbenchers to sit in the first two rows. Some rowdy sheeters would flatly refuse but a few docile, meek backbenchers obliged.

There was a joke circulating that umbrellas or raincoats should be provided by school authorities to students who sit in the first rows in his class. He was very kind-hearted and gentle. Once he was explaining conduction and convection in transfer of heat.

He would tell us, 'My mother used to wash her utensils meticulously and they would shine like mirrors. My father observed that our neighbour Rattamma garu cleaned only the inner surfaces of utensils, leaving the black carbon deposits on outer surfaces untouched. My father would tell my mother to learn from pakkinti Rattamma garu (*pakkinti Rattamma garini choosi nerchuko*), her cooking would be faster and she would consume less fuel since the black carbon surface is a good conductor of heat.'

While sincere students understood principle of conduction, not-so-sincere students joked about the roving eye of Sastry sir's father.

In college we had two colleagues, one Venu and one Ram.

Venu was super intelligent and was an incorrigible, unrepentant absconder of classes. Though we bunked classes, we had the decency to feel guilty about it and made the pretence of sincerity by tossing coins before bunking (though we cheated, we did have troubled consciences). But Venu had no such feelings; he would sit in the last bench close to the exit door, give attendance, and sneak out. Some lecturers would not even look up while taking attendance, so he would ask his friends to give his attendance on his behalf. He got away with it.

Just before exams, he would just flip through textbook pages and notes and would walk away with 'A' grades.

One day he happened to be in the class (a rare phenomenon, it could be due to lack of funds to buy movie tickets or a 'houseful' board or plain curiosity to know how it feels to sit in a classroom for the entire duration of a period).

The lecturer asked suddenly, 'Who is Venu?'

He stood up.

The lecturer stared at him. 'Are you from my class?' he asked him suspiciously.

Venu gulped and nodded.

'How come I have never seen you before?' he asked him.

Venu mumbled that he sits in back benches and so maybe he was not noticed.

'In so many exams you have been scoring consistently excellent marks. So I was curious to see who it was,' Lecturer told him.

Venu was stuck. Since he was in the limelight, he had to attend all of that lecturer's classes.

My other friend Ram always sat in first row. He sincerely believed what lecturers told us that nothing is impossible, and with sheer hard work, you can break the citadel and dethrone 'A' graders. I don't know how he could be so naïve. He never gave up. He studied quiet hard day and night, fought tooth and nail, and always ended up in our league, i.e., middle class.

We stayed in the same hostel. He is the culprit who effectively demolished any notions I had that I was the next Muhammed Rafi. When I was singing my favourite song in the bathroom at the top of my voice and actually enjoying it, he banged the door as if he wanted to break it. When I asked him what the matter was, he sheepishly told me that he thought a girl was being molested or raped or was being murdered and he wanted to rescue her.

He would wake up at ungodly hours like 3 a.m. or 4 a.m. and would study hard. Though everyone told me that early morning hours are the best time to study, it never suited me. I tried a few times. The feeling of sleep deprivation would last the entire day, and contrary to the popular belief that the mind would be fresh and would absorb readily anything you read, I would find the pages getting blurred as eyes could not focus and eyelids would seem to weigh a ton. I preferred to study till 2 a.m. or 3 a.m. and sleep for three or four hours and try my luck in exams.

But Ram was adamant; he would never give up even after a few nasty incidents. Once he kept a kettle on an electric stove to boil water to make tea. Then he went to sleep while seated at his desk. Our hostels were in a circular shape. Anil's room was diametrically opposite to Ram's on the same floor. Anil got up at 5 a.m. and came out to enjoy morning-fresh air. He was shocked to see thick smoke clouds swirling from Ram's room. He rushed, opened Ram's door, and switched the heater off, and took the stove outside. The water evaporated and the container melted. And Ram was happily sleeping.

On the second occasion, he kept piping hot tea on his table and was sipping and reading. When he woke up a few hours later, his lungi was all wet; he knocked off the teacup and spilled hot tea into his lap…and he slept through that. He told us that he was dreaming that he was being lowered into a cauldron of hot water by some tribals and he fought them and escaped but not before he was lowered waist-deep. And he thought the hot tea scalding him was part of the dream.

We could play pranks, textbook cricket or escape to the canteen when seated in the last rows. People sitting in the first row have to be attentive and on best behaviour all the time. Lecturers would be looking at their faces while teaching. I think only masochists or true seekers of knowledge prefer the first row. He never listened to us; we told him he could hear and follow as clearly in the last row as in the first row.

Once, he was very furious with a lecturer for not awarding marks for one question and thought it was unfair. Ram is very gentle and well behaved. I don't know what madness possessed him that day; he picked up the duster from the lecturer's table and acted as if throwing it at the back of the lecturer, who was writing on the blackboard. The lecturer suddenly turned back and stared wide-eyed at Ram, who was caught in the pose of throwing the duster.

He was very sincere, honest, and very industrious. But he lacked our wisdom. We realized, recognized, and accepted the fact that our many gifts did not include mercurial brains and irrespective of any amount of hard work we put in, we could never dethrone 'A' graders. We were practical and logical. Suppose an 'A' grade is awarded to two students and 'B' to ten, then it did not matter if your rank is third or tenth, you would get 'B'.

The only exception was Eashwar; he had a mercurial brain but lacked the desire or seriousness to aim for 'A's. I think he didn't like loneliness; 'A' graders are mostly a serious and grim lot and generally lead a blameless life. No movies, no entertainment and no bunking. A few exceptions to the rule were Anil and Venu.

Recently, I met Eashwar. He asked me if I remembered my roll number. I said it was 17 or 21. Not only did he tell me my correct roll number but he recited the entire list of our class, names and roll numbers of all students.

I was speechless, and when I accused him of being a freak after I recovered, he countered, saying that I was a freak and not he; when you listen to the roll call day after day for five years (discounting 25 per cent bunked classes) it was impossible, he felt, for anyone to forget.

NIGHTS OUT

I feel that the thoughts of 99.9 per cent of all average, middle-class students coming out of exam hall would be along these lines.

'Damn it, had I put in a little more effort, I could have scored twenty[or whatever] marks more. From now, I will allot two hours to read the portion covered daily. Then portions would not pile up like mountains and it is not possible to read in a day. I will be more organized from tomorrow.'

But like they say, tomorrow never comes.

The next day, he or she would go to the movies since one deserves relaxation after all the tension of exams. Then birthday parties, functions, and get-togethers follow, making postponement of the resolution a necessity. Before one realizes, again, a huge piled-up portion and a monstrous exam loom large.

I did not practice nights out. My theory was that if you cannot complete a portion in twenty hours, then you won't be able to do it in twenty-four hours. So I would sleep for four hours and tried to make the best of what I read in those twenty hours.

My Wild Bunch friend Dinesh's brother-in-law had a medical shop. So he had access to medicines to keep him awake. and he would pop one and would read the whole night.

I refused his offer and would sleep for a few hours and follow my pattern.

But one day I was tempted. The next day there was a tough Theory of Machines exam; It had a complicated lesson about cam profile design. I was able to read only a few lines and was going back to understand and it was infinitely slow. It was quite frustrating (It reminded me of the hero Psmith of *Leave It to Psmith*, a book by P.G.Wodehouse. Psmith goes as a guest, impersonating a poet, to heroine's mansion. He tries quite hard to read the poet's poems so that he could answer any questions from admirers and fans. He cannot read beyond the first stanza, 'Across the pale parabola of joy', and when fans ask for his autograph, he writes that stanza and signs).

I asked Dinesh, 'Does it really work?'

Dinesh said, 'One hundred per cent. I have used it many times. You will be awake like an owl. Even if you lie down and try to sleep, you can't.'

So we popped one each, read for a while in sitting postures, and then slowly slid onto our backs... and fell asleep. When I woke up, it was 7 a.m. I shook him up.

I shouted at him, I accused him of giving sleeping pills by mistake. He denied it. He said he didn't understand why it didn't work. We went unprepared and it was a disaster but not the end of the world, as it seemed at that time.

His theory was that my strong desire for sleep was so intense that it nullified the effects in both of us.

We used to do nights out during Maha-shivaratri in my younger years. My mother would tell us that we are expected to stay awake praying to Lord Shiva and immersed in his *bhajans* and *kirtans* and not by watching movies which would be screened the entire night on that day (Those days there was no TV). On normal days, you can stay awake till sunrise if India is playing cricket in West Indies and Sachin Tendulkar is going great guns, but if you are expected and required to stay awake, the toughest challenge will be to keep the eyes open.

One of my friends is a habitual drinker. When he travels by train, he says he doesn't have the urge to drink if he has a bottle packed in his suitcase. The reassuring thought that it is available, it seems, makes him feel at peace. But if, for some reason, he forgot to pack it, he has an insane urge to drink and would be willing to spend any amount of money for one bottle. Maybe it is the human nature.

My daughters inherited my habit of procrastination; they try to cover up and complete entire piled-up portions in one night. Their theory is that they would forget if they studied a week before the exams. Unlike me, they don't snooze for a few hours. They go to exam after a night out and score very good grades.

Maybe there is a method to the madness. In college, we used to cram as much material as possible in the brain so that it would be waiting at the tip of our noses. In the exam hall, we sneezed and filled up answer sheets with all the data collected in a heap when we sneezed. Once we came out of the exam hall, brain was relaxed and memory of previous exam was deleted, making space for the next exam material.

COMBINED STUDIES

People would like to watch horror movies in a group; not many would relish watching a horror movie alone, with few exceptions like my elder daughter and me. When you are frightened out of your wits, you can always have the comfort of reality check. You feel less scared if you have someone beside you whom you can ask if they locked the front door properly, switched the gas off, or have they completed assignment or did the girlfriend reply.

Basic principle of combined studies is same. You are scared at the enormous volume of accumulated material to study. If you have a group of three or four friends who are equally scared, it gives you confidence that you are not alone.

Theoretically, combined studies are fail-safe. A group of friends congregate and study together. When one of them has a doubt, others clarify. One does not get stranded, unlike, when reading alone. Each friend reads a couple of chapters and explains to others. So studies should proceed smoothly, efficiently benefitting one and all.

But practically, it is anything but fail-safe. Main culprits are 'moods' and smokers. In our combined studies group, we were four: Eashwar, Bikki Mubber, Jeella Babu and I. We were all from mechanical and mech marine departments. Though Anil was also from mech marine, he was an 'A' grader, and like all 'A' graders, he would hunt alone.

We would plan to start at 6 p.m. We promised each other that we would study seriously without indulging in gossip, discussions about movies, cricket and other topics. Invariably, the quantum and quality of studies would be far from satisfactory. Tea breaks, cigarette breaks, waiting time for the 'mood' to set in, Hema Malini, Jaya Prada, Gavaskar, G.R.Viswanath, several others, and other aspects make us lose focus.

Before going to exam, we all agreed that combined studies are a bad idea and in the future, we should study alone. Come next exam, we all huddle together again; fear factor brought us together.

We used to meet at 6 p.m. at Jeella Babu's house (his dad was an officer in Indian Railways and was allotted an independent house; Babu had a room of his own). We decided who would read which chapters and we planned to complete by 8 p.m., take dinner break, meet again at 9 p.m., and continue till morning.

In all earnest, we study for a full fifteen minutes when Eashwar says he is too tensed up and wants to smoke a cigarette. One by one, all would accompany him. A five minute break would not do much harm.

When Eashwar is smoking and others are walking and talking about new released movies, I suggest we have tea. We proceed to Apparao's tea shop, sip one-meter tea, and when we come back, time is 6.45 p.m (Apparao had a technique of pouring tea from one container to another, quite fast, increasing the distance between the containers to more than a meter). We are rattled and warn each other to be serious and again proceed to study.

Suddenly, Bikki Mubber would recollect a funny incident and another fifteen minutes and momentum would be lost. Then it is time for dinner break.

On resuming after break, after thirty minutes Eashwar says to hell with it, he is sleepy and asks others to wake him up at 2 a.m. or to study hard and explain everything to him in the morning. If you've noticed, a sleeping person induces envy and drowsiness in others who are trying to stay awake.

One by one wickets fall. Each feeling that he could study while reclining on the bed, and eventually going to sleep. Only Jeella Babu would fight and would be the last person to sleep and the first to get up.

It may not be as bad as this, since all of us managed to get many 'B' and few 'C' grades.

Worse was when all of us decide that since it was impossible to complete the portion anyway, we might as well go to a second-show movie to relax and overcome tension and anxiety. As luck would have it, we always ran into the lecturers who taught us the subject for the next day's exam. Our feeble explanations that we studied hard and prepared well for the exam and came to watch a movie for relaxation did not cut any ice with them. They always seemed skeptical.

On one occasion, metallurgy lecturer could not control his curiosity. He walked over to us during the interval time and asked, 'Why do you have such contempt for my subject, metallurgy? Don't you know, without metallurgy, engineering is nothing?'

Eashwar thought he was reassuring him when he said, 'No, sir, we don't have contempt only for metallurgy.'

Though he meant that we treated all subjects equally and impartially, it sounded as if we had contempt for all subjects.

I cleared my throat and asked him, 'Sir, why do you say that? We love metallurgy.'

He glared at us. 'Do you? Then why do I always find you in movie theatres a day before the exam in my subject?' he asked.

Bikki Mubber said confidently, 'Sir, tomorrow's exam is in Theory of Machines, not metallurgy.'

The lecturer fired at us non-stop for ten minutes. 'So you have been bunking classes for many days. You are not even aware that the timetable has been changed. Tomorrow's exam is in metallurgy, Theory of Machines is the last exam. You people don't even have the curiosity to ask friends…'

We didn't watch the second half of the movie. We rushed back, tried to focus on reading metallurgy.

Once, during one of our many tea breaks, Jeella Babu said, 'I feel cheated.'

We asked him why.

He said, 'I stood in queue for several hours and was the first to enter the hall on first day when the movie *Kabhi Kabhi* was released.'

'Did you buy the ticket in black? He charged exorbitant money?' I asked.

'No, you don't understand. Have you seen the movie? *Kabhi kabhie mere dil mein…* song?' he asked.

'Yes, that is the highlight of the movie. Mukesh was outstanding,' I said.

'No. I am referring to the song Rakhi sings on wedding night. *"Suhhag raat hai ghoonghat utha raha hoon main"*'(It is nuptial night and I am lifting up your veil). 'Shashi Kapoor sings but he doesn't lift *ghoonghat*,' he said as if complaining.

I was puzzled. 'What are you talking about? Of course he lifts *ghoonghat* [veil],' I said.

Jeella Babu was silent for few minutes.

'Ohhh…that is called *ghoonghat*?' he said as if a mystery was cleared.

'What else did you think *ghoonghat* was?' I asked him, still mystified.

He slowly said in a low voice, 'Petticoat.'

We laughed and laughed until our stomachs ached and tears rolled down our cheeks. Had we been in the house, we would have probably rolled down on the floor.

Jeella Babu didn't find it funny and was hurt. He was morose and accused us of making fun of him; he lectured us on how we should be sympathetic to people who learnt only the Hindi alphabet in village schools. If our schooling was not in a city but in a small village, we also would be as ignorant.

I tried to keep a sober face but it was impossible. Even now, if I meet him, I don't think I can control my laughter.

In engineering first year, all subjects were common for all the branches. From the second year, we went to different classrooms and sections. But mathematics was common to all branches. Dinesh worked in colour lab (movie processing lab) for two years after the high school, so he was completely out of touch.

Mathematics was quite advanced and he was unable to cope up. I used to teach him and in that process, I was learning. He is very grateful, and even now when we meet, he says he would have still been stranded if I had not assisted him. He says he dreams about staring blankly at a question paper with a thudding heart since he feels as if he is looking at

French script. Suddenly he wakes up in cold sweat and relief floods him when he realizes it is only a dream.

So when I stayed with my brother and sister-in-law, he would come for combined studies. My brother was in the night shift. He would leave after midnight and come back the next day at noon. My sister-in-law went to her parents' house for a few months.

That night we went to a Dracula movie (Christopher Lee), studied for a few hours, and went to sleep. After a few hours, Dinesh got up, as he was thirsty. The room was completely dark. He was paralyzed in shock and fear as he saw a white ghost crouching as if ready to jump. He sat still, sweating. Ghost also was not moving, as if waiting for him to make a move.

He whispered quietly, 'Girisam, get up... there is a ghost on your left.' I didn't stir. Once I fall asleep, it is not so easy to wake me up.

The problem was that the ghost was sitting right underneath the light switch. If he had to switch on the light, he had to reach above the ghost.

He knew that he could not expect any help from me and that my brother would come only after daybreak.

He could not wait forever. So he invoked Lord Hanuman, jumped, ran to the light switch, and switched it on in a jiffy. My brother's white lungi was draped on an egg-shaped dirty clothes basket woven with bamboo strips.

My brother shifted to another rented house. Dinesh helped us in loading and unloading all household articles. After dumping everything in the new house, my brother went to work. He was in the second shift, i.e. 2 p.m. to midnight.

Dinesh and I unpacked and arranged all the items. Finally, we fixed the ceiling fans, given electric connections and switched on and tested regulators. Everything was fine.

'Okay, now let us fix the fan blades,' I told him. I was sweating profusely and desperately longed for cool air. Our idea was to complete unpacking, switch on the fan, and study for next day's exam.

We could not find the fan blades. We searched every square inch and opened and checked all boxes. We were baffled, since my theory that we could have forgotten to unload the fan blades was dismissed by Dinesh.

'I distinctly remember, your brother was carrying fan blades and walking into the house as I crossed him to bring some other item from the truck,' Dinesh said firmly.

We scratched our heads. It was maddeningly irritating that we could not locate items as big as ceiling fan blades. It is impossible to hide them even if one wanted to.

I remember Dinesh climbing on a chair and peeping in the ventilator.

'Are you mad? Why would my brother keep the fan blades in such an inaccessible place?' I asked him.

We were frustrated, irritated, and demoralized. Dinesh refused to go home; he said that he would not be able to sleep until the 'mystery of missing fan blades' was solved.

He even asked me if it was possible that my brother could have thrown the fan blades in the well in the backyard.

'Why would he do that?' I asked him.

'You once told me one of your uncles is potty,' he mumbled.

When my brother came after midnight, he was shocked to see us awake.

'Where did you hide the ceiling fan blades?' I asked him. 'We have been searching for hours.'

He went into kitchen, pulled the gas cylinder. Fan blades were behind the cylinder. He kept the fan blades propped on the kitchen wall and on the next trip he brought the gas cylinder and put it in front of the blades, covering them.

On another occasion, we had to read many chapters of industrial psychology. We had neglected it since it was not a main-stream subject. Eashwar came to my hostel after dinner. The others were not there.

After studying for a couple of hours, I felt very sleepy. I told him to wake me up at 2 a.m. and then he could sleep.

He did not wake me up. When I woke up on my own, the sun was already scorching the world, and Eashwar was sitting at the table and studying in the same posture that I had seen him in before going to sleep.

I did not even go to brush my teeth; I yelled at him, I called him a traitor, *mitra drohi*, selfish, cunning, and a snake. When I ran out of breath and expletives, he turned towards me. Until then, I was only seeing his left profile. When he turned towards me, I stared at him.

His other cheek had bloated like a balloon, almost closing his eye. My first thought was that he must have gone out and teased a lady Olympic boxer but it seemed unlikely.

I asked him, 'What happened? Why didn't you wake me up if someone was bashing you?'

He coolly told me, 'You slapped me.'

My jaw dropped. 'Impossible. I can't even swat a fly. Moreover, I was fast asleep. From the way your cheek looks, someone had used entire strength behind that blow.'

He said, 'I was feeling very sleepy. Somehow, I managed to stay awake till 2 a.m., since I promised you. I tried to wake you up by tapping on your shoulder, you sat up, pulled your arm as far back as it would go and swung your arm in an arc, gave a massive slap, and went back to sleep. I thought I would faint as your hand landed on my cheek. Thousands of stars sparkled and birds tweeted, and I was instantly awake and all traces of sleep vanished. I did not dare wake you up again and completed reading entire portion.'

I apologized profusely. He was quite gallant. I came after a quick shower and he taught me what he read the whole night in two hours. My relaxed brain absorbed it like a sponge.

Ironically, I scored better than he did. He actually felt happy. He said it was a tribute to his teaching skills; he could cram so much information in such a short time, into a peanut-sized brain like mine.

Tailpiece:

There were two blackboards in the classroom, on opposite walls. Anil and I wrote the names of the latest movies of that time and correlated the subjects on the unused blackboard when no one was there. We expected outrage and censure from lecturers but were surprised that all lecturers including the head of the department had a good laugh. That was not erased for a very long time and we kept adding.

Movie name	Subject
The Good, the Bad, and the Ugly	Strength of Materials 1,2,3
For a Few Marks (dollars) More	Machine Design (The lecturer was thrifty in awarding marks.)
Fistful of Marks (dollars)	Electrical Technology
Hang 'Em High	Metallurgy
Blind Terror	Theory of Machines
Wait until Dark	Marine Machinery (The lecturer would come only after 6 p.m.)
Count Dracula	Industrial Psychology (The lecturer had fangs like teeth)
Dracula Has Risen from the Grave	Managerial Economics (Same lecturer)
Venkanna's (McKenna's) Gold	Building Materials (Lecturer was very liberal.)
Vengeance of She	Electronics (only lady lecturer)

Gods Must Be Crazy	Mathematics I (Professor was kind-hearted and never noticed when we escaped to the canteen after giving the attendance).
Chitty Chitty Bang Bang	Mathematics II (Professor had a vintage car like in the movie.)
Russians are coming, Russians are coming	Production Technology I (The lecturer Polonkov was fond of referring to Russian textbooks.)
Dr Zhivago	Production Technology II

Smooth Sailing... Almost

GOLDEN DAYS AS A
JUNIOR ENGINEER

In this folder, I have written all pleasant memories of sailing as a junior engineer and also with the family.

I was very fortunate to have excellent support and encouragement from all the officers and crew of my first ship. That factor alone can make or break a career in shipping.

You are leaving the comfort zone of a family, friends, and Mother Earth and venturing into a realm of unknown spheres, literally and figuratively. Some of my friends quit sea life after some traumatic experiences, not with machinery or ship, but with the colleagues and superiors.

I wish to give a brief introduction to some terminology of shipping for the benefit of readers not conversant with shipping.

Most of you have seen the Hollywood movie *Titanic*.

Imagine yourself standing at bow of the ship with hands stretched out and feeling fresh air and warm sunshine like in that famous scene in that movie (Kate Winslet or Leonardo DiCaprio as your gender may be).

Your left-hand side is called port side and right-hand side is called starboard side (I use abbreviation 'stbd' for 'starboard').

Simply put, when you are facing forward, the left side is port and the right side is stbd. Where you were standing with arms stretched out is called the bow of the ship.

Where Kate Winslet wants to jump and commit suicide is called the stern of the ship.

When the ship is going forward, it is called ahead.

When the ship is going in reverse (backward), it is called astern.

Like your cars have steering wheels, ships also have steering wheels. Steering wheels move the rudders. Rudders change the direction.

When you turn the steering wheel full to the left, it is called giving hard a port and to the right, hard a stbd.

Propeller turns, giving momentum to the ship. It can be turned in either direction at varying speeds as required. This speed is controlled by giving command to increase or decrease rpm (revolutions per minute) of propeller.

There are several tanks provided in ship for storage of fuel, fresh water and seawater. When the ship is loaded, the tanks containing seawater are emptied (These tanks are called ballast tanks). When cargo is removed, the ship would become light, so seawater is filled in these tanks to keep the propeller submerged in the water and also to maintain the stability of the ship.

Pumping in water is called ballasting; pumping out water is called deballasting.

Ballast voyage is when ship's holds are empty and the ship is going for loading cargo.

Loaded or laden voyage is when the ship's holds are filled with cargo.

Like you fill your car tank with gas, ships have several storage tanks situated in different locations to store fuel. The operation of receiving fuel into the tanks is called bunkering. Ships require thousands of metric tons of fuel for voyages. Some ships consume several hundreds of metric tons of fuel per day.

I hope this terminology will be helpful.

LUCKY BREAK

I was born lazy. Not that I am proud of it. Far from it—I feel guilty, ashamed and every day I vow to shed laziness like a wet dog shaking off water. The only problem is that I postpone it to the next day. As they say, tomorrow never comes.

When I was in the third year of my mechanical engineering studies, I suddenly saw that there were two vacancies in the marine engineering course. Two students developed cold feet when they learned of rough seas, seasickness, and other unsavoury aspects of sailing and wanted to change over to the mechanical stream. My good friend Eashwar and I decided to jump just for the fun of it. Anil, was in the marine engineering course and he would tempt us with accounts of glory, adventure, and visits to exciting and exotic places all over the world. All of which are by-products of a career in shipping. What appealed to my lazy mind was that jobs were aplenty and there was no need to apply for jobs, or appear for interviews.

So we switched over to marine engineering. After graduation, we did the compulsory training in shipyard, which we enjoyed to the hilt.

We were supposed to learn all aspects of shipping at the shipyard during six months of training. No one there had the patience or the time to teach us and shooed us away. So we used to go at 7.30 a.m., loiter around, have subsidized coffee, snacks, lunch, kill time, and go home at 5.00 p.m. Tea would cost three paisa, coffee twelve paisa, breakfast twenty five paisa, and lunch fifty paisa. We used to buy coupons every month.

Though we were not paid, attendance was compulsory. Every morning, afternoon, and evening, we had to sign in the register. The training officer was present only during the afternoon. Someone had a brainwave. We decided to work in shifts. In the morning, half the batch would go at 7.30 a.m and sign in for everyone (The training officer would not be there, so we bribed the peon). At lunchtime, all of us would be present, sign in front of the training officer. Then the morning batch would leave and the second batch would sign for all in the evening. We practiced each other's signatures and kept it very simplified.

Sometimes, guilt would gnaw at our hearts. And like a fever, the enthusiasm would last a few days, during which period we tried to learn everything about shipbuilding from laying the keel to delivery of the ship. We would burn with enthusiasm, go to the library, read manuals, go to the dry dock, and pester the machine operators to death. Then, as suddenly as it started, the fever would go down and we would go back to playing cards under the trees, gossiping, and catching naps in nooks and corners.

That was a very enjoyable transition phase. No college, no tests, no tensions. and no responsibilities. We had to live within our meagre budgets (money sent from home). We managed to squeeze in a lot of fun and laughter. After the training was over, the harsh realities of life stared us in the face.

The worst phase of recession in shipping had just begun. Jobs were drying up. There were about ten Indian shipping companies. All of them had sent regret letters but promised to employ us when vacancies arose. Damodar, Chougule, India Steamship, Scindia, Mogul Line, and Dempo—every company was prompt in sending regret letters.

Just when I was giving up hope, one shipping company sent an interview letter. I jumped in joy. My uncle's (dad's brother) close friend was a top boss in that company. So my dad gave me a letter to Mr. Swamy, my mother gave three big jars of pickles for uncle's family, and I boarded the train to Bombay in the scorching heat of May.

I got down in Dadar the next day and asked for directions to go to Chembur. I was directed to go to some other platform, catch a train to Kurla, and again change to another train to Chembur.

'It is not far, only a few stations away,' they assured me. But I had to climb up and down hundreds of steps with pickles weighing a ton. I climbed up what looked like *Galigopuram* at Tirupati shrine, got down to another platform, boarded the train to Kurla, and repeated the same exercise at Kurla and Chembur. By the time I came out of Chembur station, I was mad with hunger and anger. I resisted the impulse to dump the pickles in the garbage bin and got into a taxi. Bombay taxi drivers are good. They never grumble. He took me to my uncle's apartment.

Now the proverbial straw on the camel's back—my uncle's flat was on the third floor ... but no elevator. I was panting like a dog by the time I reached his flat and pressed the buzzer. My cousin opened the door and invited me in.

She was very beautiful, like Aishwarya Rai. She was very fair, with light-coloured eyes and was a double doctorate in economics. My uncle had passed away several years back. My aunt and cousin warmly welcomed me. I took a much needed shower, had lunch, and hit the sack. When I woke up, it was already dark.

My cousin took me to Mr. Swamy's house. He received us well. I gave my dad's letter to him. He gave it a cursory glance and returned it.

'Don't worry, go and celebrate. I will make a few calls. You are selected. Your uncle Raju was my best friend,' he said. We thanked him and came out. I was on cloud nine. My sister was also happy.

The next day, I went to the shipping company building promptly at 9.30 a.m. I was surprised to see many people, including a few from my batch. I tried to look as worried and tense as them, trying to disguise my confidence.

My name was called. I entered, wondering how I should react to an offer of coffee or tea. I expected the interviewer to hug me, shake hands, and ask me to sign on the dotted line. But the interviewer resembled an irritable bulldog with constipation, badly ticked off by his wife. There was no warmth or friendliness visible on his countenance. He looked at my application form; I expected his eyes to widen and a smile to replace his scowl, since he was sure to recognize that I was the one recommended by Mr. Swamy.

The scowl remained in place as he started bombarding me with questions: How do you de-sludge a purifier, How do you blow down a boiler, How do you prevent crankcase explosion, What will you do if it occurs? I knew partial answers to some, none to many. Then he donned the avatar of Narasimha about to tear Hiranyakashipu apart.

For those not familiar with Hindu mythology, Hiranyakashipu was a demon king who worshipped Lord Shiva with great devotion. Lord Shiva was pleased and appeared before him and granted him a boon. Hiranyakashipu asked for a boon of immortality.

Lord Shiva told him that he could not be granted immortality but Ravana can re-phrase his request to cover all angles of death.

Hiranyakashipu thought for a while and asked that he should not get killed by a human or a beast, within a house or outside the house, during the day or at night, on the earth or in the sky, and not by any weapon. He thought he covered all possible ways to cheat death.

Lord Vishnu incarnates in the form of Narasimha (lion-faced man, neither man nor beast), carries Hiranyakashipu and sits on the threshold of the house (neither in the house nor outside) during sunset time (neither day nor night), stretches him on his lap (neither on earth nor in sky), and tears his stomach with his nails (not any weapon), and kills him.

'You lot, you never bother to learn, what did you learn in the shipyard? I know what you must have done, slept off under the trees, smoked, and played cards. I don't know what will happen to this country ...' He described our activities very accurately, since he must also have done the same in his time. After a while he ran out of steam and waved me out.

I came out dazed and collapsed in a chair. My batch mate, one P. Swami, anxiously asked me what had happened. I told him. His face was ashen. In training days if I was 'bad', he was 'ugly' (reference is to the movie, 'The good, the bad and the ugly'). My conscience used to prick me once or twice a week and I would try to learn until the zeal and the steam ran out. I used to attend at least half a day of training. But P. Swami was hard-core, devoid of any feelings or sentiments. He would come to the shipyard at the lunchtime, have subsidized lunch, sign in the attendance register, and go out. His morning and evening signatures were taken care of by his friends. On the rare occasions that he spent a full day, he would be sleeping under a tree or playing cards.

His name was called and he went in. After ten minutes he came out, jubilant. He was selected. My jaw dropped. Surely he could not have answered all the questions.

He assured me that he did not. He laughed at my disbelief.

'He started shouting. I simply went on the other side of the table and fell at his feet. I told an emotional, tearful story about my poor father, who is a teacher with three daughters, and the plight of my family and my unmarried sisters. I told him that by giving me a job, he would be saving several families. Though he looks like a bulldog, he is very kind-hearted. He almost wept and would have adopted me had I shed a few more tears.' he said. I congratulated him and left desolately.

In the evening I went to Mr. Swamy's house with my cousin. Without batting an eyelid, he told me, 'Oh, I completely forgot about you. What happened? Were you selected?'

I told him that I was not selected, and if he could put in a word now, it might not be too late.

'No, no. It is of no use. Try other companies. I am sure you will get a job', he said. He was so casual and uninterested; I asked my sister if uncle and he were friends or enemies, after we came out.

She smiled. 'This is your first lesson in life. What people say and do are entirely different! Never go by the face value. What are you going to do?' she asked me.

'I don't know, maybe post-graduation or look for a shore job. My degree is basically in mechanical engineering,' I told her sadly.

The next day, I thanked my aunt and sister, took their leave and reached VT Station at noon. The scheduled departure of my train was at 3 p.m. As I was entering the station, I recollected that I had not visited one particular shipping office. In the preceding few days, I had visited all the shipping companies in Bombay that had sent me regret letters. All of them assured me that they would call when a vacancy arose.

The sun was scorching hot as it usually is in May. Like in the movies, the 'good' and the 'bad' images came out of my frame and started quarrelling. The bad (lazy) image was telling me that the sun was so hot and going to that shipping office was so futile and did I not learn a lesson even after receiving so many 'no's? The good image was reasoning that I could sleep as much as I wanted after boarding the train, but to visit the shipping office again, I would have to travel so far, besides what did I stand to lose, except a couple of litres of sweat?

I overruled the bad image, put plaster on its lips, checked my baggage in the cloakroom, and went to the office on Bank Street. I enquired and was directed to one Mr. Dhar.

I asked him if there was a vacancy for a fifth engineer and he said no. As I turned back and walked a few steps, he asked me, 'But we must have sent a regret letter.'

I said that I didn't receive one and that was the reason I wanted to check. Dhar called a peon and asked him to check in a file if a copy of my regret letter was there. My heart was thumping so loudly that I was scared the peon would hear. That shipping company was affiliated with a government department, which saved me. The peon flipped a few pages perfunctorily and told Dhar that it was not there.

Dhar checked my CV and sent me to one Mr. Om, technical superintendent. Within minutes, I was interviewed, selected and the appointment letter was given.

I rushed back to VT Station, cleared my baggage from the cloakroom, and boarded the train. I was in a daze and shock for several hours. I must have read the appointment letter hundreds of times to convince myself that I was not dreaming.

Joining Ship

I thought that nothing could be worse than the summer in Bombay during May. Madras (Chennai's name in those days) took offence and roasted me in June as I went to the agent's office to complete the ship-joining formalities.

The agent dropped me at the gangway of the ship and left. I looked up and the gangway seemed to be set at 90° to the vertical to test my stamina and strength. The ship looked huge (Later, I was C/E in ships six to eight times larger). I huffed and puffed and dragged my heavy luggage (uniforms, boiler suits, warm clothing, pickles and books) and managed to reach the peak.

My heart was beating fast not only from exertion but also from anxiety. All the stories of how the tough second engineers make fifth engineers wish they were not born were playing endlessly in my mind. I was praying to all the gods to grant me a kind-hearted second engineer (graduate, if possible, but I should not be too greedy while asking gods for favours) and entered the accommodation from the main deck. The sudden A/C cool air felt wonderful. As I looked at the deserted alleyways, I found a door saying 'Engine Room'.

I opened the door and saw a man in a white boiler suit, white cap and sporting a walrus moustache. He was putting on his shoes.

'Excuse me, sir, where can I find the second engineer?' I asked him timidly. He looked me up and down.

'I am R.Khanna, second engineer, what do you want?' He had grapes in his right hand.

My mouth ran dry. I did not know whether to shake hands (he had grapes) or smile and say hello (he might take offence) and I did nothing. So, I stood there gulping.

'Don't tell me you are the new fifth engineer?' he exclaimed.

'Yes, sir, I am,' I replied in relief.

'My God, what specimens the company sends! Okay, keep your luggage in the cabin, give your documents to the purser and report to the engine room in...' he looked at his watch, 'in fifteen minutes.'

I said, 'Yes, sir,' and came out and was lost. There was no one around; all the alleyways were deserted. I did not know where my cabin was and whom to ask. Then in the duty mess, I found one very drunk steward. Luckily he was our deck steward. So, he guided me to my cabin, I changed into the boiler suit, went on the bridge, gave my documents to the purser, one Mr. Mallik.(It is surprising how I remember the faces and names of everyone on my first ship but have difficulty in recollecting people of my last few ships).

Then I rushed to the engine room. The engine room was like an oven. Within seconds, I was lost. I caught hold of an oilman and asked him to take me to the second engineer. He walked me through what looked like an intricate maze of pipes, machinery and into the cool air-conditioned engine control room. There, second, third and fourth engineers, and electrical officers were having tea and talking about general topics.

I shook hands with them and introduced myself. They looked curiously at me as if I were a rare specimen.

I made myself tea and sat at the table.

I will use abbreviations C/E,2/E,3/E,4/E and 5/E(engineers), E/O (electrical officer), R/O (radio officer) to make writing less tedious.

There are many similarities between a new daughter-in-law and a brand-new 5/E joining a ship. The difference being, the new daughter-in-law will have one mother-in-law but a new

5/E will have more than two. The 2/E is the main mother-in-law, directly in charge of disciplining and educating (read harassing and tormenting) 5/Es. C/E is the chief mother-in-law to whom 2/E reports about the commissions and omissions of 5/Es. If 5/E is lucky, the captains can be benevolent observers like a fathers-in-law or else they can join the mother-in-law brigade, hell-bent on disciplining the new breed.

Then 3/E, 4/E, and E/O take on the mantle of the husband's sisters. This breed can be very sadistic and derive vicarious pleasure in the discomfort of 5/Es; they keep filling the mother-in-law's ears about the misdeeds and mischief of poor 5/Es. In case of a new daughter-in-law, the husband's sisters, especially if unmarried, can be a real pain in the neck and elsewhere, they keep harping on their brother, 'You have changed a lot after marriage, you used to be so affectionate,' thus forcing the poor man to take them to the movies and shopping, all the while neglecting his poor wife.

Then the engine crew takes the role of servant maids and cooks, who act as spies and whisper in the ears of the mothers-in-law about the negligence, laziness, or carelessness of 5/E, like how he didn't clean the filters, though he told you that he had done it, how he was goofing instead of tracing pipelines and how he was taking naps behind the switchboards. In daughter-in-law's parlance, it is the equivalent of being slow in bringing in the laundry when it rained, not watching over boiling milk, and being careless while peeling potatoes so that one fourth kg curry resulted from a kg of potatoes.

But the similarities end here. A 5/E has the advantage that he is not landed for life with the monsters-in-law. If he weathers the storm or is patient, either they or he will sign off. Once he is eventually accepted, he will be promoted to the in-law status; whereas a new daughter-in-law will either be trampled into submission or fight like Lady Lara Croft or Rani Laxmi Bai to assert her rights (as in *Seeta aur Geeta* and other such movies).

Then 2/E asked me the question I was dreading.

'Are you a graduate?'

I took a deep breath and said, 'Yes, sir, BE (Mech-Marine),' and waited with bated breath.

'See how lucky he is? When I joined, I was the only graduate and what a tough time I had! Now except C/E and Pal, all of them are graduates,' he told the others. I almost jumped in joy and would have broken into a dance had I been alone.

'Who is Pal?' I asked 4/E in a low voice.

'He is the other 5/E. C/E is ex-Indian Navy,' he replied, elaborating on 2/E's remark.

'Now you go to your cabin and relax. Report at 6 p.m. From today you are on night watch,' 2/E told me.

I thanked him and left. I was determined not to get lost in the jungle of machines, pipelines and equipment and to reach my cabin without seeking help from anyone.

I kept going in circles, reaching the same place every time and one oiler who was working at one place asked me rather tactlessly if I was lost and needed help. I tactfully replied that I was checking some machines and managed to avoid him in the next round and ended at the boiler platform. Finally, I managed to extricate myself from the tentacles and reached my cabin.

I unlocked the door, entered and felt like I was in heaven. I loved my room. It was to be my home for the next twenty months. It was small and compact, with a bed, a sofa, a writing table, a few chairs, and attached bathroom. I was whistling as I unpacked; this was the luxury that I had lacked. Ours is a large family, four brothers and one sister, and though we were not living in cramped quarters, I never had a room of my own. Though I lived in hostels, the common bathrooms and waiting for turns was tiresome.

Here I had a room completely to myself and I enjoyed the luxurious feeling. The best feature (which was absent in all my other ships, including when I was C/E) was the calling bell placed next to the bed, which summoned the steward. When I got up, I had to just stretch my hand and press it and the steward would come with a tea tray in ten minutes. That was a luxury I never had in any other ship.

I unpacked, got a few hours' sleep and went to the engine room thirty minutes before I was due. I made allowance for my getting lost in the maze. I went to ECR (engine control room); no one was there. Pal and the oilers were nowhere to be seen. I came out of ECR and was looking around when a blur of movement caught my eye.

I looked up and my jaw dropped as I saw a figure sliding along the railings of the staircase. He was holding the rails and with both feet in air he slid: zip… zip… zip… he stood in front of me in a few seconds with a big smile.

'Hi, I am Pal, 5/E,' he extended his hand.

'Hi, I am Girisam, new 5/E. If you slipped, you could have broken a few bones. Tell me, why were you sliding?' I shook his hand and asked him, puzzled.

He laughed. 'While going up, you have to climb, there is no option, but we can save energy and time while coming down. I will teach you. Next week, you will also be doing same,' he said as we entered ECR.

I looked at him curiously. He had Chinese eyes and was short and athletic. He had a typical British, clipped accent. It was so incongruous. He smiled.

'I know what you want to ask though you are hesitating to do so. My Chinky eyes—my mother was from Burma and dad was from Calcutta,' he told me.

'Was?' I asked hesitantly.

'I am an orphan. They are no more,' he said.

'I am sorry,' I said. We were silent for a few minutes. I didn't know how to break the awkward silence.

'Apart from sliding down stairs like Spider-man, what are the other skills you have?' I asked him.

He asked me to lift my hands. I did. With his forefinger he pressed a spot in my ribs, and I was paralyzed. I could not move a finger and I could not even scream. He removed his finger, and as I rubbed the spot, I asked him in amazement what it was.

'Karate. I am a black belt. With a light chop on your neck I can make you unconscious,' he told me casually. I said, 'Wow,' impressed. After a few minutes of apprising me about the ship, he left.

After twenty months, when I went home, I promptly joined a taekwondo school and attended the school regularly, religiously for a month, until one day the instructor made us carry our partner on our shoulders for a full round of the ground. First, I had to sit on the shoulders of my partner, a thin, lanky Muslim teenager, with my legs wrapped around his neck.

All the time he was carrying me, I was scared he would stumble and I would fall flat and break my nose and a few bones. That boy was cursing me, why I was so fat (I was not, in those days I was slim) and why I couldn't be a few kilos lighter. I thanked him and God when he safely deposited me after an anxious ride.

Then I carried him. I found his manner irritating and insulting. He was acting as if he was a king and I was his horse. He was enjoying the ride and was urging me to gallop and overtake others. So, that was the end of my taekwondo ambitions.

I am an enthusiastic starter but a poor finisher. I start something with gusto, pursue it with vigour and enthusiasm for some time, until the enthusiasm wanes. I tried to fool myself and others that it was due to my sailing; had I been employed ashore, I would have pursued them to the end.

My wife gets mad with the piling up of semi-used, unused, and intended-to-be-used-in-the-future products. To make matters worse, though my daughters inherited their mother's beauty, they refused to download her enthusiasm, capacity for hard work, or her active lifestyle. Instead, they downloaded the latest, upgraded version of my laziness, procrastination, and 'five minutes more sleep' attitudes. Their software has additional packages of no remorse, feelings of guilt, or other nonsensical sentiments.

My younger daughter is like a fly on a hot, sweaty summer day. Whatever you do, you can never discourage a fly from scrubbing its feet on your sweaty forehead, eyebrows, upper lip or make it stop its irritating droning sound. My daughter will never rest until you accede to whatever her current demand is.

She will drive her mother almost to tears (Dad is sailing most of the time, advising wife not to give in to her blackmail tactics). Once she gets what she demanded, her interest might not last even a few hours.

An easy Slim tea packet gathers dust after she consumes one teabag and she loses interest in it.

Then she hounded me till we bought a guitar after browsing through several shops. She attended one class at Mellowing Musical Institute and lost interest in the thing. Since then, the ungainly, hideous guitar developed a nasty habit of lodging itself where you want to sit or lie down. If you want to sit in the sofa, it is there; you want to lie down on the settee, and it rushes there before you. When you want to sleep on the bed, some instinct makes you look at the bed before you crash on it, and there it is, lying sideways, occupying the entire length and breadth of the bed.

I managed to convince one of my elder daughter's friends to take it. He promptly returned it after a few days, perhaps, after his neighbours complained to the police that sounds of women being murdered and tortured were emanating from his flat, mistaking the awful ruckus this sadist instrument was making, for those.

After its return, it has learned a few new tricks. It keeps quiet for the whole day; when it is past midnight, it incites my younger daughter to strum it. It enjoys when my wife, her brother, and my daughters have a big fight.

My younger daughter was enthusiastic about karate (I paid fee for full three months and she attended just one day), tennis (one week), veena (this lasted surprisingly longer), and several others. When reminded about the colossal amount of money wasted, she tells us to to keep a record of all expenditure; and that she would repay it with interest after she is employed.

But my wife somehow managed to stand firm and say no to her demands for a puppy. She managed to divert her with a newborn chicken (on rental basis) or fish or tortoise or rabbit.

My wife, poor lady, has to deal with not one, but three specimens. My daughters have a fixed belief that one needs to sleep till ten minutes before actual time to leave the house. Every day there is a mad rush, panic to find towels, hair clips, hair dryer, shampoo, black leggings or green top, earrings, and finally ID cards.

After the kids leave, the house resembles a battlefield. Clothes are flung everywhere, all items helter-skelter. It would take my wife a full two hours to get things back to normal.

Be that as it may, after Pal left, I decided to get the hang of the engine room. I wanted to reach ECR from any point without getting lost. That was my project for the night. Duty oilman was an old Muslim man, who lectured me about character, conduct, and the evils of alcohol. After roaming for a few hours in the engine room, I got the hang of the layout.

When I was having tea at 9 p.m, the phone rang. I answered.

'Good evening, ECR,' I said.

'This is Chief Engineer. Who is this?'

'Sir, I am Girisam, new 5/E,' I said politely.

'Girisam, see and tell me the position of the telegraph,' C/E asked me.

I thought telegraph was a file or something like a telegram. I looked around and told him that I could not see telegraph.

Here, I should explain what a telegraph is. In the movie *Titanic*, when the ship collides with the iceberg, the navigating officer moves the handle of an instrument to stop and then moves it again to another direction. Then they show the engine room, where they also move it and the propeller stops and then it turns in the reverse direction. That instrument is called a telegraph. Navigating officer moves the telegraph to the speed he wants: dead slow, slow, half, and full in either ahead or astern (reverse) directions. Then in the engine room, telegraph bell sounds continuously until Engineer acknowledges by moving his instrument handle to match and adjusts speed accordingly.

C/E blew his top. 'What? You can't see the telegraph? Are you blind? Ask the oilman to call me,' he yelled and put down the phone.

I called the oilman and asked him to call C/E. He called and told C/E that the telegraph was in the 'FWE' (Finished with Engine) position, put down the phone, and told me that C/E wanted me to go to his cabin.

I was sweating as I knocked on his door after a few minutes.

THE FIRST DAY

I knocked on C/E's door and waited. My heart was thumping loudly; I could not believe that within a few hours of joining, I had managed to get a meeting with C/E to get a pasting.

The door was opened by a very fair-complexioned, short lady holding a one-year-old boy.

'Yes?' she asked. For a crazy moment I wondered if India had advanced so much that a one-year-old kids' mother could become a chief engineer. Then realization dawned.

'Good evening, ma'am, Chief Engineer sir asked me to meet him,' I said politely.

'Oh, I see, you are...?' she asked.

'I am Girisam, the new fifth engineer, ma'am,' I told her.

'Are you a non-vegetarian? It is tough for vegetarians,' she said.

'I am a vegetarian, ma'am. But, no problem, I brought pickles from home. I will manage,' I told her.

She smiled.

She was smiling ear to ear as C/E entered from the bedroom, scowling.

As she was going into the bedroom, she told C/E, 'Listen, Nandu, this boy is a vegetarian. Be very gentle with him. These boys are very sensitive and get demoralized very fast.'

He told her, 'Yes, dear.' His original plan of having me fried in hot oil was doused with cold water by 'His Master's Voice.' When the door was opened, I saw a wig on his table. He glanced at it and was tempted to put it on, but decided against it.

C/E was very fair, like a European, and very bald. He was bald as an egg. His baldness was striking and attention-grabbing. When you come across bald people, some have other features like a bulbous nose, very bushy eyebrows, double chin, or elephantine ears to grab your attention rather than their bald pate. But anyone coming across C/E will look at his bald pate only and, while talking to him, cannot take their eyes away from it.

His wife, poor lady, could not escape from it. It must be depressing to have to look at it for the entire day, for in those days, C/Es were never supposed to go to the engine room. The 2/Es would feel insulted if C/E ever came to the engine room. So, C/Es were virtually confined to their cabins. His wife must have bought him that wig in a foreign country.

He had wanted to put on his wig and open the door but his wife, in her haste, had exposed her husband's bald pate to me. Now he wanted to get rid of me fast.

I looked at the floor while he gave me a mild dose of reprimands, informing me that he would keep a close watch on me and if I did not pick up in a month's time, I could pack my bags and go home. I assured him that I would not give him a chance to complain, wished him goodnight, and turned to go.

C/E's wife came out from the bedroom and told me, 'You take whatever you want from the chief steward. Badasaab [C/Es are called badasaab in Indian ships] will tell him tomorrow. Nandu, don't forget to tell chief steward tomorrow.' I could sense C/E grinding his teeth as he said, 'Yes, dear.'

I thanked her and wished them goodnight and went back to the engine room. After that day I did not see C/E without his wig, except once, when he came to ECR during an emergency and flung his wig on the ECR table. If he had hair he would have pulled it, so that was the best course of action available to him.

I could not find oiler Patel anywhere in the engine room. I searched for him everywhere and finally found him sleeping in a corner. I shook him up. He woke up startled and cursed me for disturbing his sleep.

I told him that he was on watch and he should not sleep. He laughed and told me not to teach him and to remember that I had not completed a day on ship, whereas he had been there for donkey's years. I resisted the impulse to tell him that was what made him one and I went to the ECR.

I was as nervous as a cat on a hot tin roof. Here I was in an engine room I knew nothing about, with a duty oiler lost in dreamless sleep and already warned and reprimanded by C/E. I was just counting seconds until midnight when the next oiler would come on duty. After what seemed like an interminable torture, finally, it was midnight and the next oiler came on duty, woke Patel up, and sent him to sleep in his cabin. I heaved a sigh of relief and went on deck to breathe fresh air.

Cranes were loading iron ore into the ship's holds. I peeped into the ship's office. The 2/O had switched off lights and was sleeping on the settee. I went on the deck. Seaman on duty greeted me and we chatted for a while.

I froze when I saw that the captain was returning from shore.

I whispered to the seaman, 'Have you seen that? Captain is coming up the gangway?'

He gave an uncomprehending look. 'So?' he asked.

'Are you not going to wake up the 2/O? Captain will hang him,' I told him urgently.

Seaman looked at me as if I were mad and asked 'Why should I wake him up? Poor fellow, he was out in the hot sun the whole day, shopping'.

I greeted the captain good evening as he came up. He nodded and I held my breath as he proceeded to the ship's office. I expected him to drag the 2/O by the collar of his boiler suit and jump on him with spiked boots for sleeping while on duty.

Nothing of that sort happened. Captain did not even switch on the light. He used a flashlight, quietly opened a drawer, took his cabin key, closed the drawer, and left like a cat.

I was still dazed when I returned to ECR and narrated the incident. The oiler felt that was normal.

'How can anyone remain awake, the whole night? Captain understands that,' he said and yawned. 'Okay. I am going to sleep. Don't hesitate to wake me up if you have any doubt.' he said. As he made to leave, I clutched his hand.

'How can you sleep? I am new here. At least for a few days, until I get the hang of things, stay awake,' I pleaded with him. He was unmoved. He said that there were alarms for everything and told me not to worry and he left, leaving me to my 'cat on a hot tin roof' routine. Fortunately, there were no alarms or any cause for anxiety.

At 4 a.m, the old Muslim oiler came on watch. Now, I was a little relaxed, since he had no intention of going to sleep. But he kept lecturing me about the evils of alcohol and virtues of pious living; I began to wonder if I preferred the sleeping oilers. Finally, my long vigil came to an end.

I stood outside and was looking at the stairs, waiting for Spider-man Pal. This time, he walked down the stairs. His eyes were red, face puffed up. He was in a foul mood due to a hangover. By his own admission, he had had too many drinks. Standing behind him, the oiler gestured to me 'I told you so, the evils of alcohol.'

Pal gave a cursory glance at all the gauges and instruments and, like Sarge in *Beetle Bailey* comics, shouted at me in my face, 'Why is A so less?'

I was puzzled. 'What is A?' I asked him. Now, Pal was furious.

'You don't know what A is? How can you be so stupid?' he yelled.

I told him that if he showed it to me once, I would never forget.

'You are the first person I have seen who does not know A,' he grumbled and took me out of ECR to the next deck.

'This is A,' he said, gesturing to two huge pressure vessels, which are called air bottles. Air compressors fill up air to 30 bar pressure, which is used to start the main and auxiliary engines.

I clutched my brow. 'Oh, you meant air? Air pressure in air bottles?' I asked.

'Thank God, at least you know now,' he said. His British accent made him swallow 'ir' from 'air'.

I learnt later that his mood would improve as the day progressed, and by evening, he would be jovial and effervescent. I learnt to be careful while dealing with him when he had just got up from sleep. In fact, I am always careful when waking up people who are fast asleep and those who have just woken up. Both can be dangerous, as I learnt in my college days.

I described in 'Golden College Days' how I slapped Eashwar when he tried to wake me up and I didn't even know that I did it.

I told Pal that from the next day I would be careful and would not depend on sleeping oilers. I went to my cabin, showered, had a hearty breakfast, and hit the sack. Prior to that day, if I was deprived of ten minutes of sleep from my quota of eight hours, my eyes would burn and I would be yawning the whole day, desperate to somehow regain those lost precious ten minutes. I skipped lunch and had nine hours of dreamless sleep.

That was my first day in my ship.

Practical Jokes

After I got up, I took a shower and went out. From the GPO (General Post Office) which was just outside the port, I called home and told my parents not to worry, I was fine, the ship was excellent, all the officers and crew were very friendly, and food was excellent.

I was ravenously hungry, since I had skipped lunch for sleep. I went to Saravana Bhavan and had sumptuous food and returned to the ship. I changed into a boiler suit and went to the engine room.

Pal was very relaxed and witty. There was no hint of his earlier crankiness. My heart sank when he gave me a list of jobs 2/E wanted me to complete.

'If you don't want to be called after watch, better complete all the jobs he has given,' he advised.

I panicked. 'It is impossible, how I can complete all these jobs?' I asked desperately.

Pal gave a few tips. All pipeline drawings were in a file in ECR. I could use them for guidance. To avoid creating a bad impression, he said, it is advisable to report to 2/E at 7 a.m, and explain to him the reasons for not completing any jobs left out.

By the time I finished dinner and had completed the minor jobs, it was 8 p.m. and oiler Patel came for watch, yawning. I showed him the list of jobs 2/E had given and he was very upset. He felt that he was being persecuted. He opened crankcase doors of one side of the main engine and told me he had done more than his share of work and went to sleep in his corner.

I opened the crankcase doors on the other side and looked at 2/E's job list. The second item was, tracing of pipelines and valves of the bilge system. I thought I should be able to finish it in half an hour. There would be a few pipelines and valves leading to the pump and the pump discharge going into a tank. Nothing simpler, I thought.

I took a flashlight and started from aft of the engine room. I crawled on my knees and identified the pipe from the bilge well to the bilge pump and the pump discharge line going into the bilge holding tank. I felt happy; this seemed to be an easy task, almost like a cakewalk.

The pump suction valve chest had a number of valves and each had a line going in different directions. I did not want to get my hands or boiler suit dirty, so I wanted to complete tracing lines from above. I randomly selected one pipeline and traced it. It went straight and then took a right turn. I bent and checked it with a flashlight.

It went underneath some pipes and came up. I started checking; it was going vertically up. I was puzzled as it kept going up and up and emerged on the main deck. When it ended up as an air vent of the cofferdam tank, I realized that the bilge pipe had fooled me and sent me on a wild goose chase.

I went back, removed my shoes, put on gum shoes, and lowered myself into the oily mess of engine room bilges and ran my hand along the errant pipe and found it took a left turn unobtrusively, acting falsely as if it was going up. This time I was not going to be fooled, so I ran my hand on it and moved along until it went crazy and developed many branches like a banyan tree.

After one hour, I was sweating like a police inspector general (PIG), tired, dirty, angry, and hungry. My sketch of pipelines resembled an octopus which had badly knotted, entangled, and twisted its tentacles. The ship was Polish built and the Polish are renowned for their love of vodka, so either the foreman had laid pipes when sozzled or had a pathological loathing for 5/Es. There was no other explanation for the senseless twists and turns.

The pipeline would go zigzag like a drunkard and for no apparent reason duck beneath a huge pipe and I had to crawl in oily bilges to see what it was up to. After a few feet it would again resurface. It seemed to wander aimlessly without any destination in mind, smack its brow for being foolish, and take a U-turn for a few feet and then turn right and vanish in a jungle of other pipes. One by one, I tried tracing the pipelines and abandoned them after a few metres. Only one pipeline seemed to be a teetotaller and sober; it went straight like an arrow and ended in port side forward bilge well.

I took a well-deserved tea break, and as I finished my tea, the phone rang. I picked it up.

'Good evening, engine room,' I said.

'Girisam, this is C/E. Take a flashlight and an adjustable spanner and come to accommodation A/C plant room,' C/E instructed, and disconnected the phone.

I had taken those items and was in a fix since I didn't know where the A/C room was. I only knew it was not in the engine room. I searched for Patel. He was not sleeping in his regular nook; he must have shifted elsewhere so that I wouldn't disturb him. I went to the crew recreation room, where a movie was playing on the TV screen and one fitter was dozing. I tapped him lightly on the shoulder and he woke up with a start. I apologized and asked him directions to go to the A/C plant room. He told me and went back to sleep.

C/E beamed happily when he saw me and nodded approvingly at my dirty boiler suit and disheveled appearance, when I entered the A/C room.

'I didn't expect to see you so soon; I thought you would be going in circles to find the A/C room,' he said as he took the flashlight and screw spanner from my hand. He fiddled around with some valves and nodded, satisfied.

I was staring at his wig. It was grotesque. He hadn't even donned it properly; it was skewed. I dragged away my eyes as he looked at me.

'Now, listen carefully. You should not breathe a word about this to anyone. Understood?' he asked me sternly.

I did not understand but I nodded.

'I will behead you and give your head to my son to play if you say a word to anyone.' He stressed the need for secrecy.

I assured him that my lips would be sealed, though I wondered what he had done.

Next day there was a big hue and cry. All the engineers' and engine crew's cabins were on the port side and the deck officers' and crew's cabins were on the starboard side. While port-side cabins were cozy and comfortable, the starboard side cabins had become warm from midnight.

Since I was on watch, I was grilled by the captain and C/O and let off the hook as I told them that I did not even know the location of the A/C room. For the next three days, it remained a mystery why their cabins were comfortable in the daytime but became warm after midnight. C/E got tired of his prank after three days since it lost its novelty and also it was tiresome for him to move about stealthily at midnight for this errand.

Engineers and navigating officers (deck officers) are strange bedfellows. They are like cats and dogs. They dislike each other immensely and lose no opportunity to deride each other. Yet they accept each other as a necessary nuisance.

The animosity has its origins from the days when ships with sails were replaced by ships powered by steam and diesel engines.

Navigating officers join as cadets after completing tenth standard. So, their academic qualifications are a butt of ridicule among engineers. But engineers, especially chief engineers, have to learn to eat humble pie as captains have full authority and command of the ship. Engineers are jealous of deck officers because of the glamorous nature of their job.

Any book, movie, or novel about ships will have deck officers dressed in spotless white uniforms and epaulettes as heroes. Engineers in dirty boiler suits are ignored.

Only exception was the movie *Sand Pebbles* starring Steve McQueen. I have seen that movie many times since the hero is an engineer.

Navigating officers are envious of engineers. Engineers can shift to shore jobs as there are many other opportunities for engineers ashore. Deck officers have very limited jobs ashore. Most of them have no option but to sail.

This could be compared to airlines. Pilots in their imperious uniforms dragging their luggage evoke awe and respect. No doubt they have huge responsibility of hundreds of passengers' safety. But their lives also depend on correct functioning of the equipment, which is ensured by maintenance engineers, the unsung heroes. They are never thanked for their excellent work, nor is their dedication acknowledged. All the credit is gobbled by the pilots like Bollywood stars getting all the accolades while the lyricist, choreographer, spot boys are ignored.

Anyway, after I returned to the engine room, I gave up the unequal struggle to trace the bilge line. In an exam, in spite of your best efforts, when you are unable to answer questions, in desperation you seek help from the friend in front of you and copy from his answer sheet, as a last resort. In the same fashion, I copied bilge line diagram from the plan Pal had showed me.

The next day, at 7 a.m, I entered ECR. All the engineers were having tea and planning their work for the day. The 2/E asked me if I had completed the assigned jobs and asked me for the bilge line diagram. I gave him the copied diagram.

He smiled and passed it on to others. They burst out laughing. I watched baffled, as they roared.

'Are you sure this is the layout of the bilge line?' 2/E asked me with a smile. I said yes.

Again they roared. 'Pal fooled you. He told us he would pull this prank. He made a fake drawing and was sure you would copy it,' 4/E said between peals of laughter.

I had no choice but to apologize and produce my entangled-octopus-leg drawing and explain that I had actually tried and failed.

The 2/E told me to come daily after breakfast and work till 9.30 a.m until I traced all the pipelines. He would assign one man to lift up the floor plates and to assist me.

Until then I was alone in the engine room with one oilman. When I came after breakfast, I was amazed to see the engine room teeming with people like bees in a beehive.

When I was chief engineer of the second largest bulk carrier in the world at that time, the ship's overall length was 324 metres. It could load more than 300,000 tons of iron ore and had a total complement of only 22 persons. Break up was like this:

Engine Department—C/E, 2/E, 3/E, E/O, 2 oilers, fitter, wiper
Total—8

Deck Department—Capt., C/O, 2/O, 3/O, bosun, 5 AB seamen
Total—10

Catering Department—Chief cook, second cook, 2 stewards
Total—4

In contrast, this ship, about 1/7 of the size, had 53 people. Break up was like this:

Engine Department—C/E, 2/E, 3/E, 4/E, 5/E (3 nos), E/O(2 nos), engine serang, engine cassab, 3 fitters, 3 oilers, 5 firemen
Total—21

Deck Department—Capt., C/O, 2/O, 3/O, 3 cadets, R/O(2 nos), purser, deck serang, deck cassab, carpenter, 3 sukhani, 5 seamen
Total—21

Catering Department—Chief steward, pantry man, chief cook, second cook, third cook, bhandari, asst. bhandari, 5 stewards
Total—12

I gave these statistics just for fun and for no other reason. The other ship was the latest with automation and UMS (Unmanned Machinery Spaces). Even so, 2 E/Os and 2 R/Os were superfluous in this ship.

After three days we sailed out to Rostock, then in East Germany...

FIRST EXPERIENCE
OF SEASICKNESS

F inally the ship completed loading iron ore and sailed out to East Germany.

Eashwar and I had laughed and ridiculed those two guys who wanted to shift to mechanical engineering from marine engineering and it is possible that they might have put a curse on us. We had made fun of their squeamishness about seasickness, rough seas.

The moment the ship left the protected waters of Madras harbour, she started dancing waltz, *kathakali, kuchipudi, bharatanatyam, odissi,* and though we didn't know it at that time, a few steps of break-dance also.

Charlie Chaplin, in one of his movies, sails in a ship. When the ship rolls in one direction, he tilts his body in the opposite direction by the same angle and we laughed and laughed. When his lunch plate goes from one end of the table to the other, we laughed so hard that our stomachs ached. It was so funny.

But it was not at all funny in real life. When the ship moves from side to side (port and starboard), it is called rolling, forward and aft movement (like a see-saw) is called pitching, and going round is called corkscrew motion. If ship was sensible enough to roll, pitch, or corkscrew, it would have been tolerable.

But the sea was so rough; before completion of one cycle of rolling, a wave would hit and she would pitch, and before completion of that, corkscrew motion would start. The net effect was as if you were put in a glass jar with the lid screwed on and shaken vigorously. It was not as if the sea would say, 'Poor chaps, they had a tough time, so from 5 p.m. to 6 a.m. let us stop this rough sea business.' No way! The ordeal can continue for weeks at a time.

You cannot sleep, sit, or eat. The stomach is a very sincere, hardworking organ. It tries to digest any garbage dumped in. It grumbles and complains only when we push it to its limits.

My stomach is very loyal and faithful. I used to mercilessly load *mirchi bajjis*, pickles, and all hot, spicy food items non-stop. It stoically bore it all with a stiff upper lip, never complaining, like Jeeves, the faithful butler of Bertram Wooster. It could rest only when I hit the sack, and while I could get eight hours of sleep, it got a few hours less, since it had to digest the food that I had dumped in, before calling it a day.

But the rolling, pitching, and corkscrew was too much for it to handle. When the food is sloshing all around, digestion is impossible. Not even for a second was the food in the stomach stationary.

My stomach finally threw up its hands and told my brain, 'I can't handle it. I am sending the food out.'

My brain told it to hold it for a little longer. My stomach said okay and after another thirty minutes, it said it could not hold it any longer and sent the food up. So, I sat near the bilges and vomited.

My brain reasoned with stomach: 'I will send some biscuits and tea, try to digest it.' I went to ECR, had some tea and biscuits, and ran down and again threw up.

My brain lost its temper. 'Are you crazy? Why did you send up the biscuits? He will become weak.'

My stomach was adamant: 'I will keep sending everything up. Let him get permission to lie down, then I may reconsider.'

I went to ECR and asked 2/E's permission to go to my cabin and rest. The 2/E firmly refused.

'You have to rough it out. If I give you permission to go and rest, all your life you will wish to lie down the moment the ship rolls. No, the only concession I will give you is this, you need not trace the pipe lines below bilges. Until you are Okay, check the pipelines above decks,' he told me sternly.

I went back to my place near the bilge pump, sat down with my head in my hands, waiting for the next cycle of vomiting. No one in the engine room was sympathetic or concerned and none of them seemed unduly affected by the rolling and pitching.

In fact, I watched with shock and awe as Pal, 3/E, and the others gobble food by the buckets, saying they were ravenous while the very sight and smell of food had become anathema to me.

When my stomach refused even water, my brain lost its temper. 'Why are you trying to kill him? Do you know the dangers of dehydration?' it shouted at my stomach. The stomach, which is very docile and unflappable, flared up. 'It is entirely your fault. When the vacancy came up in the marine section, you incited him to take it up. You did not consult any of us. So, don't lecture me,' it shouted at my brain. Net result was that both stopped functioning. I was totally dazed.

One E/O, Basheer, was a very kind-hearted and sweet-natured person. He took me to the workshop, made me sit in a chair, and enlightened me like Sri Krishna, and I listened with folded hands like Arjuna (Before the start of Maha Bharata war, Arjuna was dejected and refused to fight, since he has to kill cousins, uncles and teachers. Lord Krishna enlightens and motivates him).

'Girisam, there are three types of persons in this world. The first type, they are born with steel linings in their stomachs. They never feel seasick in any weather and no amount of rolling and pitching will affect them. I have seen brand-new cadets and wives and children of officers who were perfectly fine while seasoned, experienced sailors were flat.

The second type, they are seasick every time the ship rolls. Any number of years of sailing will not cure them.

The third type, they feel seasick for a few days and once the disorientation of the eyes, brain, and stomach is overcome, they will be all right. I think you belong to the third type. You will be fine in two days, have patience and keep taking food and liquids even if you throw up.' He told me about the physiology of seasickness.

'Which type do you belong to?' I asked him curiously.

He smiled sadly and took out a number of plastic covers from his pocket.

'Second. I completed two decades in Indian Navy and here. I have learnt to live with it. I keep eating, vomiting and eating, hoping and waiting for the sea to become calm,' he told me.

'Then why don't you quit this job? There must be thousands of jobs for skilled people like you,' I asked him.

'It is not as bad as you think. Once we cross Gulf of Aden, the sea will be like a lake. Once you accept it, it doesn't bother you much,' he told me and left. I thanked him for his counselling.

Sure enough, from the third day I was all right, in fact, more than all right. I seemed to be hungry all the time. A few hours after having food, I would feel hungry again, as if I had not eaten for a day. I would be fast asleep even before my head touched the pillow and it required a great effort to get up from bed. I was sleeping so well.

Since then, rough seas have never bothered me. When I board a ship after a long time, I might feel seasick for a day or two, but after that no amount of turbulence affects me.

But I was amazed to see that my wife and kids belonged to the first type. They never felt seasickness. In one ship, there were four families and six kids. All the mothers and kids were flat during a particularly rough patch of weather, except my wife and kids. My wife would go to the galley, cook food for all the kids, and feed them, since their mothers were not in a position to get up from their beds.

By the time the ship crossed Gulf of Aden into the calm sea, I was active and socializing. The cadets were my best friends. I learnt that I had a skill in table tennis, which I had never played before.

Two incidents happened which increased my stock with 2/E and C/E.

The main engine lubricating oil is stored in the sump tank and it has to be purified continuously. Lubricating oil purifiers draw oil from the sump tank, purify it, and pump it back to the sump. The purifier was not taking suction and 2/E had engaged the entire engine crew to find and rectify the fault. The crew was in the bilges, applying grease on the pipes and flanges to stop any ingress of air. After two days, everyone was fed up.

Those days, 5/Es specialized in being chameleons; they developed skills to merge in the background and be invisible to 2/E. So, it required courage on my part to approach 2/E and ask him to give me a chance to try my luck with the purifier. He hesitated, but gave me permission on the understanding that I did not break or damage the equipment.

The crew's jaw dropped when they found the purifier was taking suction and running well, after they came from their tea break. There was a lubricating oil storage tank on a higher deck. I opened the line to the purifier for a few seconds and closed it. Once the lines were full of oil, it took suction normally. It was like a Sherlock Holmes mystery; it looks like a miracle until he explains how he solved the case. The 2/E was impressed.

Basheer told me later that I should learn to be smart. I should have made it look like I had struggled day and night to solve the problem. It would have made people appreciate and notice my efforts.

I could never learn to be smart. I tried and tried, and gave up. Shailendra had written the song with me in mind and not

Raj Kapoor. '*Sab kuch seekha hum ne, na seekhi hoshiyaari, sach hai duniya walon, hum hain anari*.' (I learnt everything, but not smartness. It is true, my friends, I am dumb).

Being smart requires a lot of effort. I neither had the energy nor the inclination. In fact I am too lazy to be smart.

At home, my wife is exasperated by my lack of smartness. For instance, if one of her friends had asked her to buy her a parrot-green saree similar to the one she wore, and we had found it in the second shop on our errand, the following would be the likely conversation.

Friend: Thank you so much, you have taken so much trouble, you must have spent a lot of time searching for it.

Wife wants to say, 'It is Okay, in fact, we went from Patny's to Sultan Bazaar. Finally we found it in the last shop.'

Before Wife can speak, I say, 'It is nothing. We found it in the second shop on our search.'

Wife looks daggers at me and later I tell her that I will mend my ways.

Then on the next occasion, someone asks when I had landed at home. Before wife can say, 'One week,' I say, 'Two weeks.' Then they pounce on us, why we didn't attend some function if I was in town.

We give some expensive-looking gift. The recipient is thrilled and says, 'Thank you so much, but there was no need for such expensive gifts.' Before my wife can say, 'Don't give it a thought, you are very precious to us,' I say, 'Don't give it a thought, it just looks expensive, but it is not.'

When I follow the best policy, silence, that also irritates her. But less damage is done by silence.

What my wife suffers in this regard, words cannot tell.

When I am sailing, her mother takes care of tormenting her.

My wife cleaned and arranged and kept the house in an immaculate condition, since some guests were visiting. The guests were quite impressed and complimented her on the tidiness. Wife's mother was quick to tell them that the house was like a railway platform an hour back; her daughter had cleaned and tidied it up since they were visiting.

When my wife's friend hesitated to take the dozen chocolates for her kids offered by my wife, mother-in-law tells her not to hesitate since her daughter has more than ten kg of chocolates in stock.

But my mother-in-law is very considerate. When I am on leave, she hardly visits. She realizes that my wife can only handle her or me, one at a time.

The second incident was when 2/E was venting air from the main engine lube oil filter vent plug. I was standing close by. Suddenly the plug flew and oil was splashing in a jet. For a second, 2/E was paralyzed and plugged it with his glove and yelled to me to call C/E. I ran to the ECR, called C/E, and rushed down. The 2/E was drenched in oil and was totally black; only his eyes were white.

I offered to hold it and he removed his hand. I plugged the leak with my hand. In that short span the oil splash drenched me also. That was the occasion when C/E threw his wig on the ECR table.

The 2/E appreciated my gesture. But for the next few days, the smell of lube oil enveloped me and 2/E like an aura. People were very respectful; they used to give us ample space and would remember some urgent work when we approached them. When we were going down the stairs, if someone was coming up, normally both would turn sideways and pass but now, they would go downstairs and allow us passage.

Since we had become immune to the smell, it looked strange to us that people were treating us with unusual deference. Now, I know how Moses must have felt when the Red Sea was parting to give him way or Vasudeva, when carrying baby Krishna and the River Yamuna parted to give him passage. We had the recreation room entirely to ourselves.

Now we were a few days away from the Suez Canal.

DELUSIONS OF SINGERS

After we crossed the Gulf of Aden, the sea became as calm as a lake and everyone heaved a sigh of relief.

C/E threw a party in his cabin. So after my watch, I had a shower, freshened up, and went to C/E's cabin. I greeted everyone and sat beside Basheer. The party was already in progress; there were very animated discussions about cricket and politics.

I was ravenous. My stomach was ashamed and guilty for its unbecoming behaviour during the rough sea days and wanted to make up for lost time. It was digesting food at a faster rate than I was eating and I was always hungry. There were many items on the table. I whispered to Basheer to tell me which items were vegetarian. I put some on my plate and started nibbling.

The day before I joined the ship, my mother sat beside me and asked me to promise her something. I tensed as I was waiting for this moment. I was wondering what handcuffs and shackles she wanted to put on me to ensure I remained a good boy.

'Sure. Go ahead,' I told her.

'Promise me that you will not eat non vegetarian food,' she asked. I promised.

Even if I hadn't promised her, I would not have had non-vegetarian food any way, since I had been horrified by the sight of lions killing and devouring deer and zebras in the movie *African Safari*, which I had seen in my schooldays. I had been so upset that I had difficulty in swallowing food for the next few days.

As she got up to leave, I asked, 'And?'

She smiled. 'And nothing,' she said and left.

My parents were courageous, lion-hearted. My mother must have been upset and anxious to see me join a ship and go thousands of miles away into unknown territories. But they always bid me farewell smiling. They never tried to hold me back by sentimental shackles even when they had health problems.

Basheer and I were talking in low tones when C/E interrupted us.

'Girisam, have a beer.' He opened the cap of a Heineken beer bottle and gave it to me. I hesitated. I whispered to ask Basheer if foreign beer contained any animal products. He laughed and told everyone and all of them roared.

C/E's wife told him, 'Nandu, he is so innocent, doesn't he remind you of my younger brother?' He grumbled in assent, as I must have reminded him also of her confounded younger brother whom he could not stand and who must have irritated him.

C/E told me, 'I don't know how orthodox you are at home, but in my home we don't even eat onions. So, if I am having beer, it means it is safe, Okay? None of the alcoholic drinks have non-vegetarian stuff, now drink. Cheers!'

I said, 'Cheers,' sipped, and grimaced. In my childhood, my mother used to give us an oil bath every Sunday. Instead of shampoo, she would use crushed and soaked *kunkudu kai* (soap-nut). She would ignore our cries as the liquid would sting the eyes, and when it entered the mouth, it left a bitter, pungent taste. Beer tasted like that.

Pal told me to munch on some peanuts and take another sip. When I finished the beer, the party shifted into the next gear.

Every party crowd will have an enthusiastic Tansen, willing, nay, impatient to sing. They would comment that the party is becoming dull and that someone should sing and prompt a few reluctant people. When they dither, they start belting out numbers. Purser was the Tansen that day. After he sang a few songs, C/E suggested that someone else should now sing. All eyes turned towards me; I was the unanimous choice.

I was an enthusiastic bathroom singer. Like with everyone else, whenever I sing, my voice sounds like Rafi, Kishore, Hemant, or Mukesh to my ears. Whichever song I sang, to my ears the sound of my voice was the same as that of the original singer. Hence, I never thought that I could be torturing others with my singing until one evening in my college days.

During one particular festival holiday season, the hostel was almost deserted. I don't recall why I didn't go home. Only ten of us were there. I really enjoyed the vacant bathrooms. No need to wait or finish the bath in a hurry, so I was enjoying a leisurely bath and singing at the top of my voice.

Then someone started banging on the bathroom door urgently. I stopped the shower and asked what the matter was.

'Are you Okay?' Ram asked me anxiously (He is also sailing as C/E now).

'Yes. Why?' I asked him.

There was hesitation, and then he asked again, 'Are you alone? There is no girl with you?'

I shouted at him, 'What the hell are you talking about?'

Ram said, 'I thought a girl was being molested and was screaming. I came to rescue her. Good thing I didn't go and call the watchman and others.'

That effectively killed my bathroom-singing career and any notions I had that I was the next Rafi or Kishore. Later, Ram tried to console me by saying that my singing was not that bad and maybe the bathroom acoustics made it sound so horrible.

I chose a two-wheeler singing career instead. In a car, I don't sing; I have consideration for others. But while driving a two-wheeler, I care two hoots for the public who happen to be at the receiving end for a few minutes or seconds. I am not forcing them to suffer; they have a choice of overtaking me or falling back enough to be out of hearing distance.

But my kids and wife are embarrassed if they are riding pillion and keep pestering me to stop singing as I am drawing attention to them. I ignore them since I feel I also should enjoy certain liberties.

Now both the kids have their own vehicles and my wife travels by car. On the rare occasions when the driver is absconding and she has to ride pillion, she suffers in silence, since I point out that I tried to teach her to drive a scooty for a month and she had refused to learn after she skidded once. Had she learned to drive a scooty, she would not have to ride pillion.

I tried to dissuade C/E that the party might break up soon if I am forced to sing. Still they would not listen.

Then I sang *'Yeh nayan dare dare...'* (Hemant Kumar's song). They gave a standing ovation. They genuinely loved my singing. I had an impulsive urge to drag Ram then and there and make him eat humble pie. Later, Basheer told me that they expected me to sing some Telugu song or a badly twisted Hindi song but never expected a star performance.

I had one more beer and sang two more Rafi songs and then we played antakshari. I was again the star. I knew so many songs. Purser, who was the uncrowned king, came a poor second. Later, I took their leave as I had to go for watch at 0400 hours.

Tailpiece: We, meaning, my wife and I, are also guilty of Ram-ish folly. My younger daughter has a very beautiful voice, high-pitched and with good modulation, which I did not notice until recently.

My younger daughter evaluates parental care and love by the yells and shouts she gets per day. She cannot sleep until she gets her quota. We are also so used to it that on the rare occasions when she manages to pass two days without inciting us to shout at her, we begin to get worried if everything is Okay with her. Every day she gives us a hug and a kiss to make up for all her mischief.

On some days we are so preoccupied with other jobs that she fails to provoke us to shout at her, all her attempts like leaving a chocolate wrapper on the sofa, leaving the guitar on the bed, mobile phone on the floor for us to stamp on, and changing her mother's mobile to silent mode and so on. But when nothing works, then she resorts to singing after midnight, which is a fail-safe. Then we shout at her.

You can't blame us. Even if Nusrat Fateh Ali Khan sits on your bed and sings at 1 a.m., you will force him to shut up and get lost. His voice is meant for large auditoriums of 1000 or more people and not for a small bedroom. In the bedroom, it will have the effect of a power hammer which road repairmen use to break cement roads; I mean, like you are holding the power hammer and breaking cement blocks. It will jar every bone in your body and make the teeth rattle in your skull.

I recorded all our family videos and photos in one storing device and one day I was playing the videos while I was working on my computer. I heard a beautiful voice singing a popular number. I wondered why there was no music accompaniment, since I genuinely thought it was the original. I looked at the TV and my jaw dropped. It was my daughter singing; she had recorded a video.

I told her to utilize her skill to better purpose than to get a shout from us. Since then she has been singing at college functions and other events and is greatly appreciated.

PANGS OF ENVY

Whatever my merits and demerits may be, even my detractors will concede that I am not prone to jealousy. Yes, I may feel a pang of jealousy when I see my neighbour's 46-inch Onida LED TV, but I don't go about smashing it or lose sleep over it.

I thank my parents and God for this sterling quality. Jealousy is one emotion that works twenty-four hours a day and spoils the health and happiness of people.

Fortunately, my wife doesn't feel even a pang of jealousy when she sees the neighbour's Onida TV. So, we are happy in our bliss of ignorance, content and happy with what we have. Her cousin, who was a normal, middle-class man like us a few decades back, now invites us once in a few years to house-warming ceremonies of his palatial mansions which he constructs with clockwork precision in the most prestigious locations.

After returning from those events, I brace myself for attacks from Wife about my inability to construct even a normal house, while her cousin boasts of houses next to chief ministers and movie stars. But so far she has resisted the impulse.

But, when I was a 5/E, I was guilty of being jealous. I used to feel jealous when I saw radio officers and electrical officers. I could not stand the sight of their happy, contented, and relaxed faces.

Radio officers had the cushiest job in the ship. They would sit in the radio room from 8 a.m. to 12 a.m., send and receive any messages by Morse code, and in the evening, for a few hours they would sit and polish their nails. That is all they used to do. Once the ship comes to port, they close shop and they are free to enjoy port stay without any work. If they wanted to, they could stay outside and join the ship just before sailing.

Those days we used to have very long port stays abroad as well as in India. They could go for sightseeing until they dropped from exhaustion. The ship used to stay for months altogether in Indian ports. They were the chosen ones.

Electrical officers were a little less lucky. They didn't have R/Os' freedom and were kept in check by C/E. Still, apart from taking a morning round wearing gloves, they did precious little. Our ship had a swimming pool. You could see the R/Os and E/Os enjoying themselves most of the time with chilled beers and floating like leaves in the pool. They were expert swimmers; one E/O could stay afloat in cross-legged *padmasan* posture.

Who wouldn't feel jealous? Especially when you slog for twenty hours after a breakdown and go to have a late dinner and see them laughing, drinking, and enjoying themselves watching movies or playing cards... If your blood doesn't boil, then either you are a reptile or a saint.

One day, after a breakdown job, as we were taking a tea break, I vented out my anger.

I told Pal that I felt so angry and irritated when I see their smug faces, I wanted to tie them up, gag them, and make them listen to a metallurgy lecture by our lecturer Polonkov for two days non-stop without food or water.

Pal snorted. 'Rubbish. Do you call that punishment, listening to a lecture? I would take AK-47 and shoot them up... tatattaaat... tattattat.' He mimicked the action of shooting.

I was horrified. 'Come on, you are being unreasonable.' I tried to reason with him.

He laughed. 'You call that unreasonable? Then listen to this. I will shoot them, their family and friends and will make our purser sing all his nasal songs on their graves.'

I was aghast. How cruel could Pal be?

I reasoned with and convinced Pal. He reluctantly agreed to drop Purser's singing from the agenda.

I did a great service to mankind. The problem with Purser is that he is like Cacofonix in Asterix comics. He thinks he can sing and that everyone would wish to listen to him sing. Everyone else thinks he cannot or should not, ever, be allowed to sing.

When you volunteer or are eager to sing, even if your voice is nasal and you are off-key, you are at least expected to know the lyrics of the song.

He starts off with '*Mere sapnon ki rani…*' Midway he realizes he hasn't sung '*Kya hai Bharosa…*' He applies sudden brakes, says, 'Oh, my goodness, I forgot that stanza.' He sings that and forgets where he was and asks the audience where he was. Someone says, '*Phool si khil ke,*' other one says, '*Bagon mein…*'

Yet another calls them both idiots; they are mixing up different songs. Within no time, people almost come to blows; teetotalers like Basheer and Mrs C/E intervene and restore order.

Undeterred, Purser starts singing '*Dost dost na raha…*' and freezes after '*Tumhee to thay.*' People try to help him and without warning he would start another song.

So after convincing Pal to drop Purser's singing, I tried to make him see reason. He reluctantly agreed to let their family and friends live. I put in a little more effort by pointing out the virtue of forgiveness, the teachings of Gandhiji, Buddha, and Christ…and he finally agreed not to kill anyone.

He sadly conceded that it was not their fault that they were enjoying themselves. We were stupid to opt for the backbreaking career of engineer. I cheered him up by painting a picture of his life after becoming C/E, playing with his kids in the cabin, singing duets with his wife, and the only job he would ever do in a day is to sign in the logbook.

That brightened him.

I heaved a sigh of relief at having saved so many lives and Pal from the gallows.

I was jealous to a lesser extent of navigating officers for obvious reasons. They at least look busy as if doing something. So, for them only six hours of Polonkov's lecture was adequate.

Tailpiece: I met the E/O of my first ship again several years later. I was 2/E in a ship and we had major complications with the A/C. Next to our ship was his ship, which was a sister ship to ours. I went there to get some advice and there was this E/O. After hugs and pats on backs, I asked him about the A/C.

'Where is the A/C room?' he asked me. I was shocked. He was sailing for four months in that ship and he did not know that the A/C room was on the same deck, in fact, a few metres away from his cabin.

Later when I asked the 2/E of that ship about E/O, he smiled and said that I should not be surprised; in government organizations, such laid-back attitude was common.

SONGS THAT TUNED MY NATURE

I remained junior engineer for my full tenure of twenty months in that ship, which was unusual. Normally, as fourth engineers and third engineers signed off, we would move up the ladder and could become 3/E if we were lucky.

When I joined as the most junior engineer, Pal was senior to me by a couple of months and Venugopal was senior 5/E. After a few months, Venugopal became 4/E, Pal became senior 5/E, and we were stagnant in those positions for almost the entire time. Venugopal and Pal also wanted to complete twenty months' time so that they could appear for 2/E's examination. We had to complete eighteen months of article time (actual stay on ship in port and sailing) and 365 days of actual sailing time before we could qualify to appear for the examination.

I had no tensions or worries, nor was I unduly perturbed. I was happy-go-lucky. The 5/E has a few privileges; chief among them is that he is like a driver with an 'L' board. He is not supposed to know anything and is expected to commit blunders and the onus is on the senior engineers to ensure that he doesn't. One reason why my stagnation didn't bother me was the influence of movies and songs of that era.

I firmly believe movies, songs, and books determine the way the youth think and react.

In the present context, Rafi's song '*Main zindgi ka saath nibhata chala gaya...*' was my favourite song and I used to hum it a lot. In that he sings, '*Jo mil gaya usiko muqaddar samajh liya, jo kho gaya usiko bhulata chala gaya'* (I accept what providence has given me and I move forward forgetting what I lost). Yes, it suited my lazy disposition not to rush and achieve but to accept and be happy.

In my youth, there was a clear demarcation between a hero and a villain. The hero was studious, brilliant in studies, respectful to elders, chivalrous to damsels in distress. He rescued them from villains, and the beautiful heroine would fall in love and sing duets with him. Villains were rowdy elements, eve-teasers, and generally hated by everyone for their evil looks and grating laughter.

So, we wanted to be heroes, study well, impress girls, sing duets, that I couldn't impress girls and induce them to sing duets was not due to lack of efforts from my side but due to the absence of girls in the schools I studied, as they were boys' schools.

While we were diffident, next generation young men were boisterous. Once, I saw a chief officer and one cadet travelling in a crowded bus. In that state transport buses, conductor will not move in the bus, collecting money and issuing tickets. Conductor would sit near the rear entrance, and all passengers pass money in a chain system, until it reaches the conductor and he sends back ticket, and change in the same way.

Cadet was from Delhi and didn't know about this. A beautiful girl extended her arm and told him 'Sangeetha'. What she meant was that she would alight at Sangeetha theater stop, and wanted money and that information to be passed on to the conductor in the chain system.

Cadet's face lit up like a thousand watt bulb. He didn't see the money in her hand. He grabbed her hand in his hands and shook warmly.' Hi, Sangeetha, nice to meet you, I am Rahul'

All hell broke loose. Girl panicked and started crying, and the crowd ganged up to bash up Rahul. Luckily chief officer knew local language, and pacified them.

There was only one girl in the entire engineering college campus in my days, and with no disrespect to her, she would not have induced me to sing a solo let alone a duet. Moreover, she was in electronics section, so we hardly saw her.

The math professor had a very beautiful daughter. She was a cousin of one of our friends. We seriously thought of falling in love with her but abandoned the idea after the said friend warned that it could be injurious to our health and academic career. The math professor was a typical Telugu movie heroine's father, whose only aim would be to harass the hero, his family and friends since the hero had the audacity to fall in love with his daughter (It doesn't matter if the hero is the most eligible boy in the country). In the last reel, when he realizes the purity of the hero's golden heart, he would relent and give his blessings.

Unlike some of my friends, I didn't have the energy to wait in bus stops in sun and rain, escort the girl home, and dream sweet dreams if she deigns to fling a smile. I used to help my friends by holding their cigarettes if those girls happened to pass by because they wanted to impress the girls.

Now, the trend has changed. Heroes are vagabonds, good-for-nothing rowdies, and eve-teasers, and girls are supposed to fall for them. Those who wish to study well are portrayed as weak-kneed, soft in the head, and buffoons.

I think I took the lyrics of songs too literally. Mukesh's song '*Jo tum ko ho pasand wohi baat kahenge, tum din ko agar raat kaho, raat kahenge*' (I like whatever you like, if you say day is night I also will say the same thing) was my favourite song. I hummed it so many times; the lyrics have permeated my soul and influenced me. '*Tum din ko agar raat kaho, raat kahenge*' (If you say day is night, I will say it is night). I thought it is the ultimate expression of love and it did not occur to me that the lyricist may have discovered the hard truth after many battles of disagreement with his wife.

So, I fully agree with Wife, to the exasperation of my wife and kids. If my wife says, 'Oh, this blue saree is very beautiful,' I say, 'Yes, dear.' Then she says, 'But that yellow with pink border is even grander, what do you think?' I feel it is atrocious, but will say, 'Yes, dear.' She gets fed up and stops asking me.

If Mukesh hadn't sung that song or if I hadn't heard it, if my wife declared day to be night, I would most probably have said, 'Are you stupid or mad? When the sun is shining so bright, how can you call it night?' Or that blue and yellow sarees reminded me of Aborigine tribal dresses shown on Discovery Channel, and probably would have regretted it lifelong, since ladies' memories are razor-sharp in storing and recalling unsavoury comments.

I was influenced so much by that song, I did not know *mujhe pasand kya hai* (what I liked). I think I am a rare specimen; I honestly don't know what I like or what I am supposed to like (maybe there are many like me, but we hide in nooks and corners since we think we are abnormal).

But come to think of it, I suspect, three of our four brothers are afflicted with this ailment since one of my sisters-in-law, in a rare moment of indiscretion, commented that all of us (the four brothers) are inert masses (*jada padardhalu*). I say a rare moment of indiscretion, because an Indian lady feels that she alone has the right to criticize and castigate her husband and normally she tries do so in private but if any unfortunate soul does that in her presence, she would maul that person like a tigress saving her cubs and it would take quite some time for the scars to heal.

On a rare occasion, in fact, the only occasion, I was witness to a wife publicly declaring that she respected her husband a lot and that he was a gem of a man. My wife and I had gone to meet my friend who is also a chief engineer. Three sets of jaws fell open to the danger point of getting dislocated; mine, my wife's, and her husband's. I feel that was her way of apologizing to her husband after a massive fight. After introspection she must have realized he was right and she was wrong or she must have felt that the dose of criticism she doled out to her husband was disproportionate to his lapse or crime.

If you ask me what colour I like, I am stumped. I have no great like or dislike for any colour and wonder how anyone can be passionate about a colour. While my wife goes to dozens of shops to select even one saree for my mother, I can buy a dozen shirts from the first shop.

My wife and kids are irritated by my impatience. If we go to a shop to buy shirts for me, I Okay the first two shirts that we see and want to finish the ordeal. I know something is seriously wrong with me; you make me work for twenty-four hours in the engine room, I am not tired. You make me watch a Gavaskar or Boycott batting video for two full days, I am not tired. You make me drive a two-wheeler for twelve hours in the hot sun, I am not tired. But you leave me in a shopping mall for one hour, I feel so tired and exhausted that I want to lie down in a corner and go to sleep. It saps all my energy. I think I suffer from 'mall-o-phobia'.

Shopping malls and shopping per se exhaust me. I think the anxiety of having to choose tires me. If my wife gives me a list like 'buy 1 kg cashew, 20 gms saffron, Vaseline, so-and-so cream…' I can happily shop. But, if she says, 'See and buy things of your choice,' I am in a panic. I remember my daughters once declared war on me for having bought some apparel that would be loose even for sumo wrestlers. Did I think they were so fat?

The following shopping nightmare has haunted me from my childhood. When I was in school, I had just learnt to drive a scooter and would pester Mother to send me on shopping errands so that I could practice my new skill. Once she sent me to purchase a 25-kg rice bag. I went to the Marwari shop and asked him to show me the rice, which he did.

'Is it new?' I asked him in a confident tone. I did not want to let the shop owner know that I was shopping for rice for the first time; I wanted to show that I was knowledgeable.

'Brand new, sir, just now arrived,' he assured me. I warned him that I would return it if it was not new. I brought the bag home on the scooter.

My mother was horrified. 'But it is new rice,' she exclaimed.

'Brand new. He assured me that it had just arrived. I told him I would return if it is not,' I assured her.

My mother is a great lady. If my wife or I were in her place, we would have screamed and shouted.

She laughed and said, 'Don't you know you should always buy old rice? I pity your future wife.'

How was I to know that while everything you buy is supposed to be brand new, rice is an exception to the rule? For the next several days, everyone was cursing me for having to eat the white liquid paste that resulted from the new rice. I think later my dad went to the shop and convinced the Marwari fellow to exchange it for old rice.

My mother would give me a lunch box daily in my school days. Once she could not prepare it so she asked me to have something in a restaurant. It was a great day for me. Finally I was going to a restaurant on my own and not in tow behind Dad and brothers. So with a serious face, I studied the menu card and ordered—idli, dosa, tea.

When the waiter brought the bill, I ticked him off. Why did he bring the bill, had he asked me what else I wanted? The waiter was surprised. 'But you ordered tea!' he said.

'So? Maybe I could order something after tea,' I told him seriously. I had a suspicion he was biting his lip to control his laughter.

'Sorry, sir, what else do you want?' he asked, unable to hold in his laughter. I gave it a lot of thought but could think of nothing else that I could have after tea.

'Okay, this time I will pay the bill, from next time you should ask me what else I want before bringing bill,' I told him sternly and paid the bill.

As I was leaving, I saw the waiter and his friend having a hearty laugh at some joke. I had a vague suspicion that it had something to do with me.

If ever I open a saree or jewellery shop, I will have an anteroom with a mini-bar. While the ladies do the shopping, men can relax there and both will be happy and business will thrive on all counts. Otherwise, men are always in a hurry to finish shopping.

I was stuck as a junior engineer and I did not regret it. I used to have a lot of fun, play table tennis, swim in the pool, and while in port, would go out daily. I would work in the night shift and, in the morning, go out after breakfast. No shops would be open, the roads would be deserted but I used to go for long walks. I remember, in Sweden and Finland it would be freezing cold, still I would wear warm clothing and go out. Everyone used to make fun of me.

Tailpiece: I lost a 20-20 match with my wife over '*Jo tum ko ho pasand*' (I like whatever you like, if you say that the day is the night, I will also say the same thing).

My wife said she didn't believe that I say yes to all her likes. I told her that I said yes to everything.

Then she bowled an in-swinger. 'Okay, I like leafy vegetables, salads, and fruits. They are good for health. So from today, that will be our dinner.'

Luckily, I brought the bat down in the last second or else it would have been out LBW (leg before wicket, a cricketing term, a batsman is declared 'out' if the ball strikes the pad on leg, when the leg is in front of wickets).

'But the keyword in the song is *kahenge* [tell], not *karenge* [do]. So I will definitely agree with you and say that they are good for health, not necessarily have them for dinner.'

She thought for a minute and bowled a Yorker and uprooted all the stumps.

'I like you to say that you will have leafy vegetables, salads, and fruits every day for dinner,' she said.

As I remained silent she said, 'Though I don't sing, in my song, *karenge* [do] is the keyword. I know you don't like shopping. So, I leave you to drape yourself on the sofa and watch WWE, cricket, and Hollywood movies when you are not dozing. I don't drag you to saree shopping. I slog even when my feet are killing me.

'Every time you come home, you promise to clear the tons of garbage and useless articles that you have accumulated over the years. You postpone it all to the next day and finally go back to ship. I clear everything, you come back, and before you go, again you pile up another ton of garbage. So stop singing and start acting.'

I walked back to the pavilion, crestfallen, with the bat under my arm.

English Movies
Need Subtitles

When I joined as 5/E, I was quite paranoid about my communication skills. Though I was quite fluent in English prose (I started reading P. G. Wodehouse, Sir Arthur Conan Doyle in my ninth standard), there was not much practice in conversing in English and I used to find it difficult to follow conversations in some of the Hollywood movies, especially American ones. It always intrigued me why they couldn't speak without munching a sandwich and with their mouths full or chewing on a cigar (Clint Eastwood) or drinking. If nothing else, six of them would be speaking at the same time and you are expected to follow the conversation.

I really envied the silent-era movies and that generation. Even a child could follow what was going on. Like in the advertisement of some paint manufacturer, 'Whenever you see colour, think of us,' my niece says that she always sees my face on the TV screen whenever a Hollywood movie plays with subtitles. Poor girl, it must be gruelling to see my face staring at her until she changed to a non-subtitled channel. In her growing years, I used to always complain rave, and rant about why Hollywood movies don't have subtitles for illiterate or semi-literate people like me. Why should the majority suffer in silence and pretend that they are following and enjoying what is going on, when in fact, they are as puzzled or baffled as the next guy (who is also pretending so that he does not lose face)?

We were all hypocrites, acting as if we understood and enjoyed the film, when we could not understand a word.

I sympathize with my niece. It took some effort but I managed to get out of the hypnotic influence of the paint manufacturer and managed not to think of him whenever I saw colour (it is impossible not to see colour). The trick was not in trying to block thinking about him (it will further irritatingly remind you) but to think of something else. It was so effective, now I don't even remember who that advertiser was.

Coming back to the ship, I need not have worried. If my Hindi was atrocious, some Tamil and Malayali people's Hindi was incomprehensible and unspeakable (literally). I could be Sant Kabir compared to them.

English is a strange language. It can be like sweet music when some people speak in the Queen's English accent and slang and can be jarring if people speak English in Telugu, Tamil, Malayalam, or Hindi accents. I read Alistair MacLean's *Golden Rendezvous* and if my friend Anil had not corrected me that it should be pronounced 'rondevoo', how would I know that? Similarly 'gh' is silent in 'dough' but present in 'enough' or 'laugh'. The list is endless.

I was in the watch of a third engineer (I am now reluctant to throw the names; with Face book so active, he may come hunting for me with a hatchet) who later became 2/E. He was very uncommunicative. Initially, I thought that he was reserved or shy but realized later that his English was not so good and he was reluctant to talk with people like Pal around who speak Queen's English.

His favourite words were 'What...Bloody...' These were his way of expressing anger, shock or surprise. Then he would clam up. One day he asked me, 'Are you a vegetable?' For a few seconds I was lost and then I told him that I was a vegetarian. He nodded sagely and said, 'Good, being a vegetable is good for health.'

He was a pig-headed man. When his family (wife and two young boys) were sailing with him, he took them out in France in the freezing cold. He put on his coat, gloves, and cap but his wife was clad in saree, one normal sweater, and slippers and his sons were wearing half-pants. They were shivering and he was unmoved. I was so upset and angry with him that I wanted to remove his clothes and make him stand in his underclothing to make him realize their suffering.

My daughters tried to correct their maternal grandfather and me but eventually gave up. It seems we were pronouncing 'we' wrong. The 'tear' which rolls down one's cheek and the 'tear' when one tears a paper, it seems, should be pronounced differently, so on and so forth.

Once, while job-hunting, I was filling up an application form in an office. Sitting next to me was a very senior master. He was also filling a form and he asked me, 'Here, it says "marital status", should I write good, excellent, or average?' I thought that he was joking but when I realized that he was not, I explained to him that what they mean by status was 'married', 'single', 'divorced', etc.

When my father was transferred to a city from a small town, I was in the eighth standard. In the town school, they had just started teaching the Hindi alphabet. In the city school, we had textbooks, non-detailed stories, poetry, and prose. I panicked and refused to go to school. My dad started to teach me for an hour every day and I picked up quite fast. After that, I always stood first in class. I used to write poetry also in Hindi. But there was the same dilemma: I couldn't speak in Hindi.

Our art teacher could not speak Telugu. He gave us a topic and we had to draw and paint a picture. Now, my friend and I had doubts if the drawing paper of A4 size was OK or should we draw it on a bigger drawing sheet. I was dying to know how the question should be framed in Hindi and prodded my friend to ask the teacher.

I was standing next to him; when he asked the teacher, I was all ears. '*Itta paper bassa*, sir?' he asked. I was flabbergasted when Roy sir replied, '*Hou, itta bas hai.*'

Later, I asked my friend what was the language he had used. He was surprised. 'Hindi,' he said.

Later, I sailed with Filipinos, Thais, Bangladeshi, and Ukrainian crew and officers. We had to speak in few words without grammar to make ourselves understood. I was worried that after a few years, this telegraphic type of communication might become a habit. True enough, when I was working in Dubai, one Malayali asked me, 'You catch cold?' when I sneezed.

My daughter burst out laughing when I replied, 'Yes, I catch cold.'

My Wife's Sailing Saga

I was second engineer at the time of marriage. Though there are very few movies made with hero in a ship's officer role, my wife could have seen a Dharmendra movie where he acts as an officer in a ship. In immaculate white uniform with epaulettes, he must have looked quite handsome and dashing. So she must have assumed that all ship officers strut around in immaculate uniforms and sit behind desks and sign papers.

She joined her first ship at Cochin. Her brother escorted her to the ship. I received them at the station and took them to the ship. I introduced them to Captain, Chief Engineer, Chief Officer, and others. They were all in crisp uniforms: white shirts, black trousers, and epaulettes. I think my brother-in-law left immediately.

After she settled down, I told her it was time for me to go to work and changed over into boiler suit; it is like coveralls you see car mechanics wear, only mine was dirtier.

She was astonished. 'Why are you wearing that?' she asked me when she recovered.

'This is my working dress,' I told her. I could sense her dreams collapsing silently.

'Are you a mechanic?' she asked despondently. I think she must have had a terrible thought that I duped her, saying I was an engineer. In her mind's eye the depressing images of her washing my dirty boiler suits near a roadside hand pump outside our thatch-roofed hut while our kids were playing in mud, with runny noses and hair like dried grass, must have been playing like a movie in her mind. She collapsed in a sofa.

I sat beside her and tried explaining that I was an engineer in charge of maintenance and I can't very well do it wearing white uniform. I knew I was not getting anywhere. If her brother hadn't left, I think she would have gone back. Those days, luckily, there were no mobile phones.

Someone knocked on the door. It was Chief Engineer.

My wife's spirits sank further when she saw even Chief Engineer was wearing coveralls, though slightly cleaner than mine.

After we left, Captain and Chief Officer's wives came and met her. Captain was a Muslim and a heavy drinker. His wife was very fair and beautiful; she tried all tricks to make him stop drinking. So, he used to keep whisky bottles in others' cabins and would come and have two, three quick shots and leave. Captain's wife told my wife of his habit and cautioned her not to let me entertain him.

Chief Officer's wife Geeta had a cute two-year-old girl. My wife is very fond of children, so her heart lightened after playing with that girl. When I came up for lunch, I changed into uniform. She relaxed further when she saw we were seated next to Captain and Chief Engineer. Slowly she was reconciled to my dirty boiler suits and messy maintenance work.

We had a great time in that ship. Ship was small, cabin was small but it never bothered her since she was not aware of bigger ships and better accommodations. When I went to engine room, she would go to galley (kitchen in ship is called galley), chat with cooks and stewards and deck crew, with other ladies, and would go on bridge and chat with deck officers.

Within two days, she knew everything about everyone, where they lived, how many kids they had and about their parents, etc. She has no ego hassles and was friendly with everyone. She was like fresh air in a stuffy room. The crew never experienced an officer's wife enquiring about them, their families and chatting with them. Normally, officers' wives would be standoffish if not snobbish.

We would go out daily, catch a launch, go to Cochin and walk about the streets and beach, and go back. Since port stays were long, there was lot of free time. Captain's wife, Geeta and her daughter became good pals to my wife.

One bald sardar (he is the only bald sardar I had seen—if I were a sardar and bald, I would always wear pagri) was third engineer. Sardars belong to sikh religion, and traditionally, they are not allowed to shave or cut hair, but now, a few sardars are not following these traditions. His wife and five-year-old daughter joined him during port stay. One day we were talking to him standing on deck, when this girl started climbing the mast (Mast is a long vertical pillar-like structure).

My wife almost screamed. 'Look, she is climbing up,' I told him urgently.

He casually looked up, cautioned her to be careful, and continued talking. My wife and I had our hearts in our mouths and stopped breathing as we watched her climb up to the top and then climb down.

When I reprimanded him, he laughed.'Kuch nahi hota, in our village, she climbs higher trees all the time.'

Finally, the ship sailed out to Mumbai. The sea was quite rough and there was heavy rolling and pitching. I was very pleasantly surprised to see that my wife was not feeling seasick at all while seasoned sailors were throwing up everywhere. That was a real boon or else that would have been her first and last ship.

We anchored at Mumbai.

My wife's only complaint was the constant throbbing beat of the engine. She was happy with everything else, including food, which she used to repair and make Chief Cook's dishes tasty. She said the monotonous beat of the engine was disturbing her sleep and wished it would stop.

I immediately told her, 'Never wish for that. You will regret it.'

As luck would have it, her wish was granted and we had a blackout while we were at anchor. It happened around 8 p.m., we opened up for one engine overhaul and seawater entered lube oil sump of running engine, and we had to stop.

I requested Captain's wife to give my wife company and went to engine room to carry out repairs. Captain's wife told her many spine-chilling ghost stories, including some that originated in that ship and when Wife was properly and truly scared, she told her, 'I have to go now. My husband will take advantage of darkness and finish two bottles. Don't worry. Power will be restored soon,' and left.

My wife called the engine room and I had to go, brought her to engine room, and made her sit in a chair while we worked. She sat there, sweating. After that episode, she learnt to be grateful for the reassuring beat of the engine and never complained since.

It is interesting, this phenomenon of being afraid of darkness and ghosts. My elder daughter and I are never afraid and can sleep happily. In fact, better, after watching a second-show scary ghost movie like *Nightmare on Elm Street*, *Exorcist*. Whereas my wife and younger daughter would stay awake nervously, jumping at every squeak of a door, rustle of a curtain and at imaginary footfalls and noises.

One of my wife's brothers (he is also afraid of darkness and ghosts), who is jealous of my inability to get scared, expounded the theory that only intelligent people with active imagination are scared of darkness and ghosts. I disagree. It is more likely that lazy people do not get scared easily since it requires effort to be scared.

That shipping company was on the verge of bankruptcy, and after several visits to Shipping Master and the union, I managed to recover my wages and signed off. We were very lucky; later the ship sailed out to Sri Lanka and was arrested there for non-payment of port dues. The ship was stranded for several months and I read in the newspaper that the captain appealed to the Indian government and embassy to help them. Local people were giving them rations.

My wife joined next ship after a long gap. Lord Brahma and my elder daughter conspired to throw spanners into our plans of sailing for two years. Elder Daughter must have harassed Lord Brahma to give her a good placement and he sent her to us to get her off his back.

But no complaints. That was the best thing to have happened. Elder Daughter brought happiness and joy not only to us but to all members of both sides of the family and friends. My wife would have been bored if she were to sail alone since as a second engineer I would always be busy. I had to keep watch between four to eight in the morning and evening, and then, after 8 a.m. I had to work till 12 a.m. I would be so exhausted after work, I would fall asleep. My daughter kept my wife busy and happy.

A few words about my daughters: before Elder Daughter was born, I used to wonder how Gandhari, a queen from the *Mahabharata* epic, brought up 101 kids (100 sons and 1 daughter, Dussala). Though they were royals and could afford to keep many ayahs, still it was a huge responsibility. After Elder Daughter was born, I realized that child-rearing is child's play if all kids are as well behaved and model kids like Elder Daughter.

She was a 'user (mother) friendly' kid. She would cry only when there was a cause, like Johnson's 'no tears' shampoo entering her eyes while taking a bath or an ant biting her. After you give her a bath and dress her up, she would sit like a doll, no tantrums, no nagging. If you feed her anything and she would eat without making faces.

When we say this, my younger daughter scoffs and says, 'She was not a model or well-behaved child but a dumb and stupid one. No self-respecting child would allow her mother to dump boiled carrots down her throat without kicking up a racket and putting up a fight.'

Sometimes, elder daughter gets very angry and both sisters fight. Their mother has to intervene to prevent the fight escalating into war.

But we were genuinely worried by her 'too well-behaved' nature and took her to our family paediatrician who laughed us off. Some kids are reserved, he told us.

When we told our parents, my father said, 'Where do you give her chance to be naughty? All the time fussing. Now watch.' He took an old newspaper and tore it in front of her. That was it. Every day she would crawl and tear newspaper to pieces before my father could reach it. She always beat him to it.

In sharp contrast, our second daughter kept us on our toes and still keeps at it. Second Daughter was so naughty and mischievous, it required a whole battalion to make sure she didn't come to harm. My father-in-law, mother-in-law, wife's brothers and sister worked in shifts running behind her. We both would not have been able to manage her on our own.

When travelling by train, Elder Daughter would be fast asleep a few minutes after the train leaves station and would wake up only after we reach destination, irrespective of length of journey, whereas Younger One would neither sleep nor let us sleep. We had to be alert every minute; she would either get down, run in the compartment, or would spill something. Anyway, I will devote one post for them later.

Though Wife insisted, I also wanted to be in the hospital when each child arrived. At the same time, I couldn't sit idle for seven months; moreover I was in heavy debts at that time. Those days, all shipping companies would give contracts for nine months to one year. Only very small companies with few ships would give contracts for three to four months. I worked in such ships until my daughter was born.

In fact, my wife joined me for port stay in one ship. Chief Officer's wife was also in the family way. She also came to stay with him. Both became good friends. The manager told us that the ship was sold and we had to take the ship to Europe, hand over the ship to crew of new owner, and fly back home. Chief Officer and I insisted that we be relieved irrespective of any change of plans since wives' due dates cannot be changed. When we went to the UK, Manager told us that the sale was off and we had to sail to South Africa. I refused to sail, kicked up a racket, paid my own fare and came back. Chief Officer backed out at the last minute and agreed to sail.

When I met his wife in Mumbai, she cried and said she wished he also made a bold decision like I did. I was in time, and the exquisite feeling of holding the newborn baby will make you forget all hardships.

Shipping companies would not allow children below one year to sail. So we had to wait till my daughter was one year old. That ship's accommodation was the best to date. Our cabin had a spacious day room, bedroom with thick and very soft blue-coloured carpets with matching curtains. I can still feel the velvety smoothness and softness of the carpet as the foot sinks smoothly and we could leave our daughter freely as she was learning to run.

CLOSE ENCOUNTERS

GROUNDING OFF A CARIBBEAN PORT

I joined that ship as an additional C/E for two reasons: the first was of course the promise by the superintendent that I would take over from C/E within two to three months and the second reason was that the company had allowed me to join the ship with family even though that was the first time I was working for them.

We had to go to their office for visa formalities and my wife did not like the super and had misgivings. 'He looks like a shifty character; he is not making eye contact with anyone while talking. I do not think he is a man who keeps his word.' I allayed her apprehensions by informing her how hard work and sincere efforts are always valued and rewarded.

We joined the ship at Sibenik, then in Yugoslavia. It is a very beautiful and tranquil place. You feel as if you have been transported back to the Middle Ages. The town had neat, beautiful houses along the waterfront and a town square with tiled streets and looked as if it was lifted straight from a Hollywood movie with a Middle Ages storyline (like Dracula movies). My wife commented that she would love to live in such a place in a waterfront house. We had no inkling that all hell was about to break loose in that peaceful, idyllic place and that the country would witness one of the worst genocides in human history.

Be that as it may, I concentrated on my job and put in real hard work. There were days when I could not play with my two-year-old daughter, as she would be sleeping when I returned to the cabin or when I left in the morning. The ship went to dry dock in Greece. While everyone went sightseeing, I stayed back attending to all the repairs. Super was present at that time and appreciated my efforts. After a month, when the ship went to Ravenna in Italy for loading, I was shocked to learn that a new C/E would be joining.

I was shocked and outraged and called the superintendent. He affirmed that he was quite happy with my performance and had no objection to promote me but the company policy had changed. As per the new policy, an officer could not be promoted in the ship he was sailing and he offered me a promotion in a ship that was in New Zealand. I declined the promotion and asked for immediate relief. He requested me to sail for one more voyage. I sent my family home from Italy and we sailed to Honduras (The nature of the cargo eludes me. I did not take much interest in it).

To add insult to injury, I learnt that this was the new C/E's first promotion and that this was his first employment with this company. I found him to be quite panicky and he had the habit of clutching his head and sitting on the ECR floor, moaning, 'Why does this happen only to me?' whenever there was a problem or crisis. In addition to that, he was scared of the captain.

Once, after we sailed out, the air cooler seawater inlet pipe developed a leak and bilges were getting flooded. The new C/E was refusing to talk to the captain about the crisis and about stopping engines to effect repairs.

'Captain will get angry, keep pumping bilges into bilge tank until we reach next port,' was his stand. I overruled him, talked to the captain, and stopped the engines to conduct repairs.

To go to that port, you have to go through a narrow, muddy river. I had my heart in my mouth when I saw the muddy water with floating leaves and other debris. We had no problem while going to the port as the ship was light. After we completed loading, the return passage which lasted about fourteen hours, was one of the most traumatic, exhausting, and tension-ridden periods of my career.

About half an hour after departure, the oiler rushed into the ECR and said that the main seawater pump had lost suction. I checked and found that nothing was coming out of the high sea suction filter vent. We changed over to low sea suction and opened the high sea suction filter. It was completely choked with leaves and mud. Fortunately we had a spare filter. We had hardly replaced the filter, when the low sea filter was choked. I sensed this was going to get worse and immediately called C/O and asked him to send as many men as he could spare. The worst affected were the auxiliary engines and the cooling water. Lube oil temperatures would rise very fast as lube oil cooler tubes, being of smaller diameter, would get choked first.

We worked in three teams. One team would be cleaning only the sea suction filters. We had a very good fitter; he made an arrangement to give cooling water to the auxiliary engine lube oil cooler from the fire line (Emergency fire pumps had a separate line). The second team would be cleaning the auxiliary engine lube oil coolers. The third team comprised of me and an oiler; I could not leave the ECR because of manoeuvring. I would be monitoring temperatures and sending messages to all the teams.

I was starting and stopping the auxiliary engines, taking on load, and offloading A/Es. There was no respite. I was like a juggler in a circus, handling several items in the air, ensuring that nothing would fall. Soon enough, each team had perfected their allotted duties. C/E was conspicuous by his absence; he would call from the bridge once every thirty minutes to enquire 'if everything was under control'.

Just as when I felt we were losing the battle, we suddenly entered deeper waters, and sheer exhaustion prevented people from breaking into a dance. When I think back, I cannot help feeling a twinge of professional pride surge through me. Once everything settled down and all parameters were normal, I left instructions to 3/E and was going up to the cabin. I suddenly felt the ship listing and heard the turbocharger surging. I ran back to ECR and saw that 3/E was paralyzed with shock and was slowly reducing RPM. I immediately brought the rpm to dead slow ahead.

C/E called ECR and said that we had run aground. Captain gave full astern for an hour. Ship did not budge an inch. Meanwhile, our staff was taking soundings of all tanks to check the structural integrity. To take maximum cargo, Captain had taken much less fresh water. He assumed that the fresh-water generator would see him through the long voyage to Denmark.

The Pilot told us that nothing could be done until the next high tide and that two tugs would be sent to assist the ship. We were badly stuck; every day two tugs would come at high tide and we would give full astern and struggle until the change of tide and give up. Fresh-water rationing started; one twelve-litre bucket of water per person was the quota. Even provisions were depleting. It went on for two weeks. Everyone was becoming frustrated. Finally, as per the suggestion of some religious-minded people, all went forward, and everyone offered prayers. Hindus broke coconuts and lit *agarbattis* and prayed before pictures of gods. Muslims offered namaz, and Christians offered their prayers as per their religious norms.

Everyone must have sincerely appealed to the Supreme One to save us from that predicament.

It was past midnight when I suddenly got up from a deep sleep, as I thought I felt slight movement. I just rushed to the engine room in my night clothes, informed the bridge, and started the engines. One astern movement and we were out.

Now, when I think back, I am surprised by the casual manner in which the master, company, class, and PSCs treated the incident. We did not proceed to the nearest port for underwater inspection but embarked on a long voyage across the Atlantic to Denmark. I started the fresh-water generator and we just crossed our fingers and hoped that until the completion of the voyage, the FWG which was notorious for its breakdowns, would behave when the situation was so critical that one day's loss of production would become critical. Eventually, we reached Denmark. Underwater inspections revealed no major structural damage. I signed off and went home.

Tailpiece: We had a fourth engineer. He was very nervous and shaky, his hands used to shiver at the slightest hint of a tense situation or a breakdown. I did not give much thought to his nature, until he asked me once to place my palm on his chest. I got a jolt as I could literally feel his heart moving up and down. Luckily we were in Italy. I informed C/E and C/O and we rushed him to the hospital. I thought that he would be kept under observation and be signed off. I was surprised when he returned within an hour with a few medicines. He was advised to rest for a few days and not to do any hard manual work. Now, in addition to the numerous machinery problems, I had this burden of having to remain calm when he was around. At the hint of trouble, I would ask him to go and relax. Only after he left the engine room would we go about our frantic running to set things right. I consider the way the entire E/R staff cooperated in acting normal until he left E/R highly commendable.

STEERING FAILURE
IN SUEZ TRANSIT

M y maiden voyage as a chief engineer was on a bulk
carrier with five holds and four hydraulic cranes. My
staff consisted of a 2/E and a 4/E with six months' experience
and three brand-new junior engineers. Electrical Officer was
quite efficient and was one of the best E/Os in the fleet.

That shipping company was very generous and permitted
my wife and daughter to sail with me, even though I had
been recently promoted. They probably allowed it because I
had already sailed in the ship as an additional C/E for three
months.

I had no premonition of what was in store. Like any newly
promoted C/E, I was brimming with enthusiasm and fervour
to show good results and to prove that the confidence placed
in me was justified. I was working quite hard, spending a good
deal of time in E/R and going through the previous history
and old files.

The ship sailed out from Goa, carrying iron ore to
Rostock and Hamburg. As luck would have it, E/O fell ill
with malarial fever. He could not even get up from his bed.
With inexperienced staff and a sick E/O, my hands were more
than full. I was quite watchful and we sailed to Suez without
any incident.

The Suez and Panama canals are two major arteries for
world trade and economy. Both save astronomical costs and
time for the ships. If the ships were to circumnavigate the

African and South American continents, the additional costs and time delays would cripple the world economy.

The Suez Canal crossing is an exciting and enjoyable experience. A convoy would start in the morning, with fast ships (containers, tankers, etc.) leading and old ships with slowest speed coming at the rear of the convoy. Convoys would start from both ends of the canal and midway, at Great Bitter Lake anchor area, ships would weigh anchor. The upstream convoy would be cleared first and then the downstream one.

For some strange reason, that shipping company had the policy which required C/E to be on the bridge during maneuvering or stations. The logic behind that policy always eluded me as C/E's presence in E/R is critical during emergencies (I should guiltily confess that I enjoyed my stint on the bridge, as I had the opportunity to see many breathtaking, picturesque scenes, like the Suez, Panama, Kiel canals and Bosphorus channel crossings and docking and undocking at various ports).

On that particular day, everything went smoothly and we were approaching Great Bitter Lake anchor area. I went to the cabin for a few minutes to relieve myself. Just as I was about to unlock the bathroom door, my wife started banging on the door. 'Hurry up, Captain called, he says it is an emergency,' she was shouting. I rushed to pick up the phone. 'Badasaab, steering failed, we are heading for collision,' Captain screamed and put down the phone.

I ran to the steering room. Even as I was running, I could make out that the ship was beginning to list. When I reached the steering room and saw what was happening, I was paralyzed with shock. Rudder was stuck at hard a port, and the screeching sound of the steering motors was deafening. I quickly recovered myself and tried the emergency steering on both motors. Nothing was happening. As the ship was madly turning, the roller-coaster effect was increasing.

Suddenly, I did not know why I did it, but I switched off the port steering motor. The rudder immediately swung to midship.

We narrowly missed colliding with a container ship. My wife, who was watching through the porthole, told me that it was a very, very close thing. The captain later told me that he had given full astern and was praying to God, as there was nothing else he could do.

Later we found that the port steering motor directional valve spring was broken and the broken piece had jammed the valve.

While everyone patted each other's back, congratulating each other and rejoicing on a providential escape, I had a nagging feeling that someone had either cautioned me or I had read somewhere about the course of action that I had taken. The reason for my switching off the motor was eluding me. It was like a nagging and irritating feeling that a solution is within grasp and, yet just out of reach.

The next day when I went on the bridge, the caution note posted on the steering panel jumped at me.

It said, 'WHEN BOTH STEERING MOTORS ARE ON AND STEERING PROBLEMS DEVELOP, SWITCH OFF ONE. IF PROBLEM PERSISTS, STOP THE SECOND ONE AFTER STARTING THE FIRST ONE.'

Why do many officers only look but don't see?

Near Miss—Avoiding Collision at Vizag

I relied on and believed in my sixth sense. On several occasions when I would suddenly woke up from a deep sleep, I never tried to go back to sleep. If the ship were a UMS, I would go to the engine room, take a careful survey, and come back after satisfying myself that everything was normal. In ships with manned engine rooms, I would call up ECR and ask the duty engineer or oiler to take a careful round and call me back. While in some instances it turned out to be a false alarm, more often than not, I would find some abnormality or a leak that could have developed into a disaster.

We were sailing out from Vizag anchorage. After the pilot disembarked, Captain gave full away, I increased M/E rpm to sea speed, calculated fuel and LO ROBs (remaining onboard), gave instructions to 2/E, and left ECR. Normally, I would call the bridge and give oil figures on the phone. But, on that particular day, I thought that I would go to the bridge and give oil figures to Captain and go to the cabin, since time was closer to 5 p.m..

As I was opening the door to the bridge, the seaman who was steering became unconscious and slid to the floor, right in front of my eyes. The steering wheel, in the process, had shifted to starboard side. I could see no one on the bridge. I was caught in a dilemma: should I attend to the seaman or find someone to steer the ship? I could see many ships in the anchorage area; the captain had given full away as soon as the pilot got down, without waiting for the ship to clear the restricted waters.

I ran to the port bridge wing; no one was there. Then I ran to the starboard wing and found the captain there. I screamed at him to come over, he rushed in and took over the wheel, while I called for help on the PA system.

We went quite close to another ship at anchor, so close, in fact, that I could see panic in the faces of the crew as they were shouting and waving. Captain, who's also from my place and a good friend, always recalls this incident whenever we meet.

Incidentally, that seaman was fasting that day (Saturday was his *upvas* day) and was working in the hot sun, leading to weakness. Since that day, I have always discouraged people (especially Muslims) from practicing fasting rituals while onboard.

REFUSING TO SAIL IN AN
UNSEAWORTHY SHIP

This was my second ship with that company. While sailing with an Indian company, though I had several offers to migrate to foreign companies, I was reluctant to leave my comfort zone. One of the superintedents had left and joined this shipping company and convinced me to follow suit.

To my surprise, my first contract with that company was quite enjoyable on all fronts. Good company support, harmonious on-board conditions, and very good port visits (my family sailed with me for most of the contract) made that stint on the first ship quite memorable and I was totally unprepared for the jolt of the second one.

I joined the ship at a port in the Red Sea. I was surprised by the biting cold. I had always thought that was a hot, humid country. But the climate was different from the chilling weather of Europe in winter. This cold was like being covered with an icy wet blanket, the chill biting into the bones. This depressing climate was probably an indication of things in store.

The ship was of course quite old. The age of the ship did not bother me, since I was of the age and mindset that gives you the supreme confidence that no obstruction is insurmountable, nothing is impossible and that with hard work, diligence, and intelligence, any problem can be solved. I was in for a rude shock.

It was well past midnight as I went up the gangway and proceeded to the C/E's cabin. My apprehensions began to

133

grow. The ship had a depressing, neglected, and ill-maintained look. Alleyways and floors were dirty and the lighting was poor.

C/E opened the door to my knock, and said, 'Thank God you came!' My spirits sank another foot. He offered a beer which I gratefully accepted. He was from my state, a couple of years senior to me. We talked about common friends. He was sailing with his wife, who also participated in the conversation.

After some small talk, he assured me that everything was in order, though they had many problems and breakdowns in the preceding voyage. But his obvious relief at the prospect of going home was disquieting. I should have taken a quick round of the engine room, but I was quite exhausted; I bid them goodnight and went to the spare cabin and went to sleep.

Next day, C/E's flight was at 10 a.m, so the agent came to pick him up at 8 a.m. In two hours of available time, Raju handed over fuel oil, lube oil statements, pending repairs and jobs. We took a cursory round of the E/R. Dirty would be too mild a word to describe that E/R. As explained earlier, I was young, brash, and overconfident and believed that any problem could be solved. I had to pay dearly for my foolishness in not asking for sufficient time for taking over.

After seeing him off, I observed the following deficiencies.

1. There was no spare M/E cylinder head. The ship had a history of frequent breakdowns due to cylinder head failure. Raju assured me that a new one would be connected.
2. M/E flywheel was submerged in E/R bilge water up to 1/3 height. There was thick black oil deposits in bilges.
3. HO settling and service tank drains were led to E/R bilges with fabricated pipelines.
4. The bilge pump was not working.

5. Only one GS pump was in working condition and it was used for pumping out bilges, deck water, winch cooling. No spares for any of the pumps.

6. The incinerator was not working; once you started it, oil would splash all over the bulkheads and on the auxiliary boiler.

7. Accommodation blower had a breakdown, cast-iron bearing kept getting cracked, no spares onboard and on-board repair not possible.

8. The domestic hot-water heater had a breakdown. Spare heavy oil purifier heater was installed and you would get oily, lukewarm water for bath.

9. Air pressure reducer was malfunctioning, causing blackouts without warning.

As can be expected, I was very disturbed and talked to Captain. I asked him how he had allowed things to deteriorate to such a condition and that I wanted to call the head office, and inform them of my decision to go home. He asked me to sleep on it and the next day we could talk to the office.

The crew was from a non-seafaring nation and they had no seamanship or basic seaman qualities. I was horrified by the ignorance, carelessness, and the dangerous practices followed in that ship by the crew and officers.

I went to the bridge and told the captain that I could not delay my decision to leave the ship any further and wished to talk to the office. He made the call, talked to the superintendent, and handed the phone over to me. Before I could say anything after formal greetings, the superintendent told me, 'Chief, there is a small problem. We ordered a new cylinder head to be connected at Gibraltar. It is on the way. But, we have realized that we ordered a wrong model. You have to manage till South Africa without a spare.'

I told him that I was not ready to sail till Gibraltar, let alone South Africa. I told him that the ship was unseaworthy and she should go to a lay-up berth for adequate repairs. He was shocked and asked me to give details. I explained everything to him. He had one trump card. He told me that had I asked for Chief Engineer to stay for one more day or until I was satisfied, it would have been possible. But with the ship sailing the next day, there was no time to arrange relief. He requested me to take the ship to Gibraltar, where I would be signed off. I had to reluctantly agree.

We sailed out he next day. After sailing, I noticed that intermediate bearing oil was contaminated by the seawater. There were so many problems I did not know where to begin. We were very lucky that we managed to cross the Suez Canal without incident. During the entire transit, I kept 2/E near the air pressure reducing valve to prevent a blackout.

A few days after Suez, the weather became very rough. The 2/E reported that exhaust smoke smell was observed from M/E cooling water expansion tank vent. It was either the cylinder head or the exhaust valve housing that was cracked. My worst nightmare became a reality. In those very turbulent weather conditions, lifting and checking heavy items exhausted us all.

It was a very old Mitsubishi engine with three very heavy exhaust valves and massive cylinder heads. Disconnecting and lifting these in rough sea with heavy rolling was very taxing. A little miscalculation or lack of focus can seriously injure people and ship. We found out that the cylinder head had cracked in the combustion chamber area, rendering on-board repair impossible. We had an old cylinder head with a burnt exhaust valve pocket. I replaced the cracked one with this. With the unit cut out and at less speed, we were moving at a snail's speed.

Wind and weather refused to die down. Though I was physically exhausted, I was very alert. I must have traversed from E/R to bridge at least a hundred times. Finally we convinced the company that the ship should be diverted to repair the cylinder head with the burnt exhaust valve pocket.

We anchored at a port in Italy. One young superintendent boarded the ship with a local workshop. After landing the cylinder head for repairs, I told Super that he had to wait until I completed my sorely missed sleep for any discussion. I must have gone without sleep for at least three days. The reserve energy that was driving me suddenly deflated. I just collapsed on the bed.

After I woke up and freshened up, I told the super to take care of his baby and to allow me to go home from there. He pleaded with me that Gibraltar was only a few days away and my reliever was all ready to fly and requested me to cooperate. Whether he was acting or not, I do not know, but he looked devastated by the carnage. There is no other word to describe the state of affairs. We received repaired cylinder head after twenty-four hours and we sailed out to Gibraltar. Weather improved miraculously and the sea was like a lake. Looking at the placid waters, it was hard to believe two days back it was trying to gobble us up.

En route to Gibraltar, a message came from the company that the South Africa charter was cancelled and the ship had to proceed to the USA on ballast. While I thanked God and my stars for taking a firm stand, I could not but help feel sympathy for the incoming C/E. To embark on a transatlantic voyage without a spare cylinder head and numerous problems, that too to the USA, would be the ultimate nightmare for any C/E. Super could read my thoughts, so to prevent my scaring away the new C/E, he escorted me to the boat at Gibraltar anchorage immediately after I handed over the oil figures. I managed to tell the new C/E to read my handing-over notes as soon as possible. The new C/E was lured with a promotion and I was further depressed. An experienced, seasoned C/E may manage but what chance would this raw, inexperienced C/E have?

While I was waiting in the boat for Super, the C/E managed to extricate himself from the super and came into the boat. 'Badasaab, tell me honestly, why are you going in such a short time, is it due to family problem as the office told me or is it due to the condition of the ship?'

I could not be dishonest. I told him. 'There is no family problem. I just felt that I cannot do justice. You are much younger, more energetic, and you should be able to tackle the problems. But before you leave, inspect the liner, the engine was running for several hours with an exhaust leak and the cylinder lubrication could have been affected.'

He was worried and distraught.

'Do you think I should refuse the promotion and go back?' he asked me. 'I did not expect this scenario.'

Before I could answer, Super came into the boat, shook hands with C/E, wished him all the best, and saw him off the pilot ladder. The boat pulled away. As the ship was disappearing into the horizon, I asked Super if the workshop would attend to urgent repairs and liner inspection before sailing. Though he was courteous and pleasant, he told me that ship would sail out after bunkers and I need not have any apprehensions since I was no longer in charge. I kept quiet.

All the flights were overbooked. We stayed in a hotel for two days and then flew home. The company bore all my expenses. Super was very polite, and thanked me for bringing the ship safely to Italy, when we were parting company.

About a week later, I got a shock when my friend, the personnel manager of my previous company, called me and informed me that I was blacklisted in FOSMA (Foreign Owners and Ship Managers Association). When I called the India office, they said they had no idea as to why and that I had to contact the head office. I directly called the big boss and demanded an explanation. At first he dodged and tried to shift the blame to Indian office. I told him recruiting agents can take no such action without the principal's instructions.

Finally he came out with the truth. He told me, 'Do you know that the ship had a major breakdown right in the middle of Atlantic? The liner cracked, they had to change the liner in rough sea.'

I asked him, 'Have they managed to change the liner? Is the ship safe? Where is she?'

He told me that after a lot of struggle they managed to change the liner and the ship was sailing and that the management was very upset that signing-off C/E did not advise Super or the incoming C/E about necessity of liner inspection.

Suddenly, I lost my temper. I asked him to check all the telex messages from the ship. I reminded him that I refused to sail after joining and everyone in HO had thanked me for taking the ship safely to Italy. My hotel stay and air ticket expenses were borne by the company to show their gratitude. I asked the GM to look directly into the eyes of Super and ask him whether I had advised him, or not, to inspect the liner and carry out minimum urgent repairs at Gibraltar, not that any super worth his salt needed someone to tell him that after such grave breakdowns. I reminded him that Super did sail in the ship from Italy to Gibraltar and he should take blame for commissions and omissions. The least that the company could do was to talk to me before deciding to blacklist me.

The GM conveniently escaped, saying he had an urgent meeting. Before he could hang up, I challenged him that not only would I get back into foreign shipping but would earn such a good name that he would regret having lost such a fine officer.

I was in a state of severe depression for the next two weeks. Blacklisting in FOSMA did not bother me at all. I kept asking myself whether the ship could have been saved from all this ordeal had I told the incoming C/E about everything and advised him not to sail or had I apprised the harbour masters of ports of the ship's deficiencies. Every day I prayed for the safety of crew and ship.

I slept peacefully after a crew member called me from the USA and informed me that they arrived safely.

NEAR MISS—AVOIDING COLLISION AT CHINA

We had loaded iron ore in Australia and were waiting at Mazhishan anchorage for our turn. Engines were on thirty minutes' notice. We did not take up any jobs on the engine, but opened up the ballast pump for a routine overhaul. In Cape-size ships, ballast pumps are quite massive and the entire engine crew was engaged there.

It was just after teatime, about 11 a.m. I was in the ECR preparing messages, when Captain called. He told me that a ship was dragging anchor, he had called them, and they had assured him that they would start their engines and move clear. But he just wanted to keep me informed and assured me that he would easily give ten minutes notice for engines if required.

My sixth sense told me to be ready for an emergency. Without waiting for any notice, I started another Auxiliary engine, taken on load, disengaged the turning gear and closed indicator cocks. As I was closing the no.6 unit indicator cock, the phone rang.

Captain was screaming, 'Badasaab, give engines, that ship is very close, she is bearing on us.' I gave bridge the controls; he immediately gave full astern and hard a port on steering. He told me later that we were saved literally by the skin of our teeth. A few seconds delay could have been fatal.

I asked him why he had thought that he could give ten minutes' notice; he said that he had misjudged the strength of the current. That other ship could not start their engines because of some problem and the strong current pushed that ship very fast on to us.

The captain was so shaken up, he quit sailing and is now working as director of a reputed training institute.

GROUNDING OFF BAOSHAN

Captain and I landed in Hong Kong for a briefing prior to joining one ship as observers. Our company was to take over the management of that ship from another, as per the new Japanese owners' preference. As the vessel's berthing was delayed, we were put in the company's guest house. Every day we had to go to the office at 9 a.m., stay till 5 p.m., and return to the flat in the evening.

In the office, I had to assist one super. I was shocked by his lack of computer literacy. I would complete whatever jobs he would give me, within an hour, whereas he would struggle for hours to complete the same amount of work. I could sense his unease that I could edge him out of his job, had I continued to do it. I assured him that I would never opt for an office job.

It is true, I can never sit at a desk for six hours. During weekends we went sightseeing; the most memorable experience was seeing the huge Buddha statue on an island nearby. Unfortunately Captain misplaced or lost the photographs. Slowly we were getting bored to death, until finally we got news that the ship had berthed. Prior to leaving, the Japanese owners met us and the director of our company introduced us as 'the best captain and C/E of our fleet'. Though it could have been a publicity stunt, nonetheless it made us feel proud and happy.

To our pleasant surprise, we were received very warmly onboard the ship. Normally, observers are viewed with suspicion, rightly so, since the duty of observers is to find deficiencies (apart from learning about the ship) and report these to the head office so that they can have more bargaining power. An observer's job is very delicate; he has to gain the maximum information without ruffling the Master's and the C/E's feathers. Here, Captain and I differed in our approaches.

I told C/E that I perfectly understood his position, since I had the experience of being the handing-over C/E when a ship was sold. I would only observe what he was willing or was ready to show. I told him that I was confident that I could run the ship, the logic being that if you can do it, so can I, but my only request was to give me some tips before he left, about critical issues like blanked pipes, temporary repairs and patchwork, which are not readily noticeable. That C/E was from Kerala, a thorough gentleman. I never went snooping around, I was present in the ECR during tea breaks when all were present, and we talked about everything except the ship. Slowly the ice thawed and all of us became friendly. I gained more knowledge than I had hoped for.

In contrast, Captain was breathing down the necks of the master and C/O and he was oblivious of their exasperation and displeasure. They were avoiding him and he was agitated.

The ship discharged cargo and sailed out to Australia to load iron ore. We were to take over at Baoshan after unloading the iron ore. It was a unique experience, sailing as a paid passenger or a tourist. I thoroughly enjoyed the carefree feeling. There must have been a huge stock in the bonded locker, which they wanted to consume before handing over. So, every evening, on port bridge wing, there would be parties with flowing liquor and antakshari, games, and snacks. Captain Rajan was an excellent host; he would make us sit till the early hours, since others had watches and duties. We could get up when we wanted to, watch movies at any time, which was a luxury not experienced even at home.

One striking difference that I noticed in the set up on that ship from our company was the quality of crew and officers. Engine department had 2/E with I class, 3/E with II class, and a very competent 4/E. The fitter was one of the best I had come across. I asked him why, with such skill and knowledge, he was not aiming to become an engineer by passing exams. His reply was that his English was very poor. I told him his English was better than Shakespeare's when compared to that of some Bangladeshi and Filipino 2/Es that I had sailed with.

I have no complaints about Filipino crew; any day they are better than crew of any other nationality. They are sincere, hard-working, and do not complain. But Filipino officers rise from the ranks; 2/Es start their careers as wipers and as such they lack initiative. They follow orders, but solving problems and seeking solutions was not their strength, in those days. But over the years, Filipino officers have evolved into fine officers and are much sought after. In those days, C/E had to wage a lone battle. This engine room complement was the dream team I would love to have in any ship.

After a pleasant and event-free voyage, we returned to China, Baoshan anchorage. By the time we anchored, it was 1 a.m. All crew members and officers were very excited and in a festive mood as they would be going home soon. Their flight details and tickets had already been received.

Pilot boarded at 3 a.m. We were to shift to alongside a mother ship which was a few cables away, part discharge, and then proceed to berth after lightening. I was in the ECR, having coffee. It was the usual routine. M/E was tried out, controls were transferred to bridge. Anchor stations were called, C/O started heaving up anchor. Suddenly there was a huge bump, a phone call from bridge, and all hell broke loose. Like a light switched on, there was sudden hectic activity; everyone was running around, starting standby generators, starting ballast pumps. Though I knew something went terribly wrong, I neither interfered nor asked questions.

After thirty minutes or so, the ship was tied up to mother ship, then C/E told me that the ship had run aground and starboard ballast tank was ruptured and both ballast pumps were unable to empty the tank. It seems that the ship was anchored quite close to an unlit island. The pilot and captain were unprepared for the strong current or proximity of the island when they heaved up anchor. Within no time, the ship banged on the rocks and by the time the engines pulled the ship away, starboard ballast tank was damaged. Efforts to empty the tank were discontinued after realizing its futility.

The crew was crestfallen, as their schedules and plans had gone haywire within a fraction of a minute. After discharging was completed, the ship was taken to a floating dry dock. We got the shock of our lives when we saw the extent of damage to the shipside plate and frames. The size of the hole was about half the area of the mess room. The web frames and plates were torn apart by the rocks as easily as a child would tear apart a newspaper.

What we were privileged to witness was not only the amazing strength of nature and the fragility of solid steel but also the tenacity, ingenuity, and expertise of man, or rather of Chinese man.

A repair of that magnitude would have taken at least a couple of months in any yard in the world. But it was accomplished in less than two weeks in front of our unbelieving eyes. Hundreds of workers were working like ants, in what appeared to be a chaotic system. Welding cables, gas hoses were entangled all over the place, scaffoldings were erected crudely, pipes were tied with ropes, everywhere sparks were flying, welding cables and gas hoses were lying in the slushy mud. Welders were working standing precariously on a ledge, gas cylinders were shifted very close to scaffoldings, sometimes even banging. There appeared to be no safety officer around. But what mattered was that the job was completed to the satisfaction of the class surveyors within two weeks.

Flooding of Engine Room

If there is someone more dangerous to a ship than a 24/7 drunkard captain, it is the young, brash 2/E or C/O who has just cleared MEO I class or master's exam. Their overconfident, super-inflated ego is matched by their conviction that their superiors are doddering idiots. Like cricket, marine engineering is also a great leveler. Australia's cricket team is humbled by Bangladesh; India is brought to earth by Ireland. These brash young officers will eventually be brought to earth, but whether they wreak havoc before that happens is decided by luck and the alertness of seniors.

That ship was a 28-year-old OBO converted to an ore carrier. She was a deep-drafted 200,000 tonner with two Burmeister & Wein engines and numerous problems. My staff had only two Indians (2/E and E/O); all the rest were Filipinos. We completed loading at Brazil and pilot boarded the vessel.

While taking a round, I noticed that water was dripping continuously from seawater inlet expansion bellow flange of the starboard engine. When I entered ECR, 2/E asked me if I had noticed the leakage. I told him that I had noticed it and warned him not to touch it, since I suspected he would be itching to rectify it. He gave me a morose look and told me that the water was dripping from the flange and can be arrested by tightening nuts and bolts of the flange. I told him that though it appeared to be so, the leak could also be due to a crack in the expansion bellow and a repair can be attempted only after dropping pilot and once we were in the open sea.

In those ships, I used to carry a walkie-talkie during maneuvering and port stays to monitor activities. I realized that I had forgotten it and went to the cabin to get it. It would not have taken me more than three to four minutes, and when I returned to ECR, there was commotion; 4/E was all wet and shivering. The 4/E was not shivering because he was drenched, but from dread of how I would react to the news of flooding. The bellow had cracked when 4/E tried to tighten nuts and bolts under instruction from 2/E.

I went to check and found water pouring with the force of a half-opened hydrant. It was bad but not catastrophic. I estimated that we would be able to manage for about two hours before the bilge tank would be full. I went back to ECR, gave a dressing-down to 2/E and warned him not to do anything without my knowledge or consent. I instructed the oiler to keep transferring bilges to bilge tank and keep me posted of the soundings.

Bridge control was not working. Both engines had to be manually started one after the other. Skill was required to start the engines without consuming excess air and I performed manoeuvring while others would be adjusting temperatures and taking rounds. I was tied up and could not leave ECR. Once I overheard on the walkie-talkie that pilot had disembarked, I went outside ECR to have a look. I had the shock of my life when I saw one fitter working on the bolts and nuts of the flange on the other end of the pipe connected to the bellow. Before I could shout to him not to do anything, he gave a hammer blow to the spanner holding the nut. The shock transmitted to the weak bellow and water started flooding the engine room. Now it was a catastrophe.

I ran back to ECR, called the bridge and informed them that I had to stop the engines and main seawater pump as the engine room was flooding. Captain started telling me that we were in the channel and we could not stop and to hold on for thirty minutes. I asked him to come down. Meanwhile,

I stopped the main seawater pump and reduced engine rpm. Captain had one look and his jaw dropped as if it had become unhinged. I stopped the starboard engine and tried to isolate it. We found that some of the valves were leaking and water force was not coming down. Somehow, we reached a reasonably safe zone. By that time, water filled up to nearly two feet below the floor plates, submerging two Pielstick engines provided on tank top level for ballast pumps.

We stopped the engines and main seawater pump, and shut all the valves. There was still considerable force in the water since the overboard valve was leaking and as the ship was fully loaded and overboard valve had considerable head pressure. I really thank my fitters and engineers (except 2/E, who was a mere spectator) for their raw courage and determination, which saved the ship and our lives. Ore carriers normally do not give chance for survival as they tend to break and go down in seconds. They blanked the lines with great difficulty, as the seawater was splashing into their faces with full force. Fortunately, it was a tropical zone. Then with one engine, we moved further into the open sea, where we stopped to fabricate a pipe (the spare bellow was not available) and fitted it to starboard engine.

Later when I asked 2/E what madness prompted him to ask the fitter to work on the bolts of the pipe, his answer was that he wanted to save time and he wanted to reclaim some of the lost prestige due to his first mistake!

Pollution in Fos on Christmas Eve

On that Christmas Day, everything was quiet and peaceful on all fronts. The ship was in Fos (France). Only one shore crane was operating and the Filipino crew was given the day off after lunch. They were having a party and celebrating. I told 2/E and E/O to knock off after trying out the starboard engine. The 2/E had already started all the pumps before lunch and was waiting for me in ECR.

I was near the completion of logbook entries, when I chanced to overhear a conversation between the duty seaman and C/O on my walkie-talkie. The seaman was reporting that there was oil sheen between starboard stern of the ship and the wharf. C/O told him not to bother as shore people were washing their cranes and the oil traces could be from there. I got up and watched through the porthole, and sure enough, several people were hosing down their cranes and water was flowing into the water.

A sixth sense prodded me to take a closer look. I put on my helmet and went out. I met C/O in the alleyway on main deck, conversing with E/O. When he saw me, he mockingly said, 'What, badasaab, you get unnecessarily worried, that oil sheen is not from our ship, it is from the cranes.' I smiled and told him that I preferred to be safe than sorry.

I stood on the jetty, watching carefully the water between the ship and the wharf. There indeed was a sheen of oil. After about ten seconds when I was about to abandon the vigil, I suddenly saw one bubble and then oil spreading in that area. I immediately called C/O on my walkie-talkie and asked him to tell 2/E to stop all M/E pumps.

I rushed back to the ship, called all crew to the engine room, and explained the emergency. I told them to isolate each lube oil cooler, close the seawater inlet and outlet valves and check from vent or drain for oil traces, and report. The 2/E and I started changing over generators and checking the coolers. Within ten minutes, one 4/E told me that oil was coming from starboard main engine camshaft cooler. The cooler is very small, measuring about 3 feet long and about 30 cm in diameter. For some strange reason it was made of aluminium; its end cover was eroded and oil flowed past the O-ring. Camshaft LO tank was also small, about 500 litres. I could not understand why the low-level alarm did not sound until the duty oiler informed us that he kept supplementing the oil as he observed that the level was going down. His reply was a sheepish grin when asked why he did not inform 2/E.

Main seawater pump was off, but the overboard line was filled with oil. Had I started the seawater pump, the entire basin would have been coated with oil. We found an old original cooler (with brass tubes) with some tubes plugged; we pressure-tested it and kept it ready.

I strictly forbade anyone to touch anything. I went up and broke the bad news to Captain. He was also my colleague during the flooding episode (He is the cousin brother of police officer Hemant Karkare, who was martyred in 26/11). His face was ashen. 'What, badasaab, this New Year can we see our families, or will we be counting prison cell bars?' Though he joked, I could see he was worried.

I put up a brave front and said, 'France is a maritime nation and whoever is in charge of PSC (Port State Control) would be some experienced captain or C/E, who would understand that we had not polluted but actually helped in prevention.' We called DPA (designated person ashore), a Brazilian C/E, and apologized for ruining his Christmas and apprised him of the situation. I admire him for his stand. He did not tell me to cut corners or 'do something'. Without hesitation, he told us to call the agent, PSC, and class. 'Don't worry, it is not your problem anymore,' he assured us.

We followed his directive; within half an hour, the PSC Chief boarded the ship. I took him to the engine room, showed him the cooler and spare cooler which was holding the pressure test. He complimented us on the course of action and said that had we tried to dismantle the cooler or in any way tampered with the so-called evidence, we would have been in the soup. I explained to him about the 200–300 litres of lube oil that was there in the pipeline. He took photographs and left.

After a few hours, a boom was placed around the ship. The pollution containment truck arrived. It looked like an ordinary tanker truck with three compartments and had a powerful vacuum pump. A diver blanked the opening of the overboard valve on the ship side. Local workshop personnel removed the overboard valve, emptied the oil contents in the pipe to our waste oil tank with their pump, and fitted back the valve. Once the diver removed the blank, the pollution containment team was ready with their pump and chemicals. As per Captain's instructions, I started and stopped the main seawater pump, running it for a few seconds. The containment team would mop up the oil discharged. After five to six times, once pure water was discharged, the operation was called off.

The captain and I felt that we got away lightly, since the event took place on Christmas Eve, when people would be in a forgiving mood and thoughts of kindness to humanity would be overflowing in their hearts.

NEAR MISS—AVOIDING COLLISION AT SINGAPORE

I joined the PSV as an additional C/E. Since I wished to change over to an offshore fleet, I thought joining a new ship at the yard before delivery was an ideal option. We checked into a hotel in Fuzhou, China and the next day we went to the yard. There I met the C/E, who was sent two months earlier to acquaint himself with the ship and equipment. I had not come across a fatter man on any ship. He was highly experienced in offshore field and had worked only in foreign companies and mostly in the North Sea. We changed into boiler suits and went to the ship.

I could not imagine how the ship could be delivered within a week as projected by the office. In the engine room, all equipment was covered with plastic, all floor plates were out, and the bilges were full of welding rod pieces, and junk. The engine room bulkheads were not painted, and everything was in a haphazard state and. cabling was still underway.

I asked the C/E how sea trials were completed when so much work was pending. He told me that only painting and small jobs were pending, sea trials had been completed satisfactorily and all the equipment was tested. The ship was teeming with workers. I went back to the yard to study manuals and drawings so that at least theoretically I could know about the ship.

Lunch was atrocious, even people who relished non-veg food could not force themselves to eat what looked like worms, insects, and probably pieces of snakes floating in the soup liquids. That day we starved; from the next day onwards, we brought fruits and biscuits from the hotel. One Chinese supervisor who could speak a little English explained to me about starting of M/Es, thrusters, etc.

After four days, Super told us to go back to the hotel, check out, and bring our luggage to the ship. We did as we were told. The engine room floor plates were still wet with paint and shore supply was still on. The next morning, all the equipment was started and shown, except the stern thruster, which was not starting. The manufacturer's service engineer came the next day to rectify the fault and we sailed out.

I was on the 12–6 watch. Once we sailed out, I was shocked to find several deficiencies which made the ship unseaworthy. But no one was unduly concerned, especially C/E and E/O, who did not come to ECR even once during my watch.

Some of the deficiencies were

1. E/R alarms and phone bell were audible only in ECR. If for some reason the engineer and oiler were not present in ECR, E/R the alarms and phone could not be attended to by anyone, as any provision for audio/visual beacons outside ECR were not there. This was highly risky in case the bridge wanted to contact E/R in an emergency.
2. The fire and general alarm was not activated. In case of a fire, only the red indicating lamp of the sensor would be lit. None of the general alarm call points were working or connected.
3. CO_2 alarms and trips were not activated.
4. Emergency generator would start but did not come on load.

The ship sailed to Hong Kong. I was the only one perturbed by a possible PSC (Port State Control) inspection.

Everyone was supremely confident that PSC would inspect only the big ships of the main fleet and would not bother about PSVs and OSVs. To my amazement, they turned out to be right; no one came to inspect and we sailed out to Singapore. Considering that this was the maiden voyage of the ship, I found C/E's disinterest baffling. When ship reached Singapore, the superintendent, warranty engineer, and workshop boarded the ship. Super was quite frustrated with the indifferent and casual attitude of C/E.

When the near-miss incident occurred, C/E, Super, and I were in the ECR. It was around 11 a.m. The shore workshop and the cleaning gang were working in the engine room. The engine room bilges and areas under the flywheel were being cleaned. The phone rang. I lifted the receiver.

Captain just screamed, 'Give ST and BT, urgent,' and put the phone down. I could sense an emergency situation was developing. I just told C/E that the bridge wanted engines urgently and went and called all workers out, asked their supervisor to take a head count and started the engines. I came to ECR, took engines on load, started ST and BT, and informed the bridge.

During all this, C/E was screaming at me. 'You should ask what is the cause of such urgency, you should tell them Okay but give engines leisurely, otherwise they will always expect engines instantly.' He told the Super that he was not responsible for my actions.

I held my temper and tongue in check and was silent. Then we felt a bump. The phone rang.

Captain at the other end was ecstatic and said, 'Thank you for giving engines promptly, the other ship dragged anchor and gave only a glancing blow, had you delayed by a few more minutes, she would have hit us squarely in the amidships.'

When I relayed this information, C/E's jaw dropped. Later, Super told me that C/E told everyone that he urged me to give engines fast and that I was dragging my feet and grudgingly went about the business slowly.

I asked Super whose version would he have believed if he were not present. Super just laughed and told me that the crew was with the company for decades and kept him informed of everything. He said that C/E would be replaced within the next few days.

Near Miss—Blackout Near Rigs and Steering Failure

This is a continuation of the previous ship experience. As Super said, C/E was replaced. The new C/E was active, knowledgeable but suffered from a massive ego. I was quite happy as this C/E was on my wavelength and we rectified several deficiencies.

Suddenly, a few days before sailing to the oil field, he became distant and hostile. It was just like switching off a light. I could not understand, I tried to recollect what I could have said or done which caused this shift. I could think of nothing that could be termed as offensive. Finally, I zeroed in on one conversation where I asked him if he were from DMET. He replied that he was a port apprentice. When he asked me, I told that I was a BE (Mech-Marine). Suddenly he became aloof, which I found odd. Either he was suffering from a complex or he must have suffered at the hands of graduate engineers.

Whatever the reason, he started to ignore me to the extent that he would look through me as if I did not exist, when I greeted him or asked him a question. He would discuss only with 2/E, totally ignoring me. I also slowly kept to the sidelines, kept my watch and duties, and did not interfere.

That ship had two small Caterpillar engines for ship load. For ST (stern thruster) and BT (bow thruster), two Yanmar engines were there, which could be coupled to the propellers, shaft generators, and FiFi pumps. There was an inherent problem. The ship load could be transferred to the shaft generators but before starting ST and BT, ship load had to be transferred to the Caterpillar generators.

If you start the CT, BT when the ship load is on the shaft generators, the sudden dip would cause a blackout. When we reached anchorage at Rangoon, in spite of his hostility, I told all this to C/E, who did not want to start Caterpillar engines. I warned him of the danger of a blackout; he brushed me aside.

I went up, and promptly after some time, there was a blackout. Power was restored and I thought he had learnt the lesson the hard way. But he took it as a prestige issue, and to prove me wrong, he kept trying the same thing and caused blackouts close to the oil rig, while in Burma channel where strong currents could have grounded the ship. Finally, when the captain wanted to report to the company about the number of blackout incidents, C/E finally relented but despised me all the more.

Emergency steering was complicated with many cocks to be arranged in a particular way. I prepared the instructions and posted it in the steering room. I had accompanied the service engineer and understood the system.

One day, I finished my lunch and was going up. When I saw 2/E and C/E running down, I asked them what had happened. The 2/E said that port steering had failed. I also went to the steering room, found that they had changed valves correctly to enable the starboard steering motor to operate both rudders and went to the bridge.

E/O was there; I asked him if everything was under control. He told me that starboard steering was now moving both rudders but port rudder was off by 15 degrees. Unless they were synchronized, steering could not be controlled.

Because of C/E's antagonism, I was hesitating to intervene, when E/O urged me to rectify the fault since he knew I took keen interest and could take the correct action. I went back to the steering room and asked C/E politely if I could give it a try.

By that time they were at their wit's end. I isolated the port steering by arranging the valves, brought the rudder to zero position by pushing the solenoid valve with a welding rod, then put the system back to normal.

After a few days, I found C/E going out of his way to ingratiate me, talking sweetly. Later, I learnt that he had had a major fight with Captain and wanted support from any and every quarter.

CLOSE ENCOUNTER OF
A DIFFERENT KIND

This story is different from others in the sense that it does not involve machinery, equipment, or anything related to the ship.

We signed off from Brazil and were coming home. That ship was the second largest bulk carrier in those days. It was so huge it could enter only a few ports in the world. Some ports in Brazil, Rotterdam, and Japan had the required depth to take our ship in when fully loaded.

We were eight in our group; I and Electrical Officer were officers and the rest were crew. Our flight was to Mumbai via Amsterdam. There was not much of a waiting period at Amsterdam; we would have to rush to catch the connecting flight.

We passed through immigration, security and were seated in the waiting lounge near our boarding gate.

I saw the girl who was at the check-in counter run towards us.

'Excuse me, you are Indian, right?' she asked me breathlessly.

'Yes, why?' I asked her, puzzled.

'Please help us, we are having problem with a passenger,' she requested me.

I told her I didn't mind helping but I might have trouble with immigration, scanning, and security. She assured me that she would personally escort me and I followed her. We still had two hour's time.

While we were walking, I asked her what the problem was.

She shrugged and told me, 'He is standing like a statue; he is not producing any passport, nor air ticket. We thought maybe there could be language problem, I hope you can help us out.'

When we reached the check-in counters, she pointed out a young man to me. He was in his early twenties, of medium build and height, and bespectacled. He wore a half-sleeved shirt and jeans. In one hand he was holding an orange. He was mumbling something inaudibly. He had applied *kumkum* (vermilion) on his forehead which was quite prominent.

I smiled at him and asked him what his name was and where he was going. He did not even look at me. He was staring straight ahead. I tried English, Hindi and Telugu. I could see his passport and air ticket in his shirt pocket. There was no reaction from him when I pulled them out.

His passport gave his name as Kumar and address as a village in Karnataka, India. His immigration papers showed that he was a trainee electrical officer employed by a reputed Indian shipping company.

I suddenly recalled that my E/O (electrical officer) was also from Karnataka and told the girl to send for him, since this young man might respond to E/O as he spoke his language. I told her that India was like Europe with as many languages and dialects, if not more.

When E/O came, I apprised him of the situation. E/O put his hand over Kumar's shoulder and spoke to him softly in Kannada. Kumar did not speak or smile but he allowed himself to be led to the check-in counter.

I saw his ticket; he was also going to Mumbai. I discussed the situation with E/O and he volunteered to assist the poor young man. My idea was to take him to Mumbai, call his office, and hand him over to them.

We did not realize we were undertaking a herculean task.

Kumar seemed to trust E/O. He allowed E/O to lead him by hand; the girl accompanied us and she talked to immigration and security so we went to our boarding area quickly. E/O was continuously talking to him, trying to elicit a reaction or comment. Kumar just stared blankly, murmuring something inaudibly.

One of our crew members remembered having seen Kumar with a group. He walked around for a while, came back, and told me that they were sitting in a different section.

We took Kumar to them.

I asked them, 'Is Kumar your colleague? You signed off from the same ship?'

They fidgeted uncomfortably. Some looked at their shoes; others pretended not to have heard me. They were scared that I would palm him off on them.

I lost my temper, 'How can you abandon your colleague?' I shouted at them.

One of them retorted defiantly, 'It is not our problem. Master, shipping agent, and the company should look after him.'

I was shocked. How could people be so heartless?

Before I could say anything angrily, a senior man among them took us to seats a few rows away, and when we were seated, he told me, 'Sir, we are almost illiterate. Normally an officer accompanies us. This time they sent Kumar. He is a trainee electrical officer. We were sure he will be detained by immigration or security. If they find us with him, we will also be in trouble. You officers can talk and convince authorities. We can't. We are also concerned about him but we thought it would be better for him to be detained by authorities so that Agent and Master will take corrective action.'

I could partly agree with his logic, and later I was to acknowledge his profound wisdom.

I asked him, 'Now that we brought him this far, will any of you take him to Mumbai?'

He said that none of them was going to Mumbai. Many were going to Cochin, a few to Chennai, and others to Delhi.

I asked him to give us both office and residence phone numbers of the manager in India. He went back to the group and came back after a few minutes and gave the numbers of one Mr. Atul.

As he was about to turn back, I asked him, 'How long has he been like this?'

He gave a pitying look at Kumar and said, 'Sir, he was jovial, active, and hardworking. He mixed well with crew and officers. During our last voyage, we encountered very rough weather and the ship was rolling and pitching heavily. Kumar went on deck and had one look at the huge waves and rough sea and went into shock. Since then he has been like this.'

I salute E/O. He did not give up. He kept trying to engage Kumar in conversation, tried to elicit a reaction during entire duration of flight to Amsterdam.

When we were waiting to alight at Amsterdam, he told me, 'Sir, I think we made a mistake.'

I asked him why.

He said, 'I am worried. He has not sipped a drop of water, has not taken a bite. Worse, at Amsterdam airport and here in flight, I tried to make him go to the restroom. He is not budging. Maybe we should have left him in Brazil. The agent would have been forced to look after him.'

I reassured him, 'Don't worry. As soon as we get down, I will call Mr. Atul, tell him everything, and ask him to send someone to the airport to take care of him. In Brazil if he gets lost, no one can help him.'

In those days we had to buy telephone cards. I called Mr. Atul in his office, told him about Kumar and he assured me he would send someone to Mumbai Airport to receive him.

When we stood in the queue for boarding the Mumbai flight, suddenly I heard E/O exclaim, 'Oh, my God... No.'

I asked him what the matter was.

'Sir, this is a disaster. His flight is to Mumbai but not ours. His flight number is different. Departure time is also after two hours.' His voice was shaking and he had become pale.

I took Kumar's boarding card and looked. E/O was right. We assumed he was coming by the same flight since the airline was the same and the boarding passes also looked similar. Even the flight numbers were similar; only the last two digits were different.

I was in a fix. Our flight boarding had already commenced. We rushed to information desk, I told E/O to explain Kumar's condition to the lady at the desk and request her to ensure he boarded his flight. I ran to a shop, purchased a phone card, and called Mr Atul. I told him that he was coming to Mumbai by a different flight and gave him Kumar's flight number and scheduled arrival time.

I rushed back to the information desk; the lady assured us that she would personally see that he would board the flight. We left him sitting in a chair, staring ahead blankly and mumbling incoherently.

That was the last I saw of him.

I arrived at Mumbai at midnight and boarded a flight to my city at 4 a.m. By the time I reached home at 7 a.m., I was dead tired. Long flight travel, lack of sleep, and sheer fatigue were making it difficult to keep my eyes open.

When I reached home, I called Mr Atul even before I removed my shoes. I did not hesitate to disturb his sleep. What he told me made my sleep evaporate instantly.

'He did not board the flight at Amsterdam. We checked with the airline,' he told me, yawning.

I collapsed on the sofa. Cold fear gripped my heart like a vice.

'So where is he? Did you find out?' I asked him, when I recovered.

'No idea. We are making enquiries,' he told me casually.

'Please... do you understand his predicament? He doesn't eat, drink, or sleep. He needs immediate help and assistance,' I told him.

'Thanks for all your inputs. As soon as I go to office, I will make enquiries and keep you informed,' he told me.

'Can you please start making enquiries now?' I pleaded with him.

He assured me he would keep me posted with progress and disconnected. All vestiges of sleep and tiredness vanished.

My wife asked me why I was looking so worried. When I told her, she too was quite upset. I think she must have prayed for his safe return.

I kept calling Mr Atul every hour or two.

Finally at 2.45 p.m., he lost his temper.

He shouted at me, 'Please let me do my job. We are grateful for your help and assistance. You have informed me and it is no longer your problem. You are a chief engineer, so you should know about our company's reputation. We care for our staff and don't try to teach me how to do my job. I have many other important, urgent matters to attend to.'

All my pent-up anger, frustration suddenly burst out.

I shouted back at him, 'If there is a more urgent and important matter than the plight of an unfortunate employee, then your company has no right to exist. Your master and chief engineer were inhuman and dumped him mercilessly. Your crew were equally heartless. You should have pressed the panic button and involved everyone from the MD to the office boy when I informed you yesterday. Even after so many hours, the fact that you didn't trace him shows how much you care for your employees.

I will not teach you how to do your job. But if I don't hear from you by 4.30 p.m., I will make calls to the MUI [Maritime Union of India], the DG [director general of shipping], and the MMD [Mercantile Marine Department]. The high court judge is our family friend. I will file a PIL [public interest litigation] tomorrow at the high court. Now, I will not disturb you again.' I slammed the phone down.

I had no illusions. Matters like these will be on low-priority list for government agencies. I was completely demoralized.

The phone rang after half an hour.

'Good news. We traced him. He is detained by immigration in Amsterdam,' Mr Atul told me. There was no anger in his voice.

'Thank God and thank you. Hope he is not in prison?' I asked him. I felt relief surge through me.

'No. Within the airport they have a room where they keep people without a visa, he is there,' Mr Atul told me.

'So what is the next course of action?' I asked him.

'We are sending a doctor and an employee who speaks Kannada to Amsterdam to bring him back. The employee will take him home from Mumbai. We have made all arrangements,' he said.

'I thank you very much and I have one more request. Please give me Kumar's home phone number,' I asked him.

Mr Atul laughed. 'Still you don't trust me? Anyway, write this down…'He dictated the landline number. I jotted it down.

'It is not that I don't trust you. I can sleep peacefully after I hear from his family that he has reached home safely,' I told him and disconnected the call.

I called his home number; no one could speak English or Hindi. His brother could speak few words of English. I gathered that they were under the impression that he was in a ship and would be coming home after six months. There was no anxiety or concern in his voice so obviously they were not aware of his condition.

I was very restless for a day. Even though I was tired, sleep eluded me.

The next day when I called his home, his brother was quite incoherent, agitated. They must have been shocked to see him in that condition and relieved that he reached home safely.

I asked slowly, 'Is Kumar at home? When did he arrive?'

His brother replied, 'Yes. He… come…last night.'

When I thanked Mr Atul later, I sensed his ego prevented him from thanking me for waking up his conscience. He might not have imagined the situation to be so grim. But he thanked me nevertheless for my perseverance.

I crashed on the bed and drifted into sleep within seconds.

FEATHERS IN THE CAP

FEATHERS IN THE CAP— SUCCESS STORIES

Here are some of my success stories on the professional front. To quote myself, 'A feather might fall on your cap while you are walking under a tree, still there would be a feather in your cap for all to see.'

After joining as a junior engineer, we had to complete 18 months of article time (actual time spent on ship) and 365 days of propelling time (actual days of sailing) before we could qualify to appear for the examination for promotion to second engineer's position. These exams are conducted by the Ministry of Transport (MOT) and are quite tough. There were written exams followed by viva voce. Examining surveyor had full authority to fail you even if your written papers were very good.

These exams were called MOT class II and for chief engineers were called MOT class I.

As you will see, success is often a combination of perseverance and the blessings of the Divine.

CLEARING MOT II CLASS
ON THE FIRST ATTEMPT

Though I can claim that I cleared the MOT II class exam on the first attempt due to my brilliance and sheer hard work, I will not do so, for I wish to be candid and forthright in these stories. A feather might fall in your cap while you are walking under a tree, still there would be a feather in your cap for all to see.

In the late seventies, passing on the first attempt was almost unheard of. Even the most brilliant, gold-medal-calibre students had to go through the grind of making a number of attempts. I was staying at the Fairhost Lodge in Chembur. Like in my college days, I was carefree. I used to study when I was in the mood and party for any, every, and no reason whatsoever (Partying was often. As many friends or acquaintances would fail in the oral exams, we shared their grief and buried pain in their beer and whisky or occasionally someone would pass and the partying would be harder).

There were three MMD surveyors conducting the oral exams for II class candidates. They were called Good, Bad, and Ugly. Good had a heart of gold and would pass any candidate whose written exams were fairly good. So he was Good.

Bad was tough and would pass someone only if his written papers were very good and he fared very well in the oral exams. So he was Bad. Ugly was a sheer terror; he had a strict 'no pass' policy. He would rarely pass a candidate on first oral exam with him, which meant that if the candidate had come to him for the first time after several attempts before other surveyors, he had no chance. So, he was Ugly.

In those days, there used to be about fifteen sets for each subject. If you had prepared for about 70 per cent of the questions in each paper, you were adequately prepared. Even with meagre effort, I could do very well in the written exams, thanks largely to the grind and tricks learned in college (ours was a five-year course, six subjects per semester and two semesters per year with countless exams and tests).

After the exams, it was time to visit temples and pray to God to arrange the orals with Good, or at the very least, not with Ugly. After several days of suspense, my prayers were partially answered; my oral exams were to be conducted by Bad.

When D-day came, I arrived at MMD, properly and immaculately attired with tie and all.

The candidates' feelings before entering the surveyor's room can only be understood by persons of the Roman era who had to enter the circus in the coliseum where hungry lions would be waiting.

Even the waiting area in MMD sported a dejected, gloomy look of gladiators' waiting room. The tense, gulping, sweating candidates hardly talk to each other and would be busy referring to last-minute notes.

When my name was called, I knocked, entered, and froze. I expected to see only Bad, but there was another smug, smirking gentleman with him. In those days, each surveyor's pet questionnaire sets were available and I had prepared well for Bad's set. Bad waved at me to take a seat and told me that the apprentice surveyor (he didn't say 'apprentice') would be conducting the orals. This fellow was rubbing his hands in glee and could not wait to pounce on me. He must have been dreaming of this day, since his own II class exam days. He started bombarding me with questions and I started answering reasonably well. Then he started asking questions that were beyond my scope and his sneering and ridiculing way of conducting the orals was pushing my mind into numbness. I wished this grilling would end and was mentally already preparing for my next attempt.

Then Ugly walked in to discuss something with Bad and, before leaving, casually asked, 'How is this fellow doing?' Before Bad could answer, Junior replied, 'Not too good.'

Bad gave a sharp, murderous look at Junior. Junior finally told me, 'I am sorry, you have—'

'Passed,' Bad cut in firmly. Junior's jaw dropped.

'But...' he was stammering.

Ignoring him, Bad told me, 'Your written papers are very good. You have scored high marks. I think you know all the answers to the questions asked by the surveyor but you are too tense and worked up. I am passing you. You can go.' I thanked him, ran out, gave the attendant *baksheesh*, and did not hang around for a second longer. I hopped into a cab and rushed to Chembur to celebrate.

Tailpiece: There was an unwritten cardinal rule, 'If the surveyor tells you, "Passed," don't hang around by thanking him and engaging in small talk and give him a chance to change his mind. Just blurt out "Thank you, sir" and vanish.'

The background story is that once at office closing time, a surveyor passed a candidate. As they were leaving, it started to rain heavily. The candidate offered to drop him at his house. He dropped the surveyor at his home in his magnificent brand-new car.

During the ride, the surveyor had continued the orals, and when leaving the car, he thanked the candidate and told him that he had failed him and wished him better luck next time.

CLEARING MOT I CLASS ON THE SECOND ATTEMPT

It may seem strange how clearing an exam in the second attempt could figure in this section, considering our obsession with immediate success and contempt of failure. But, like a famous person said, 'Show me one man who has never failed and I will show you a man who never attempted anything.'

My first shot at I class can be termed as not even a half-hearted, maybe a hundredth-hearted attempt. I still cannot fathom why I attempted the exam with hardly any preparation. I just went to meet some friends in Fairhost Lodge and they brainwashed me to have a go.

When I protested that there was less than a month for the exams, they told me, 'See, we have also not prepared well. You prepare only for a few sets, if they click, then 'Good' takes your orals, and you are through.'

I was convinced that there was no harm. Honestly, I did not put in any hard work and I was not surprised that my written papers were horrible. This time, God granted me orals with Good, who had the decency to look embarrassed while failing me.

'I know you have not prepared well, why have you even attempted the exam? Honestly, do you think you deserve to pass?' he asked me.

I confessed that I did not, thanked him, and came out. My friends went to Ugly, with the expected result. Later, they confessed that their reason for encouraging me to take the exam was to give their sagging morale a boost. They wished to have a psychological advantage of being slightly better prepared over someone who had not prepared at all. I laughed and told them that I had no ill feelings and went back on ship.

If I have to dedicate my I class success to someone, it would have to be to my best friend Eashwar, who is now the senior vice president of one of the top companies in India. After signing off, when I reached home in April, my wife told me that Eashwar was calling daily to enquire if I had arrived and to call him without delay. When I called him, he told me that he was coming over and came on his scooter within fifteen minutes.

After the formalities of hugging, slapping of backs were over, he asked me, 'Have you unpacked?,' I replied 'Not yet, I have just arrived.'

'Don't unpack. You are going to Chennai by the evening train,' he told me. My wife and I were puzzled.

'But why? He has just arrived. He must be tired after all the hard work in the engine room. Let him rest,' my wife protested.

He told us firmly, 'Look, there are three reasons. First, God has been reincarnated in the form of an MMD surveyor by the name of Paul. If you write your papers reasonably well, he will ask questions, answer them for you if you cannot, and will pass you. The second reason is that he will be retiring in July, i.e. three months from now. Third reason is you have just one chance in June. In May, the exams will not be conducted. If you delay, you may not get a slot for June.'

My wife was still trying to convince him about the need for me to rest but he mercilessly told her that I could rest as long as I wanted after June.

I landed in Chennai the next morning and booked my seat for June. I took a room in a lodge in Santhome. I can confidently affirm that I studied for the next month with as much concentration and dedication as a yogi performing *tapasya* in the Himalayas.

Jokes aside, Chennai was excellent for educational purposes. At the Mumbai Lodge, there were many distractions and temptations to make you lose focus. You just go out for a cup of coffee and end up going to a movie or a party, since your friends would not take no for an answer. In contrast, in Chennai, you need not step out for anything. A boy used to bring tea, breakfast, lunch, and dinner to the room.

My daily program used to be like this: I would get up in the morning, complete my bath, pooja, breakfast, and study till lunchtime without break. I would have lunch, take a short siesta, and continue my studies till sunset. Then I used to go for a long walk from Santhome church to the other end of Marina beach and back. During this time I would revise everything I had studied along with diagrams and sketches. By the time I reached the hotel, all the matter I studied would be indelibly imprinted in my mind. There was no internet; only two DD channels were there. This time I was truly prepared on all fronts.

I did write my answers to the exams very well. Still the butterflies in my stomach would refuse to stay still on the day of the oral exam. Paul kept me waiting for a full two days; every day in the evening, he would apologize that he could not spare time. On the third evening, the inevitable moment arrived.

I need not have worried. After the attendant called my name and I entered, I could see my answer papers were on Paul's table. The marks on the papers were above 80. That was his way of hinting not to be tense. He asked some questions about bunkering, oil pollution and told me that I had passed the exam.

Completing a Voyage
with Unpumpable HFO

This incident happened in the same ship that figured in 'Close Encounters'—steering failure during Suez transit incident. My first ship as chief engineer literally tested me by sword and fire.

We arrived at Port Said with a few days' reserve of fuel oil and we received heavy fuel oil bunkers to complete the voyage to Poland. The old stock of fuel was consumed in the next few days and we were in the middle of the Mediterranean Sea when 2/E called to inform me that HFO transfer pump was not taking suction. The time was around 7 a.m.

I went to the ECR and asked him for details. He told me that in his watch he had transferred once to the settling tank, and when he tried to transfer the next time, the pump was not taking suction. He tried this with all the storage tanks with no luck. I got the pump suction filter opened up and was shocked to see that the filter contained not oil, but a thick grease like paste. I immediately rushed to settling tank and drained some oil. Initially, the oil flowed but slowly solidified before reaching the scupper. You could scoop it.

Now we were in the soup. I did not have any good fuel left and we were in the middle of nowhere. I called the bridge and talked to Captain. I apprised him of the situation and asked him to divert to safe and sheltered waters before our settling and service tanks were empty. He deviated from the course towards the nearest area where we could anchor.

Meanwhile, I studied the scenario. All the fuel was in double-bottom tanks. The pipes to the pump from the tanks pass through the ballast tanks. Normally, steam pipes (called tracing steam lines)are laid along these fuel pipelines to keep the fuel in warm condition to prevent the problem that we were facing. But in that ship, tracing steam lines were not provided, since pipes were passing through ballast tanks, which contain sea water. The tank heating steam lines were routed from the main deck and into the tanks. So, the fuel was warm, in fact, hot in the tanks. The problem was that it was solidifying by the time it reached the pump.

When I am faced with crisis situations like this, when a brain wave is required to find a solution, I go to the cabin, inform everyone not to disturb me unless there was an emergency, lie down on the sofa, close my eyes, and relax. The brain is an amazing organ; it works at it's best when you are not driving it crazy to provide solutions.

Within ten minutes I had the answer. I went to the engine room, changed valves of the transfer pump so that hot oil from the settling tank was directed into the bunker tank. For a few minutes, nothing happened. Hot oil was trying to force solidified cold oil back into the tank. The pump's relief valve was lifting at set point so that pump was not damaged. Suddenly pressure dropped.

I stopped the pump, changed over the valves, and transferred oil from the bunker tank to the settling tank and informed Captain that we could continue our voyage. I monitored the main engine parameters and all were normal. The only problem with the fuel was that it would solidify below a certain temperature.(Later lab analysis showed it had very high wax content; other values were within limits). I left clear instructions to keep transferring from one tank to the other once in thirty minutes to prevent the oil from solidifying.

We had no problem until we turned at Gibraltar and were going up north. Seawater temperature was steadily dropping and a time came when we had to keep the pump running continuously, transferring from one tank to the other.

Somewhere in 'Close Encounters,' I mentioned how extra-smart second engineers and chief officers can create havoc. That was my first ship as a chief engineer and I had a second engineer who had just cleared his exam and was promoted. He kept complaining that we were unnecessarily running the pump and it would be spoiled. In no uncertain terms, I told him that if he did not wish to follow my orders, he could stay in his cabin and face disciplinary action. He was following my orders grudgingly.

We had almost reached our destination. We picked up Pilot for the last leg of the voyage. In the evening, I left ECR after giving night orders. At around 4.30 a.m., I suddenly woke up for no reason and called ECR. Second Engineer coolly told me that settling tank level was very low and he had stopped the purifier. I was shocked and asked him how it had happened, because if the transfer pump were running continuously from one tank to another, this would never have happened. There was a pause, then he told me that he left instructions to the fourth engineer to stop the pump at midnight since he thought we had almost reached or destination and he wanted to save the pump.

I rushed to the engine room and found that even the service tank level was low. I called the bridge and was informed that we still had fourteen hours of sailing. There was no option but to change over to diesel oil and complete the rest of the voyage on diesel oil.

The next day all hell broke loose. The company was frantic about using diesel oil, and about sailing to the next port of bunkering, since, nothing was available in that small Polish port, not even bunkers. I got fed up of going up and down from the bridge to the engine room to talk to the office and told the captain to inform the superintendent that I would call him after solving the problem. These futile trips would serve no purpose except the draining of energy.

I was very upset and angry at the second engineer, more for his insolent attitude than for his stupidity. When I asked him why he did not inform me at the first hint of trouble, I still remember his arrogant reply, 'What could anyone do? What could you have done?'

Though I vented out my anger by blasting him, I realized I was deviating my focus from the main issue.

I sat in front of the pump and was staring at the lines. Suddenly I had an idea. I set the valves so that the diesel oil service tank was directed into the bunker tank. I called one 5/E (by the name of Ganesan, whom I met at the last revalidation course; he is a C/E now) and asked him to sit on a stool and keep looking at the pressure gauge. The moment it dropped to zero, he was to stop the pump, change valves, and fill up the heavy oil settling tank from that bunker tank.

Nothing happened for one hour. DO was unable to push the solidified mass into the tank. I increased relief valve setting to 4 bar. No change. I slowly increased it to 7 bar. I crossed my fingers and waited. I was aware that if any gasket would burst, it would be a herculean task to clean the tanks and to repair them. Suddenly pressure dropped to zero; an alert and dependable Ganesan immediately stopped the pump and transferred the heavy oil to the settling tank.

My efforts were highly appreciated, and though I was not due, three increments were sanctioned with immediate effect.

REDEMPTION AFTER
BLACKLISTING IN FOSMA

This is a sequel to 'Refusing to Sail in an Unseaworthy Ship.' I mentioned that being blacklisted in FOSMA did not really bother me, since I was confident that all shipping companies would know the standards of that company.

Before signing off, Captain suggested that a two weeks entry in the CDC would not look good and that I would have to explain my reasons for leaving all the time. I agreed with him and hence there was no entry in my CDC of service in that ship. In my job trials, first I went to one reputed company. They appreciated my stand in leaving and reasons, but they were a conservative company, hence they told me that they would get in touch if there was a vacancy.

My next stop was the next best shipping company. Capt. Khanna listened attentively to my version and left without saying anything. He returned after what felt like an interminably long time and told me that I was approved by the principals. I was surprised and suspicious. I did not wish to land in the soup again. I asked him frankly if their ships were seaworthy; if not, we might save ourselves all the trouble. He laughed heartily and assured me that this ship was a four-year-old PCC (pure car carrier) and it belonged to a reputed Japanese company.(After a couple of years, Capt. Khanna told me that they had made thorough enquiries and received excellent reports about me from my previous employers.)

This ship was a four-year-old car carrier. Though the ship was new, life was hectic and tough. She sailed at 27 knots/hour and had very fast turnaround voyages. There was hardly any port stay, with the ship calling at several ports in a few days. Loading cars from Japanese ports would be completed in a few hours and off loading them in 6–8 ports in the Middle East or Europe or the US took even less time. A major headache was the log sheet which was quite complicated and had to be filled up for every port. We could rest only during the voyages. We were always under pressure to keep up with maintenance schedules.

Jacket cooling water was leaking past O-rings of two liners of the main engine. About 200 litres of water was drained from the scavenge spaces daily. This was an old problem which none of the chief engineers wanted to highlight and rectify. Car carriers run on precise schedules for several months in advance. Hence it was kept under wraps.

After initial hesitation, I informed the technical manager about it and told him that my concern was that if the O-rings gave way in the rough sea, it would be quite risky to pull out liners. He asked me how much time I would require to pull out and change the O-rings of two liners. I committed to twenty-six hours, which could go either way by a few hours depending on how easily the liners could be pulled out (sometimes liners can get badly stuck).

He arranged twenty-eight hours at a lay-up berth in Japan. I was surprised to see several big shots turn up. They were sitting in the ECR, smoking and monitoring the situation. Well in advance, I meticulously planned about the teams (2/E and 3/E were in two teams with allotted crew), rest hours, and sequence of operations. It went off safely and smoothly because, though I was under pressure, I never shouted or screamed but gently prodded my crew and encouraged them with appreciative gestures, refreshments, and brief rest periods. Luckily the liners came out easily and we could complete the job in twenty-one hours. Full credit should be given to the Japanese technical manager and other top brass for not harassing me or interfering in the work.

This effort was highly appreciated and my stock went up by several notches. Within less than a month after signing off, Capt. Khanna called me up and told me that I have to join back urgently. When I protested, he told me that the owners had specifically asked that I be sent for taking over a new Cape-size bulk carrier, from the Hyundai shipyard Ulsan, Korea. It was an honour that I could hardly refuse.

TAKING DELIVERY
OF A NEW SHIP

The irony or beauty of life is that a fall from the crest or a rise from the trough can be sudden, unexpected, and spectacular. One shipping company felt that I was a danger to shipping and warned all foreign shipping companies by blacklisting me in FOSMA. Within a short duration, one of the most prestigious companies in the world wanted, or rather insisted, that I take over delivery of a new ship from the yard.

My company was a management company and their role was limited to supplying qualified personnel to the owners of the ship. They must have lined up a few of their best chief engineers for this prestigious assignment but had to give in to the request of owners. Capt. Dev and I first went to Hong Kong for a briefing, then to Tokyo to meet the top brass. That was one of the few occasions I was attired in a suit. We were received with traditional and customary Japanese courtesy. They then briefed us about various aspects. Though ISM Code concept was not even thought of, their vision and thinking was progressive and ahead of the times.

After the briefing, we flew to Ulsan, South Korea. Since I was a vegetarian, I had a tough time. I managed to teach the cook to prepare vegetable fried rice and had the same diet for the next three weeks. We would go to the yard daily and observe the progress and report to HO. One Superintendent, Mr. Fuji was in charge of supervising shipbuilding. He must have been at least seventy-five years old but was extremely fit and agile. One day the lift had a breakdown in the yard. We climbed all the stairs to reach the main deck and went down all the stairs to engine room and then into crankcase to inspect main bearings. While I was panting, he was not even out of breath.

Ulsan shipyard was amazing. In those days they used to deliver fifty-two ships of all types in a year, which translates to delivery of one ship every week. Like kids building with blocks or grown-ups with a pack of cards, Koreans used to build ships with similar ease and lack of fuss. One day we would observe the superstructure of a ship in initial stages of fabrication. After a few days it would be already fitted on a ship. It was like magic. Only one welder would be working without helpers, operating a cherry picker on which he would be riding with a remote. Even our ship was being completed seemingly effortlessly.

Attending sea trials was a rich experience. In all ships, the sea trial records are the guiding factor or reference point for checks. I used to wonder if I would ever get a chance to be a part of the team during sea trials. It is physically demanding. Without respite, everyone wants you to witness their equipment's performance. The main engine's indicator cards would be taken, vibration levels would be measured by another technician, noise level would be recorded by another, and steering tests would be conducted. The class surveyors, Captain, and I were on our toes for more than twenty-four hours. Finally, Captain and I took a break and slept for a few hours. But, the Japanese Technical Manager and his assistants stoically sat through all the trials, never batting an eyelid, smoking cigarettes and drinking black coffee.

After we returned from sea trials, 2/E and C/O arrived. The 2/E was young, energetic and was to take over from me. He was tall, gangly, and unattractive (I am reluctant to use the word 'ugly', but small kids would have been frightened and cried if they saw him at close quarters). After he arrived, my workload reduced, as I found him taking interest and initiative. C/O was tall and handsome and a Casanova. Both have joined the office now.

Finally the day of taking over arrived. Management companies are notorious for their cost-cutting techniques. The crew arrived two days before delivery. For the first few days, anyone will be confused with the new environment. It would take some time to reach mess, cabin, engine room, or bridge without getting lost. All stores, provisions, etc. arrived immediately after the crew came on board. One can imagine our plight in receiving and storing all items with a new crew. The problem was compounded by a language barrier. The Bangladeshi crew understood very little English or Hindi. C/O was a Bengali and 3/E was Bangladeshi. So we somehow managed to confine confusion from escalating to panic or chaos.

The vice president of our company came with his entourage for the ceremony. Like in India, a pandal was erected on the jetty. Captain and I were resplendent in full uniform, black coats with epaulette stripes and caps. That was the first and last time I donned the coat. It was too bulky to carry to ship and you could not wear it for social occasions. We were seated on the dais. After the customary speeches, the champagne bottle was broken. The vice President went on a tour of the ship. I still have photographs of discussing some aspects with him in ECR. The electrical Officer brought coconuts from India, which we broke in the bridge wings and ECR entrance. After the vice president gave long blasts on ship's air horn, the ceremony was complete. There was a gala lunch afterwards. The superintendent kept murmuring in our ears that pilot was booked in two hours' time, so not to have too many drinks, even though everyone kept offering toasts.

We were told that the program was aired live in Korea and Japan, as this was the first ship of that series, class, and design.

After lunch and farewells, the vessel sailed out. Service engineers and technicians shook hands and disembarked with pilot after breakwater.

Now, we were on our own. Though the ship was of UMS (unmanned machinery spaces) class, I decided to stick to watch keeping for at least one round trip voyage. Taking charge of the delivery of a new ship is a very cumbersome, laborious, and challenging experience. How the main engine and other equipment would perform later would largely depend on care taken during the initial running in period. The rpm should be increased very gradually; cylinder lubrication should be gradually reduced from maximum position to normal over the next few months, after observing the liner condition at each port. I told 2/E to come the next day at 4 a.m and kept watch and monitored all equipment. My other assistants were a brand-new engine cadet, and a 3/E. The first day was uneventful and smooth.

The 2/E came at 4 a.m but he did not come alone; he brought a disaster with him. He told me that he was feeling feverish and that he also had boils on his chest and torso. One look and I knew it was chickenpox. Immediately, I told him my diagnosis and told him to go to his cabin and not to talk to anyone or linger around in the mess or the bridge. I called Captain and told him about 2/E's condition. There was no option but to keep him in complete isolation, since chickenpox is highly contagious. I put accommodation A/C on fresh air. Until our ship reached Australia after two weeks, he was locked up. He had to wash his plates and clothes himself. Food would be kept outside his cabin and he would take it after the steward left. He was bored to death and tears and was pleading with me to give him at the least some paperwork.

My life had become tough. I could not rely on the cadet, and though 3/E fortunately turned out to be reliable, I had no means of knowing that initially. For two weeks, I used to sleep in the ECR and would leave the engine room only for a shower, food, and sending messages. Since this was the first ship in its series, both the shipyard and the office wanted me to check many aspects and to report to them. Twice, every day, I had to calculate the BHP by taking indicator cards and filling up the format of engine performance. In addition, warranty claims had to be made for all deficiencies observed.

Fortunately, all the equipment worked smoothly.

I had a good sleep on a proper bed in my cabin, after 2/E was given a clean chit by the doctor in Australia. Again, my efforts were highly appreciated. By the time I signed off, the number of warranty claims crossed 100. While the shipyard was unhappy, the owners and managers were jubilant, since they had leverage in the negotiations.

Scoring a Point Over the Service Engineer

Like all reluctant seafarers, I was also determined to quit sailing in my mid-forties and settle down in a shore job. A footnote to the above resolution would be achieving financial freedom and arriving at a comfort zone.

I did arrive at my mid-forties but financial freedom and comfort zone were still a distant dream. When I was on leave, I saw an ad looking for a chief engineer for a captive power plant in a foreign country, and so, I sent my application. I received an interview call and went to Mumbai.

I was the first candidate to be interviewed. One Indian and one foreigner were conducting interviews. The Indian, manager, was in charge of the cement factory where the power project was to be installed. He resembled an irritable gorilla with constipation (I realized later that my surmise was correct, he was a drunkard and had a hangover). He stares at one unblinkingly like a lizard. He is an IIT-ian (Indian Institute of technology, a very prestigious college) and was brilliant. Physically he resembled the B &W movie villain K. N. Singh and I was to learn later that he was indeed a mean villain.

The foreigner, the general manager, had an engaging, affable smile. You would automatically trust all your life's savings with him; such was his aura of warmth and kindness. Since it was not possible for them to find a more suitable candidate, they promised many things to lure me: a villa, a car (if and when I got a driving license), and airfare for family once a year. I had no misgivings and accepted.

I joined in the month of January and did not take warm clothing, since I thought that country's climate would be hot and humid. It was quite cold and my work timings were 7.15 a.m to 3.15 p.m. But, I ended up working several hours more than the normal working hours due to the utter foolishness and stupidity of the manager.

I thought life would be cool since the engines were brand new, and for the first few years, life would be smooth and relaxed. My heart sank when I saw the plant. To save the expenses of cabling, Manager had opted to install the plant right in the middle of the cement factory, where cement dust could be dense like a fog on windy days. If some of the cement particles managed to enter the engine, breakdowns were inevitable. It is still a mystery to me how the engine manufacturers approved the location. At that point of time, the engines were installed and the cabling was in its finishing stages.

I value my experience in that plant for the exposure and confidence it has given me. I was never in awe of a white man or Japanese or Chinese man but had the feeling that Europeans were far superior to others due to centuries of technological exposure. Two commissioning engineers were already present when I arrived. One was tall, grotesquely obese and I had not seen him to do any constructive work other than pulling out tack-welded support frames and yelling at welders.

I still remember the sad face of the works contractor, who was always on the verge of tears when he saw him.

'You tell me, sir, he plucks my supports like an elephant plucks a small plant with its trunk. Let him try plucking those beams,' he would say. I could not interfere since it was not my domain.

The other engineer was a tall, athletic, blond man with a lot of energy but very inversely proportional intelligence.

When I asked him if he had sailed as a chief engineer, I was reminded of Saif Ali Khan's advertisement of a mobile phone. A tall man brags about his latest phone. Saif keeps asking if his mobile has certain features. The tall man keeps shrinking with each "no" until he diminishes to the size of a baby.

David, the other engineer, said no. His swagger had diminished somewhat.

'Then you must have sailed as a second engineer?' I asked him. He shrank further. 'No.'

'I sailed as fourth engineer for a few years, then quit. I didn't like sailing,' he said after a pause.

'And you?' he asked me.

When I told him that I was a chief engineer for more than a decade, he didn't actually shrink to the size of a baby, but his swagger was definitely less pronounced.

One day he was draining water from the boiler. He was draining water into engine room bilges and then was pumping it into the waste oil tank. Not only was it time-consuming, it was very avoidable. He brushed me aside when I tried to talk to him. After many hours, he came and asked me what my suggestion was. I simply opened the nuts and bolts of a pipe flange and drained the water into an open area outside the engine room.

His jaw dropped. He must have mentally kicked himself for not having thought of such a simple thing. I gave several suggestions which saved time and effort for him but he was too proud to acknowledge them.

The plant was commissioned, and as I suspected, cylinder head valves started to burn out, camshafts were getting damaged within six months of commissioning. Whatever protection the oil-bathed louvers were expected to provide from cement dust turned out to be ineffective and insufficient. So, service engineers came again and started overhauling all the cylinder heads and other parts. After a week of toil, they assembled all the parts, and the engines were ready to be started.

The blond service engineer came in the morning full of vigour and energy and went about trying to start the engines. The engines refused to budge. Slowly his shoulders started to droop and he came to the verge of pulling out his hair. Of course, I tried to point out what he was doing wrong.

He snarled at me, 'I will struggle till 5 p.m., then it is your baby. You stay here for the whole night and break your head. I don't mind. But let me concentrate now.' So, I left him.

At 5 p.m., he literally washed his hands off the engines.

He called the manager and told him, 'All the fuel pumps and fuel valves of your engines are damaged. The engines cannot be started. We have to wait for spares.' As he was leaving, I asked him if I could have a go.

'By all means, be my guest. You can stay the whole night. I don't mind,' he said and left smirking.

There was nothing wrong with the engines. He did not set the valves in the fuel line correctly and did not vent the system properly.

His car might not have reached the gate when I started both the engines and called the manager and told him to call David back. Manager's typically mean reaction was as expected, neither congratulations nor pat on the back, only a cool 'Oh, I see. Tomorrow when Service Engineer comes in the morning, I will tell him.'

The next morning, David came directly to the plant. He could not resist the urge to have fun at my expense.

'So, when did you go home? Or did you stay the whole night?' He was mocking.

'I left ten minutes after you left, after starting, checking, and stopping the engines,' I told him coolly.

Blood drained from his face. 'Impossible. The fuel pumps are worn out,' he protested.

I did not move from my chair. I asked my watch-keeper to start the engines. He pressed the start buttons, and one after the other, the engines roared and started. The service engineer's face was ashen.

He was quite morose when we met the manager later. He need not have worried. Manager's meanness saved him. Any other person in Manager's place would have taken Service Engineer and the manufacturer to task. The so-called expert service engineer declaring an engine impossible to start and the chief engineer of the plant starting it in a jiffy would have given enormous advantage to the client. Manager treated the incident as of no consequence and my effort as insignificant.

I put this feather in my cap myself.

BLOW PAST AUXILIARY ENGINE LINERS

I decided to quit the company that gave me a break on a matter of principle. When I joined the ship, I had informed the company well in advance that I required relief in four months' time. All management companies will grant any wish and are sweetness personified until they get you onboard. Then amnesia sets in. They cannot recall any promise made or assurance given. Though I sent emails, I did not keep copies. When the time came to relieve me, the people who promised me were no longer in the office and everyone declined any knowledge. I signed off in protest, paid my airfare but told them that I would not be joining back.

I went to another reputed company in Chennai office. One captain interviewed me and a computer test was conducted. It was just a formality. As soon as I reached the hotel, all the top brass of my previous company started calling me, apologizing and promising to refund my airfare and enhanced salary. I politely declined. Later, Captain told me that rarely do they get such excellent reports, when they contact previous companies of candidates.

I joined the ship at Rotterdam. The 2/E was Bangladeshi, crew was Filipino. The ship was not very old; all the equipment was in good condition, except the generators. That particular manufacturer had gone bankrupt and spares were no longer available. The company got hold of a firm in Italy who were making liners, pistons, rings, and were reconditioning cylinder heads.

Changing of the cylinder liners used to be a regular feature. There was always blow past into the crankcase due to worn out cylinder liners. When checking sump level, there used to be a continuous flow of gas, which was considered normal. But, when it came to a stage where it was not possible to pour oil into the sump because of the force of the gas, they would need to change liners one by one. It was just like lottery. One liner would be changed and the engine started. If the flow had reduced, they were lucky. If not, one by one all the other liners would be changed. Liners would not last more than 6,000 to 8,000 running hours, in normal conditions, cylinder liners will last tens of thousands of hours.

I thought it was madness. I told 2/E that there must be a way to identify the defective liner. He gave me a defiant look and told that there were three sister ships having the same problem and none of the chief engineers or superintendents or experts could suggest a way to identify it. There was no option but to go through the routine. I myself tried by taking peak pressures, but in four-stroke engines, it is impossible to identify which unit liner is worn out by this method.

The 2/E meanwhile was laughing to himself and told me that there was no way of singling out the defective liner. That was a watch keeping ship and I started my experiments on 3/E's watch, i.e. between noon and 4 p.m. I did not want 2/E to have an inkling of what I was doing.

The 2/E was hard working, had a chief engineer's certificate and was in line for a promotion. But, I had not seen a more reticent person. Extracting a monosyllabic reply from him was as difficult as tooth extracting is for a dentist. When I told him to do something, I did not know whether he would do it or not, whether he agreed or not to my suggestions. Finally, I told him that once he was promoted to C/E, he could not keep quiet when Super asks questions on the phone and he had to develop conversational skills. Today, he is the technical manager of that company. Once something is forced on you, you will have no choice but to conform, like the reticent 2/E learned to communicate well.

I found a way of identifying the worn-out liner. I connected an air hose with a cock; the other end of the cock was connected to an indicator cock by a pipe and fitting. A pressure gauge was fitted on the pipe. I chose one unit which was recently overhauled and had a new liner, piston, and piston rings. I turned the engine so that this unit was in firing TDC (inlet and exhaust valves would be shut). I connected the arrangement, opened the air for a few seconds, and closed the cock. I noted the time taken for the pressure to come to zero. I checked all the units and noted the time taken for pressure to drop to zero. For units with worn liners, pressure would drop very fast.

When time had to come to change the liners due to heavy blow-past, I told 2/E to change the liner of one particular unit. He thought that I was selecting at random, which was the practice, and changed the liner. The blow-past stopped. He thought I was lucky. The next month, I also identified it correctly. The crew was thrilled. Their job was reduced by many times.

Finally, 2/E swallowed his pride and asked me how I had identified the liner. I told him that I would tell the next C/E and Super but not him, because instead of assisting me in finding a solution, all he did was pass snide remarks.

Super was thrilled and very happy. Not only had the spares requirement come down drastically, problems of downtime, logistics of connecting to the ships, chasing supplier, had become manageable. The managing director called me on the satellite phone and thanked me, and talked at great length. All sister ships were instructed to follow this procedure in the future.

Avoiding CO2 Release to Atmosphere

This was the same ship that figured in 'Flooding of the Engine Room'.

All ships are provided with systems to fight major engine room fires. The most preferred fire fighting system is total flooding by CO_2 (carbon dioxide); since it is heavier than air, it will settle down and extinguish the fire by smothering it. It is normally stored in many 50-kg cylinders in a room outside the engine room; the number of cylinders would depend on the volume of engine room.

But, in that ship, 5,000 litres of CO_2 was stored in a huge tank in liquid form at a temperature of -25°C. Refrigerating compressors would be running to maintain that temperature. As a chief engineer, my major focus and attention was on that tank since it was a vital piece of equipment. If the compressor had a breakdown or developed a problem, it did not take much time for the temperature to rise. Though alarms were provided, it was always monitored closely and parameters recorded.

There was a gauge glass provided to monitor the liquid level which was showing that the tank was ¾ full. We went to Hamburg, and the company arranged a workshop to carry out routine checks. Because of some blockage in gauge glass line, the liquid level was not showing in the glass at that time. The service engineer immediately jumped to the conclusion that tank was empty. I tried explaining to him that tank was

¾ full and pressures and temperatures were normal and I also showed him logbook entries.

He refused to believe and informed everyone. All hell broke loose. CO_2 is an oxygen-depleting substance and losing 5,000 litres is a very serious matter. Moreover, Port State Control Authorities would not allow the ship to sail in that unsafe condition. Procuring 5,000 litres of CO_2 was not so easy, even in Hamburg. We managed to sail out mainly because our shipping company was a German one based in Hamburg. Therefore, they managed to convince authorities to give them time and allow the ship to make one more voyage. They provided many fire extinguishers at every 10 to 15 feet in the engine room to assure authorities that ship's safety was not compromised.

Though Service Engineer convinced everyone that all the CO_2 leaked out, I was sure it was full. But how could we physically check? Since the tank was pressurized and at -25°C, it was very risky to attempt anything.

We sailed out to Brazil, loaded iron ore, and were returning to Germany. The company was moving heaven and earth to procure 5,000 litres of CO_2. Superintendent told me to vent out remaining CO_2 to the atmosphere while we were still at sea, since in port, it would be impossible to do so. I was most reluctant to knowingly commit a crime of releasing thousands of litres of CO_2 into the atmosphere.

One week before arrival in Germany, I made a decision. I would try to clear the gauge glass passage. It was, of course, risky. A blast of CO_2 with pressure at that temperature can maim or cause serious injury. In large quantities, it can suffocate and can be fatal.

I took two Filipino fitters to assist me. I never asked or expected others to do what I myself was not willing or reluctant to do. In their ignorance, they might injure themselves.

I closed both valves to the gauge glass on the tank and they carefully removed the gauge glass. I asked them to go out of the room and keep a watch over me. I opened the top valve a little; gas came out with full blast. So it was not choked.

I opened the bottom valve slowly; nothing came out. The passage into the tank was blocked. But how to clear it?

If I pushed a thin rod or wire, it might clear the passage but the sudden blast would burn away my hand and so I would have to be lightning fast in taking out the rod and closing the valve. I did not know what would be the pressure and force. I wore thick gloves, told the fitter to bend a thin rod into an 'L' shape.

I pushed the short leg of the L-shaped rod into the passage, holding the long leg of the 'L' so that my hand was not in the way of jet and gave one sharp blow to the rod with a hammer. It went in and a full blast of white CO_2 liquid blew out in a jet. I quickly removed the rod and closed the valve.

We fitted back the gauge glass and opened the valves. CO_2 nicely rose to 3/4 level. Superintendent and the company were quite thrilled and thanked me profusely.

Since I was employed by a management company and not by owner, their gratitude did not translate into monetary benefits.

But I have no complaints, I am very happy and contented with my small contribution to saving the ozone layer.

MY FAMILY AND I

My Family and I

When I see many people carrying heavy negative baggage about parents and siblings, I always thank God for clicking on my parents' icon and sending me into that folder.

I am blessed to have enjoyed a wonderful childhood with adoring and loving parents, brothers, and a sister. Our family was just like those you see in TV soaps, always laughing, enjoying, and having fun.

Of course, my father was like a grim lion, sitting under a tree and watching sternly at his cubs frolicking, never interfering. He did not actively participate in our pranks or fun but did not restrict us. Mom was always jovial, laughing heartily at our jokes and general banter.

Once Dad retired into his bedroom, we used to sneak out to second-show movies. We used to wait nervously for him to retreat and then rush to Taj, Zia, and Prakash theatres, which had ordinary benches and chairs not bolted down. You could shift them where you wanted and take a nap if you liked. Our cousin was the leader of our gang.

After we returned, we used to tap lightly on the door. Mom would be waiting for us without sleeping and would allow us in. We used to tread on tiptoe lightly and quietly go to sleep.

Once, Mom fell asleep as she was very tired, and Dad opened the door. We expected fireworks but he quietly went back to his room.

The next day, Mom told us he was aware of our sojourns and turned a blind eye purposely, and when Mom hinted to him about our plans, he would go inside until we went out. That way everyone was happy.

If we came home regularly late at night for a week, Mom could specifically guess on which days we went to a movie. She said our clothes stank of cigarette smoke on those days.

In those days there were no cable TVs and we used to visit friends and vice versa. I am also very fortunate that my wife and kids are the best any man can hope for. They appear in most of the sections, even if fleetingly.

My Wonderful Parents

I have misgivings about the title of this entry. Once, a court jester remarked that the king's youngest wife was very beautiful and it incurred the wrath of the king's other wives, who wanted him to be beheaded for insulting them by implying that they were not beautiful. By proclaiming that my parents were wonderful, I am not suggesting others' parents are not. It might sound bizarre since everyone might feel his or her parents are the best in the world.

But sadly, such is not the case. I have seen many, many individuals with very negative feelings about their parents. If they are successful, it is entirely due to their own hard work, brilliance, and intelligence: their parents have no role in it, and if they are not, the blame is put squarely at the parents' doorstep.

Hence, I have no hesitation in calling my parents wonderful. It is likely that many might feel that I am prejudiced, and because of my love for them, I overlook their obvious failings. I am not implying that they were angels without wings and were absolute saints. No human being is one-dimensional. For example, I am a son, father, husband, brother, friend, and of course, chief engineer. I may be exceptional in one role and a dismal failure in another. I am focusing only on my parents in their role as wonderful parents.

They may not have been perfect and, indeed, they were not. My dad never hugged or kissed us, never took us on fabulous holidays, and never showered us with expensive gifts.

But what they gave us, I could not give to my kids. Many parents are incapable of achieving what they did.

It was this—never having an argument, heated discussion, or a shouting match in the presence of kids. How they managed it, I could never understand. Houses were smaller, families larger, and not a day passed without invasion of the house by guests. How and when they had their quota of arguments is a mystery to me. There was always tranquillity, peace, and joy in our home. We always felt happy to be home, unlike some of my friends, who would wander and reach home late to avoid the tension-filled atmosphere. We, as kids, were completely shielded from any problems, worries, tensions, or financial crunches that they must have faced.

When I grew up, got married, and failed to manage what they did, I thought of doing some research. When I asked my dad, his reply was that Mother was very cooperative and supportive and there was no need for arguments or fights. When I asked Mother, she said that Dad was very stubborn and he would not listen to her and she didn't push after a certain point. Then I asked my brothers. I was the youngest, so I thought maybe they had seen some fireworks. They also had not seen it.

Finally, I asked my uncles and aunts (my mom's brothers and sisters). One aunt told me that my parents had massive fights and sometimes would not talk to each other for months. I did not believe her; if such were the case, it would be impossible to hide it from the kids. Is it possible to imagine a husband and wife not on talking terms for months altogether and not even one among five kids gets to know of it?

I confronted Mother with this information. She laughed and conceded that there were such instances but they were very careful not to make it noticeable as they did not want us to be troubled or tense. That was what made them unique, a mutual agreement to shield the kids from disturbance of any kind.

That single trait has elevated them several notches higher above other parents. If both were saints like Mother Teresa, then it was no big deal. But having their quarrels when kids were not around and maintaining a normal peaceful atmosphere until a truce was declared required strength of character beyond the scope of ordinary mortals.

By any yardstick, they were very successful parents, with well-settled children and grandchildren. When we celebrated their seventieth marriage anniversary at my home, it struck me that such an event may rarely be witnessed in the future. They never lectured us on good parenting nor interfered in how we brought up our kids. That was another achievement.

They loved each other deeply, though they never expressed it in conventional ways. Their tastes, likes, and beliefs were diametrically opposite in many aspects, yet they respected each other's sentiments.

For instance, my mother was very religious and would perform pooja for a long duration every day. She never skipped or missed any function, *vratam*, *nomu*, and would fast twice or thrice a week. She would invite several ladies for numerous festivals and functions. She had her pet superstitions.

Father was not an atheist but was not religious either. We have not seen him perform pooja, let alone do *namaskaram* (folding palms so that all fingertips touch each other) to God on a daily basis at home. I had not seen him praying to God or visiting temples and offering *mokkubadi* (Promising God to offer certain things if wishes are fulfilled; it could be donation, tonsure of head, gold. Daily, millions of rupees in cash and kind are deposited in Tirupati Hundi, making the shrine richer than the Vatican) even when he or mother faced very serious, life-threatening health issues. My parents had immense courage and willpower. My father was a staunch follower of Jiddu Krishnamurti. Dad would say that Jiddu Krishnamurti taught that one should search for truth without a guru. I could never follow the concept.

Dad was also very critical of superstitions and rituals. Though I often heard him say that Hinduism made death rituals very complicated and prolonged, he would perform the yearly ceremonies of his parents with utmost devotion and love, even when he was into his seventies.

He never criticized or interfered in Mother's religious activities. She never made an issue of his lack of interest or faith. They did not try to box one another into corners and accepted each other for what they were. He took her to all the shrines and temples in India and performed all the rites to her full satisfaction.

Only once, when I was maybe seven years old, I heard him having a little heated conversation with Mom. Sri Sathya Sai Baba was visiting our town; I accompanied Mom to have his darshan. There was a huge crowd and he waved at us from a balcony. After we returned, Mom joined hands and was doing *namaskaram* to a container half-filled with milk.

'What are you doing?' Dad asked, puzzled.

'Why, can't you see the shape of Sai Baba's head?' she said, pointing out an M-shaped design on one side of the container.

'Are you mad? It is just refraction of light. Light rays are scattered from the surface of milk,' he told her.

'I have my beliefs and faiths. I am not asking you to follow them,' she told him a little tersely.

He didn't say anything but later told me that Gurajada Apparao, his maternal grandfather and a renowned scholar and social reformer, had fought to make people shun superstitions and told me to study and apply science and reason and not to fall prey to blind superstitions.

In later chapters I will discuss my childhood experiences which will show why they are truly wonderful parents.

EXPLOITS OF A MISCHIEVOUS IMP—MY CHILDHOOD MEMORIES, PART I

I was Dennis the Menace and Budugu (a Telugu version of Dennis the Menace) rolled into one. I was a hyperactive child, driving my mother up the wall all the time, since most of the time Dad was not around. It is amazing how my parents, especially Mother, never raised a hand nor raised their voices a decibel higher while reprimanding me. It requires superhuman effort to remain calm when faced with situations that I created for them.

All my memories start from my age of five, from Vizag. About Cuttack, from where Dad was transferred, my memory is blank. I remember, in front of our house there was a dilapidated fort, in which only a few walls remained standing. We were staying on the first floor. On the ground floor, telephone cable rolls, telephone poles, and other items were stored. There was a huge veranda, a hall, big rooms, and a huge balcony. I remember the ceiling to be very high.

A few years back, I took my family to see the house. I was surprised to see the house. It had shrunk in size to normal levels. Since I was very small, everything may have looked huge.

The best part of the house was the bathtub. I don't remember why my brothers didn't compete with me for it. They allowed me free access and I used to enjoy soaking and playing in it. One day, as I was frolicking in the tub, my sister came crawling and managed to stand up holding the edge.

'Do you also want to play?' I asked her. She must have nodded in innocence as infants do while playing. I pulled her in, holding both her hands and she promptly landed headfirst in the tub. I was in a panic. I wrapped a towel and ran. My parents were talking to some guests.

I waited for a few seconds and ran to my mother and whispered in her ear that sister had fallen in the tub and she was blowing bubbles. My parents rushed in and pulled her out. I have no recollection of their shouting at me or reprimanding me and certainly there was no punishment. They treated the incident as normally as you would treat a small boy pushing his infant sister while playing, for fun.

But I took full advantage of the incident till high school days. I would emotionally blackmail my sister, emphasize that I had saved her life and she should gladly give her share of whatever mouth-watering dish Mother had made or obey whatever my demands or commands were at that time. Poor girl, being innocent, she would fall for it.

If she were a boy or had as much exposure as the Net-savvy girls of today, she would have said, 'Buzz off, Parents saved me. You give me your share or else I will press charges for attempted murder.'

When I finally stopped teasing and tormenting her in my high school days, I told her I was stopping all that, as I was grown-up, wizened and she could relax. But the fact was I had outgrown the craving for Mother's dishes, since I was introduced to *mirchi bajji*, *pani puri*, and *masala dosa* of Taj.

I think I took my cue to blackmail my sister from my second brother. It seems when I was almost a toddler, my second brother and my cousins went to see a lake. I accompanied them. When they were frolicking in the water, I refused to stay put on shore and walked into water and promptly fell and the current was pulling me away. My brother grabbed me by my feet and pulled me to safety at great risk to his life. He also would accuse me of being ungrateful if I did not agree to do his bidding.

A few days after the first incident, a white lady in a frock and bobbed hair visited our house. Who she was and why she came to our house, I don't know. Neither did Mother remember. She gave Mother a gift-paper-wrapped package for safekeeping and told her she would collect it later.

Mom kept it on a suitcase in the bedroom. As luck would have it, my clothes were kept in that suitcase. I took a bath, ran to the bedroom, and found this packet.

'Mom, there is something kept on my suitcase,' I shouted.

'Wait, don't do anything. I am coming,' my mom shouted and came running from the kitchen.

I was like Vinayaka in that story where he is entrusted with an *atmalingam* (a boon from Lord Shiva) by Ravana. The story goes like this. Ravana was a mighty demon king, and also an ardent devotee of Lord Shiva. Ravana meditates and prays for Lord Shiva with such sincerity and devotion that Lord Shiva is pleased, appears before him, and grants him a boon. He gifts *atmalingam* to Ravana but cautions him that he should not put it down until he reaches home. The news spreads like wildfire and the Gods become worried. If Ravana can install *atmalingam* in his kingdom, Ravana will become invincible and evil forces will rule the universe.

They approach Lord Vishnu and pray to him, to save them. Lord Vishnu instructs Lord Vinayaka to intervene. Vinayaka transforms himself into a small boy. Ravana is deeply religious and does not wish to miss his morning prayers, which involves taking dips in the river.

He sees the boy and asks him to hold the *atmalingam* until he returns after completing his morning prayers. The boy agrees, but puts a condition. The boy tells Ravana that he will hold it as long as he can, and will call 'Ravana' three times and Ravana should take it back. Unsuspecting Ravana agrees. When Ravana is in the river and taking dips, Vinayaka calls 'Ravana' thrice in quick succession. and Ravana rushes. Just before Ravana reaches, the boy puts down the *atmalingam* and vanishes... *Atmalingam* settles there permanently.

Ravana, who could lift mount Kailash was unable to move the *atmalingam* even an inch. Now 'Maha Baleswar' temple on the beach is a famous shrine.

I asked Mom, 'When are you coming?' three times and lifted the heavy packet and promptly dropped it. Mom was just a few feet away when it crashed, breaking the dinner set into many pieces.

My mom was exasperated but did not shout at me.

'Why couldn't you wait for a few minutes?' was the only sentence she spoke impatiently.

She called Tata, a peon designated for household duties (those days, officers were given some privileges). He took the broken pieces and went around the town, fortunately found and purchased another set which was exactly the same, he got it packed in a similar paper. He returned just in time. Mother gave that lady her packet when she came again in the evening.

Who that lady was and why she visited us will forever be shrouded in mystery.

This Tata was allotted the duty of being my chauffeur, dropping and picking me up at school and taking me on the bicycle to wherever I wanted to go. He used to smoke cigarettes and blow rings of smoke.

I was fascinated. 'Give it to me, I will also blow rings,' I asked him. He panicked and extinguished the cigarette. I kept on pestering him and he got fed up and asked me to get Mother's permission.

I ran to my mother and complained to her, 'See, Mom. Tata is refusing to allow me to blow rings with his cigarette. Please tell him to give it to me.'

There is a technique called 'key' designed for peace-loving parents like mine who do not beat their children. It works like this: hold the child's ear and turn it clockwise or anticlockwise like you would lock and unlock a door with a key and keep twisting until you extract a promise from the kid.

My mother used it and extracted a promise from me that I would never smoke a cigarette. After I left, rubbing and massaging my ear, my resolve to smoke had intensified.

In those days, bathwater used to be heated on wooden fires. I rolled a piece of newspaper like a cigarette, lit it, and inhaled it like I would a cigarette, burning my lips. I went howling to my mom.

For the next few days my mouth was like Lord Hanuman's (Lord Hanuman, when he was a baby, saw the rising sun and thought it was a ripe fruit, leaped to grab it. He approached quite lose to the sun and burnt his mouth).

Lord Hanuman is the Indian mythological Superman.

It permanently cured any fascination I had for smoking. However, in later years, I held a cigarette many times to rescue my friends when their parents, elders, or beautiful girls happened to appear on the horizon suddenly (Those days, drinking, smoking, and teasing girls were associated with 'bad' people or villains. Girls would fall in love with only 'good' men).

My mother's family was quite large. She had three brothers and four sisters. We had many cousins. So, during the holidays we used to go to my grandparents' village or aunts' and uncles' places and play with our cousins. My dad also had three sisters, though we used to go to only one sister's house in a nearby town.

A few years later, this Tata picked me up from station and was taking me to my aunt's house on his bicycle (My dad was courageous. He allowed me to travel alone by train).

After a few minutes I asked him, 'Do you know why Gandhiji became such a great man?'

He said he didn't know.

I told him, 'My teacher told us. He used to drink goat milk daily.'

He asked me, 'Do you want to become a great man like Gandhiji?'

I said sure, who wouldn't want to be?

He stopped the bicycle, got down, and led me by hand to a tree. A goat was tied to that tree.

Before I knew what he was doing, he milked the goat, collected milk in his palm, and forced it in my mouth. I had no option but to gulp. After two helpings, I struggled, freed myself from his grip, and ran away.

Awww… It tasted awful. As I was pulling a couple of hairs from my mouth and spitting, he was laughing his guts out.

If to become great like Gandhiji, one needed to drink this awful stuff, no, thank you, I would rather be ordinary, I thought.

My first memory of a movie is that of *Vinayaka Chavithi*. The movie is about Lord Ganesh, an elephant faced God. We, four brothers, went to that movie. In those days, movie patrons were treated like cattle. Creature comforts were never a priority for cinema owners. Poorna theatre had wooden chairs and benches with a lot of bedbugs to give you company and to ensure you don't fall asleep during the show. In addition, they provided a thin wooden strip to serve as a backrest, leaving a huge gap through which I fell into the back row and cried my lungs out.

I was more scared than hurt and my eldest brother took me out and pacified me with chips and ice cream.

This is the background for the next story.

One day, I was engaged in my destructive work for the day but observed that my second brother was behaving strangely, looking at the clock and at me anxiously.

'*Something's afoot*,' I told myself and acted as if I didn't notice. After a few minutes, Tata stood at the door and motioned to my brother to come out. My brother went on tiptoe silently like a cat, and once out of the room, they ran downstairs.

I left my work and shot out like an arrow after them, in time to see Tata riding his bicycle, taking my brother away. I ran behind them barefoot. They tried to vanish but I must have been like Usain Bolt. After a few minutes, they reluctantly stopped and took me onboard. They couldn't very well leave me in the middle of nowhere because they would then have to answer a lot of questions.

It turned out my brother wanted to see a Laurel and Hardy movie peacefully. He was worried that after that *Vinayaka Chavithi* experience, I would make the movie going experience a nightmarish one, so I should be avoided at all costs. The seats in Leela Mahal were good (they didn't have large openings through which kids could fall out) and the movie was very funny and enjoyable. People of any age can enjoy Laurel and Hardy movies. I let him watch and enjoy the movie in peace.

As I said earlier, my mother's family was quite large, so she had to attend many functions. Managing her other children was child's play so she would take them and leave me with Dad sometimes for a few days. The usual bribes were movies and chocolates.

Once, my dad took me to a movie called *Daiva Balam*. In it NTR was thrashed mercilessly and he kept howling and I started crying. Anyone else in my dad's place would take the child out, buy ice cream and chips and wait for the traumatic scene to be over and resume watching.

He took me to the projection room, knocked on the door, and requested the operator to show me the projector. Dad explained its mechanism and how the film reel turns and how the light is projected. He told me that what I was seeing on the screen was just an image and NTR was hale and healthy and maybe having dinner at home with his family.

That was a very important lesson. Later on, I enjoyed watching ghoulish movies like *Dracula*, *Nightmare on Elm Street*, *Exorcist*, and after a night show, would walk back alone to my college hostel.

After a few days it was time for the next instalment of bribery. My dad took me to watch *Chivaraku Migiledi*. This time I was not alone. Half a dozen of my dad's friends and colleagues also accompanied us. This movie had no violence and the songs were good. So I was happily watching the colourful 'EXIT' boards and whirring fan blades and sometimes the screen… and the weeping friends of my dad.

My jaw fell open as I looked at my dad's friends. Some were wiping tears with their hand and some were blowing noses into handkerchiefs and they were all crying.

With seriousness in my voice I said to my dad, 'Dad, they are thinking it is real, take them to the projector room, and show them.' I had the typically loud voice small kids have and it must have been audible to the first row, since a silent sad scene was in progress.

This time Dad took me out for chips and ice cream.

Chivaraku Migiledi is a real tear-jerker of a movie and well worth seeing. If one sees it without interruption, eyes are bound to become moist, irrespective of how hard-hearted one is. I term such movies as 'dry cleaning' movies. Our minds, souls, and hearts become accumulated with a lot of dirt from watching senseless action, horror movies and TV serials. So once in a while if you see movies like *Chivaraku Migiledi*, they purify the mind and soul, and your heart will overflow with milk of human kindness and noble thoughts.

More Exploits of a Mischievous Imp— My Childhood Memories, Part II

Budugu boasts in an episode, 'Many tuition teachers worked for me.' He implied that none of them could cope up with his naughty antics for long.

Since LKG-UKG (pre-school, Lower Kindergarten.and upper Kindergarten) concept was non-existent, my dad must have arranged tuition for me to get some preschool training, or it could also have been to give a few hours' respite to Mother. Like Budugu, I too packed off several tuition teachers.

My first tuition teacher was one *Kukka Moothi* (dog's snout) *Mastaru* (in Telugu, a male teacher is called thus).

'I don't want to get tutored by that *kukka moothi mastaru*,' I told my dad firmly when he finished talking with him and came inside. Everyone broke into laughter for that teacher's protruding mouth had a distinct resemblance to canine anatomy.

Dad also laughed but convinced me to give a few days trial.

How I tormented him! My dad was very firm in his instructions—beating or use of cane and ruler to discipline me was not allowed. He had to bring to me into line patiently. It was unfair, of course; his hands were itching to clout me on the head and I don't blame him.

First, KMM (the teacher) thought he could win me over by reciting a tale. He chose to tell the story of the crow and the jackal. The crow is sitting on a tree branch, holding a piece of meat in its beak. The jackal wants to steal it. So, it praises the crow's sweet voice and singing prowess and incites it to sing. As soon as the crow starts to sing, the piece of meat falls down and the jackal grabs the meat and runs away.

Halfway through, I told the teacher, 'You are a liar. Animals and birds cannot talk or sing.'

He smiled. 'Not now. But in those days they used to talk and sing. Remember, this is a "once upon a time" story.'

I was not convinced. 'If they can talk then, they should talk now also.' Then a crow landed, as if on cue, on the veranda wall and said, 'Caw, caw.'

'Now, you make it talk,' I challenged him. I pestered and hounded him.

My uncle (Mother's brother), who was watching, the fun burst out laughing (even now, he recites this story to his grandchildren).

After a few days, I told him that I was not in the mood to study and would like to go and play.

He challenged me, 'Oh, do you? Try it. I will see how you can leave this place.'

I told him, 'Okay, see,' and before he realized what I was doing, I got up, ran, opened the door to my mother's room, closed it noiselessly (Mom was sleeping), crawled under her bed, and waited. My sister was a few months old. I still remember, some betel leaves were placed on my sister's stomach as she must have been crying because of a stomach-ache.

I waited with bated breath. KMM coughed softly and tapped the door gently, called a few times, *'Emandi, emandi,'* and left after five minutes. Mom was sleeping soundly and he was too much of a gentleman to disturb her.

I felt sorry and guilty for my behaviour after I attained enlightenment several years later and asked Mom and Dad to give me his address; I wanted to apologize. They also did not remember anything about him except the name Kukka Moothi.

He left after some time. I don't remember much about my other teachers. But there was one other that stuck out. One gray-haired teacher came and gave me a lot of chocolates and told me he hated studies, liked to sing, dance, and play and I immediately liked him. He had enormous patience and slowly started teaching me.

My father put me in the best school in the city, every child's dream school. We were not forced to sit and listen to teachers. We could get up anytime (no need to get teacher's permission) and play on slides, see-saws, and swings. Teachers and ayahs would be on their toes, running behind us kids, like hens behind chicks. After lunch we were forced to sleep on small folding cots. If the cots were full, a big mattress was arranged in the hall. They forced us to sleep for a few hours after lunch and then woke us up. We would play and go home.

I tried my best to analyze why I used to cry every day before going to school. I should have been impatient, jumping, and rearing to go to such a beautiful school. I finally arrived at an incident which could be the root cause for my reluctance to go to that school.

One afternoon I had to go to the toilet urgently and I told the teacher. She was a young nun and she panicked. For some reason, the ayahs were absent, absconding, or on strike; I don't know.

She took me to the restrooms, and as I stood there silently crying (I had a typical reversed 'U' mouth while crying, as can be seen from my childhood photos), she was frantically pacing up and down wringing her hands and saying, 'Oh, sweet Jesus… what should I do…' She had opted for this noble and pious way of living with dreams of serving poor, sick, and needy, like Florence Nightingale, but never thought that she would be required to attend to the toilet needs of small boys.

From here my memory is blank; the next thing I remember is Tata taking me home on the bicycle. So I must have been reluctant to go to school from the next day to avoid embarrassment and ridicule as I could not avoid the young nun and did not want to face her after the humiliation.

My dad got fed up and told me that I didn't deserve to study in such a magnificent school and put me in a small school across the street (I don't know why such schools are called *Dumpala Badi*, probably because at lunch break, small vendors used to sell sweet potatoes, aka *chilagada dumpalu*).

Sending me to school daily was a cumbersome task. It used to drain the energy of everyone in the house. Finally, one day, my dad lost his patience. I crawled under the bed in my attempt to avoid detection. He pulled me by my hair (of which I had plenty—like Super star Rajnikant, I also lost hair later at the same rate as he did) and gave me one hard slap on the back (that was only time he did this).

This had a miraculous effect. From then till college, my attendance never dropped below 90 per cent. Even on the few occasions when I was absent, it was due to pressure from my parents to attend some family functions, marriage. (But in college, attendance hovered around 75 per cent, the required minimum. We used to calculate, plan, and bunk classes).

I learnt a bitter lesson that same medicine cannot cure everyone and may, in fact, be counterproductive. I gave such a slap to my elder daughter when she was crying daily to go to school in her LKG. (History is never tired of repeating itself. Again, one of the best schools a child can hope for, and she didn't want to go). My wife was horrified and she neither forgot nor let my daughter forget.

Once in every few days, when there is not much to talk about (which is more often than not, after twenty-five years of marriage and when one of the couple is a 'silent' partner), she wonders how my conscience allowed me to beat such a sweet, innocent, and delicate child. She keeps wondering how one can be so 'cruel' and 'heartless'.

Anyway, so I started going to school regularly. The carpeted area of this school was not even half of the playground of my previous school. There were no tables and benches. We had to sit on the floor. Still, I liked this school. I was the brightest, smartest kid in the class, liked by all teachers.

In fact, one day, one of the teachers once asked me to sit beside her and took *upma* from her Tiffin box and placed it in my cupped palms and asked me to eat. It was most embarrassing. While I was happy about being singled out and honoured, to eat it when so many pairs of eyes were watching was very uncomfortable. I could not dare to anger the teacher by refusing to eat it.

Once, I was late for school as my mom could not get me ready in time because of unexpected guests. I refused to bunk school. So she woke up my uncle and asked him to drop me off. He put on a shirt, combed his hair (in those days he also had many combs of it and used to style it like Dev Anand), and walked with me to the school across the street. He was to explain to the teacher the reason for my delay so that I was not punished.

I entered the class.

He said, 'Excuse me, teacher.' The teacher who was facing the blackboard turned and her face was flushed with anger and embarrassment. The kids also turned back to look at him and howled with laughter.

He didn't understand. He looked down and had the shock of his life.

He had not put on his trousers. He was wearing the striped half-pants like underclothing (half pajamas, like Dada Kondke's with cords hanging to the knees). He turned and ran back home. He says the few hundred yards' distance to the house felt like many kilometres and the few minutes felt like interminable hours.

My eldest brother was very good at mimicking a barking dog. One day I was watching the road from our balcony. I saw my brother running frantically with two barking dogs close on his heels, snapping jaws at his legs. Like in the movies, he rushed in and slammed the doors shut on the faces of those dogs in the last second like in movies. They barked for a few minutes and then left.

He was panting heavily. I asked him what had happened.

It seems when he was coming home, he saw two dogs barking furiously, quarrelling about some domestic matter. The female dog was dressing down male dog, and the male dog was not taking it lying down; he was trying to bark louder to drown out her voice.

My brother chose a most inopportune moment to try out his skills. He barked.

Both dogs suddenly stopped their shouting match, looked at each other, and charged at him. By his intrusion, my brother wanted to broker peace and pacify them. But in their language it must have sounded quite insulting and demeaning (It happens; the most courteous welcome word in Telugu is an obscene abuse in Hindi). So they changed the direction of their anger towards him and attacked him.

After that, he never practiced his art. We could not force him to try it out even behind the closed doors of our home. He was worried that a dog passing by on the street outside might take offence, lie in wait, and attack him when he stepped out.

Once, my second brother and I were asked to stage a play in my dad's office anniversary celebrations. It was a scene from the play *Kanyasulkam*; my second brother was playing role of Girisam and I, Venkatesam.

As luck would have it, after two days of rehearsal, I was down with chickenpox. My third brother was roped in for the Venkatesam role. On the day of the function, I had a very high fever. My dad told Mom to keep a good eye on me, since I had been nagging them to allow me to see the play.

Chickenpox is highly contagious so my mom refused to allow me to go. I was a very stubborn and mulish child. I kept crying and throwing tantrums and finally Mom got fed up.

She told me to wait; she would call Dad and ask him to send a peon to take me. I did not believe her and I ran into the street, barefoot. My mom panicked as she could not run after me on the streets.

Dad was on the dais, in the middle of a speech. His assistant went and whispered in his ear that I ran away from home. He told him to send a peon to bring me and maintained his composure and completed his speech.

Tata met me midway and took me on his bicycle. I enjoyed the play from the first row. Both my brothers excelled in their roles and had the audience splitting their sides.

My parents did not give lectures or make a scene later. They treated my rash behaviour as a minor matter.

During that period one doctor came to treat me. He was short, bald and was sweating profusely. My reputation could have preceded me to make him nervous. When he declared that he wanted to give an injection, I ran away and bolted myself in the bathroom. I started giving him choicest abuses at top of my voice. My mom sent Tata to climb over the wall of the bathroom (that bathroom wall did not go up to the ceiling) and jump inside the bathroom to open the door. I fought tooth and nail but Tata overpowered me and the doctor took sweet revenge.

My second brother and his friends used to play a game: each would hit the others with a rubber ball. The one who had the most hits was the winner. One day, none of his friends turned up. He wanted to lure me into playing. I refused since I was small and would be an easy target and he could easily dodge my throws. It would be an uneven contest.

He told me, 'Just think. It may save your life. Suppose a thief enters our home when you are alone. He will throw knives at you, if you play this game, you can easily dodge and save yourself.'

I bought his story and received nasty blows on body from the rubber ball. In those days we wore half-pants and the rubber ball can really hurt you if it lands on the exposed parts.

Finally, I withdrew and told him that I would never stay alone in the house and would take my chances with the knife-throwing thief.

One of the few prizes I won in school days was a small pinkish soap bar for coming in first in a running race. That bath soap had no brand name and had the picture of a camel on its cover. Every one teased me and said that I was presented with dog soap.

My eldest brother never experienced a headache and wondered what it felt like. A few of his friends told him that if he watched movies non-stop from morning to midnight (morning show, matinee, first show, and second show), he was bound to have a severe headache, 7 on Richter scale.

He and a bunch of his friends started this exercise on a Sunday morning. By the end of matinee, a few wickets fell. Halfway through, everyone retired to the hostel with severe headaches. Only my brother completed watching all four movies and still wondered what a headache feels like.

About Bodhi Tree and Mom's Culinary Magic

Millions of books and articles have been written and seminars have been conducted about the ill effects of deforestation, global warming, and ozone layer depletion but not a word is written about the catastrophe and havoc caused by the depletion of bodhi trees in the country.

Siddhartha failed to find a solution to the causes of human misery, suffering, and sorrow despite reading several books and talking to several learned people. He finally received enlightenment while meditating under a bodhi tree and became Gautama Buddha. Buddhism was born and spread all over the world.

If I were to become a prime minister or at least a minister for education, I will ensure planting of bodhi trees in school and college campuses and tie up problematic students to the tree trunks. All the students will be required to sit under the tree for a few hours regularly. The results would be amazing; everyone would be smiling, at peace with one another and in a state of eternal bliss.

In my teens, I was at my raucous naughty best (or worst, depending on which side you take), teasing and tormenting my sister and harassing Mom to prepare *chegodilu*, *jantikalu*, *palakova*, and other savouries which required back-breaking efforts. Suddenly one fine day I got up in the morning and was a changed man (or teenager). I became the role model for 'Rama is a good boy' instantaneously. My suspicion is that I must have sat under a bodhi tree for some time on the previous day. There is no other explanation for such a sudden change as if someone had flipped a switch. When I mentioned this to my good friend Eashwar, who is famous for his repartee and one-liners, he asked me incredulously, 'What? You never sat under a bodhi tree till you were a teenager? My mom told me that I used to crawl and play under a bodhi tree when I was a baby. That's why I am so matured and wise compared to you ignorant idiots.'

I used to harass my sister by pulling her plaits or pinching her and running away. She would run after me to hit me but could never catch up. I kept laughing, further maddening her. If and when I came within striking range, I would block her blows with my forearm. Her palms would land on the hard bone of my forearm, further hurting her; she would bawl louder. My poor mom was handicapped by her 'no violence' policy and I was already taller and out of reach for her 'key' (twisting the ear) strategy. She would keep repeating patiently, 'Don't harass her.' Sometimes I would instigate my sister by calling her some unimaginably irritating names like, 'Hello, Udrushini [or Shadruchini], why are you so dull?' Why and how I invented such names escapes me.

The art of savoury preparation at home has come to an end with my mom's generation. When you have shops selling Haldiram's *bhujias* across the street, where is the need to toil? My mom used to make the yummiest *chegodilu* and *jantikalu*. She used to put garlic juice and the aroma would waft across several streets. I used to joke with Mom that when I grew up, I would patent, prepare, and market her recipes and they would be such a hit across the globe that people would give up their pizzas and hot dogs and queue up for her items. She would laugh and brush aside my compliments. Present snacks manufacturers are quite lucky that I am lazy and tend to procrastinate.

Just a few sentences about *chegodilu*: My mom would first boil the ingredients (rice flour and other spices). Then she would roll the paste and make small rings (like onion rings of McDonald's) and fry them. No sooner was the first lot out of the frying pan than it would be consumed in seconds. We had appetites like Bakasura and Ghatotkacha, and Mom used to keep up her production with our consumption. Finally when our stomachs refused to be loaded any further, she would continue preparing them until three or four big aluminium containers were filled up (which would also be devoured pretty fast).

Those who haven't tasted my mom's *chegodilu* cannot imagine the exquisite taste. It is impossible to describe it in words, but let me try. They were golden brown in colour, crisp and hollow. If you broke one, you would be amazed to see the inner texture. When you crunched it between your teeth, ohhhhhhhh...it was heavenly!

But after my conversion to 'good boy', I never asked her to prepare *chegodilu* nor did I allow her to make even if she wanted to make. I was like a dictator; I declared that from that day on, said item would not be prepared and we should be ashamed to put her to all that trouble. (It is amazing why my brothers didn't clout me on the head for being so sanctimonious, since until a few days back I was the major culprit.) If someone takes a politically correct stand, others have no option but to agree.

Preparation of *palakova* is also very cumbersome. I had no difficulty in banning the item since I was not enamoured by it totally. You have to stand and continuously stir the milk and ingredients. If you stop for a few seconds, the homogeneity would be gone, resulting in lumps. My mom would stand and keep stirring for what seemed like hours. But the taste was just out of this world. It would just melt in the mouth.

I confess that even after becoming a 'good boy', I pestered Mom to make *jantikalu*. It is not as elaborate and taxing as the other items and I used to help her. However, one weakness I could not overcome was for *bajjis* when it rained; we used to sit at the sit-out and watch the downpour through the grill and munch piping hot *bajjis* made by Mom. It was a tradition we never broke. There was no compromise for that.

My mom herself never complained nor was irritated about all her hardwork in the kitchen. Anyone who knows her will recall only her smiling and laughing face. She was always pleasant and actually derived happiness in receiving and entertaining guests. I used to help Mom in the kitchen; and when guests landed up suddenly at inconvenient timings (read siesta hours), I used to grumble. She would admonish me and tell me that they visited us because they had affection and love for us.

My mom didn't like one vegetable, bitter gourd (*karela*) but would make three or four varieties with this vegetable, all exceptionally tasty. She would ask me to taste it and tell her if any changes needed to be made. She used to juggle the menu to satisfy everyone. While others were not so fussy, I was quite demanding.

For instance, Dad liked *upma* made with wheat granules (*godhuma nuka*). I asked Mom how he could like that; it tasted like sawdust. I liked *upma* in semi-liquid state; if you take it in a steel cup and invert on your plate, *upma* should retain the shape of the cup. We used to call that *pelli upma* since only in the marriage feasts the cooks could achieve the correct texture. One brother liked *upma* to be dry and another wanted ginger pieces. On many occasions, Mom made four varieties of *upma*.

Once my mom made three types, but not the one I liked. I protested and refused to eat any of the other types. My brothers got angry. They told Mom that she pampered and spoiled me; I should be taught to be considerate and accommodating and today was the best day to start. They told her to be strong and that I would not become weak if I skipped one snack. I put on my best petulant, martyr expression and watched morosely as they helped themselves.

A few minutes later she signalled to me to come into kitchen. She was super-fast; she made my *upma* and told me to eat it there in silence to avoid trouble with the others.

After waiting for such a magical day for a long time (like when I turned over a new leaf), I sincerely tried to locate bodhi trees to make my daughters sit in their shade for a few hours. Now my wife tells me that there is a garden maintained by a swami ji which has all varieties of trees. I told her to ask him about bodhi tree. However, it is true that making them sit under that tree, even if I found one, may not be an easy task.

You can take the horse to the water but you cannot make it drink it. One such horse is my wife's relative. He is and has always been two-dimensional, much to the envy of self and daughters, who tend to bloat just by breathing air. My younger daughter once commented that he would not get hurt if he was pushed from the top of a multi-storey building.

'Why, he will land just like anyone else,' my wife remarked.

'No, he will float like a leaf and will land gently,' my daughter explained.

Once, my elder daughter's friend Miss Trisha visited us. Just then Vijay passed by, wearing a new bright blue shirt. He moves fast like a blur and Miss Trisha was left wondering who it was.

My second daughter told her, 'That blue *patang* [kite] is my uncle.'

Miss Trisha is not your regular demure, shy type of girl. She is fun-loving and has a boisterous, hearty and had a high-decibel laugh. She laughed so much that my wife rushed from the kitchen to see what the matter was.

Miss Trisha and my elder daughter were employed in an MNC and were in night shift for some time. The company's policy was that the male member of the pickup car had to be dropped last, after ensuring all the girls were safely dropped at their homes. It was the turn of Mr Akhil to drop them. Miss

Trisha had to collect a book from his flat, where he was staying with two other friends.

They entered the flat, she collected her book, and they recollected a funny incident in the office and she laughed with her trademark gusto. After she left, Mr Akhil opened the door to his bedroom and was shocked to see both his friends white with terror.

He asked anxiously, 'What is the matter?'

'Thank God, you are safe. Come in quickly and close the door. There is a *bhootni* [female ghost] in the house,' one friend said, his voice trembling. The other friend had curled himself into a ball, completely covered in thick blanket and was reciting *Hanuman Chalisa* (hymns to ward off evel spirits) loudly. Both were terrorized by the high-pitched female laughter coming from the hall. They did not even have the nerve to get up and lock the door.

Coming back to the bodhi tree, if my wife's two-dimensional relative was locked in a park having only bodhi trees and told that he would be released only after sitting under a tree for a few minutes, he would stand on his feet and refuse to sit since he was in no mood to sit and would sit when he felt like sitting and not when he was told by someone.

In contrast, his brother would sit under every tree, hoping this was the magical bodhi tree. Unfortunately, till reports last came in, he is still searching for the bodhi tree. He must have sat under several trees. His luck is such that if he bangs his foot on the root of the bodhi tree and falls flat, he is more likely to cut down the tree than realize that it was the tree he was searching for.

MY FATHER'S
AUTOBIOGRAPHY

FOREWORD

My father lived to a ripe age of ninety-four. He was the grandson of Sri Gurajada Apparao the famous social reformer and pioneer and architect of modern Telugu literature of the nineteenth century. Those not familiar with Telugu society, if and when you visit Hyderabad, please see Sri Gurajada Apparao's statue on Tank Bund (it is the first one near traffic signal at the boat club end of Tank Bund or Dwarakanagar Junction in Vizag).

I know the secret of my father's longevity. Though timely meals, five- to seven-kilometre daily walks, and careful monitoring of health parameters were contributory factors and are achievable targets for many of us, what is almost impossible for us to achieve is his attitude and his philosophical thinking.

He told me several hundred or maybe a thousand times, 'Accept people as they are and never expect them to be what you want them to be. That is the only way to remain happy and healthy.'

He was not just preaching.

I think I should take credit for his autobiography coming into being. I have inherited his reticence. He would never discuss any of his experiences and would say there is nothing to tell. I kept pushing him to write his experiences since his command of Telugu and English was excellent and I gave up after some time. When I bought my video camera, I recorded my parents' interviews, I requested my friend who is very talkative and has a skill in making people open up to him to try to breach my parents' walls of reticence and make them share their experiences, thoughts, and feelings. He did an excellent job. I distributed the copies to all my brothers, sister and nieces and nephew.

So it came as a surprise when his autobiography was unearthed by my sister. I am translating it into English for the benefit of many who cannot read Telugu or at the least handwritten script.

Two things impressed me while I was translating. First was his handwriting; he must have written it when he was in his eighties. His handwriting was strong, bold, and confident. There was not one strike through or correction; it felt as if words just flowed from his pen (in contrast, if I write ten sentences, I will not be able to read my own handwriting after the eighth line).

Second was complete lack of bitterness or anger. His narration is quite balanced. He lost his father when he was three years old. He did not have a normal childhood like many kids. He doesn't blame or judge anyone.

After reading this, I realized he missed out on appreciative gestures of parents. Every child celebrates all achievements with parents and basks in their joy and appreciation. He had missed all that. That was why he would taunt my mom when she didn't praise him by saying words like, 'Excellent, you are a genius. You have done a great job,' when he repaired something or had done something which he was proud of.

She would just laugh and taunt him back that he never praised her finger-licking-good dishes either but she would learn how to praise. I don't think they learnt the art of praising.

I am not altering or changing names since all characters mentioned in the articles are no more and he didn't write any derogatory things about anyone. This might be interesting since it gives an insight into life and times in early twentieth century of India.

A Few Sweet Memories in Our Lives
by my father

When I was three years old, my father left for his heavenly abode when he was at the peak of his career and position. It seems he went to Bhimuni patnam to attend Polipalli goddess's festival. My mother told me that he died there suddenly after drinking a soda and that his entire body was found to have turned black.

My mother and sisters told me that he was poisoned because he refused to accept a bribe from a man involved in a murder case. This speculation is imaginary and there was no concrete proof. In those days, mafia gangs could not have been so prevalent or powerful. He could have suffered a massive heart attack.

My grandfather passed away few years back. It seems my father was quite worried how my uncle (Mother's brother) would manage such a large family since he was very innocent.

My father already got my three sisters married and he had to take loans since he was very honest and had no other source of income. He managed to send my sisters to reasonably wealthy families. He spent all his hard-earned money, accumulated by honest means, and borrowed for the shortfall.

He did not save for future requirement; he had no bank deposits or any policies like LIC. He invested his remaining savings on his passion, manufacturing of Ayurveda medicines. He did not bother about his family's future requirements as it never occurred to him that untimely death could be in his destiny.

To compound this, he practiced his medicine assisted by his dumb nephew who did not study even up to the fourth standard. Since he was a government employee, he honestly felt that he was not supposed to have private medical practice and practiced medicine in his nephew Mallaparaju's name.

Though my mother was also not well educated and was innocent like my uncle, she acquired some knowledge about medicines my father was making. I had occasion to experience the effect of my father's genius in healing because of an accident. One day I was standing with one foot on the veranda and another on a wooden support for jasmine plant (jasmine vines crawl and climb on supports made with sticks). I might have done this acrobatic stunt to reach out to pluck some flowers. Suddenly the fragile wooden support collapsed, and my left leg landed on a stick (a thin slice cut from a toddy palm tree's trunk) which was used to keep the support intact.

Four or five thorns pierced and penetrated deep into the calf muscle. I was rushed to the hospital. They extracted three thorns that were visible and accessible. I was in severe pain which didn't diminish even after four days as two more thorns were deeply embedded. Then my mother heated one black ointment prepared by my father and applied that warm paste and put a bandage. After two hours, two 2-inch-long thin thorns were pushed out. My wound healed quite fast.

Afterwards, I never experienced any discomfort but the marks on skin were permanent. Whenever I look at those indelible marks, tears well up in my eyes as I am reminded of my mother's presence of mind and her love.

She led a royal life until middle age and suddenly her life was plunged into darkness. I always wonder at her courage and tenacious, buoyant spirit. She had to return to her mother's house with four young boys and one grown-up, marriageable age girl, pulled herself up, brought up, educated, and settled her children, all before she turned fifty. She passed away in her fiftieth year.

When my father worked in Koraput and Navrangpur areas, he searched for and collected many rare medicinal herbs with the help of tribal people of the forest areas. He prepared medicines with those herbs. Oriya and Bengali languages have many similarities. He learnt those languages, studied many books, and prepared notes. My uncle and my father's nephew had neither knowledge nor interest to use or capitalize on the invaluable treasure and sold those precious medicines at throwaway prices.

They did not even preserve his books and notes.

When I was six years old, I had a boil on my chest and it was quite painful. My second brother Venkata Rathnam took me to a doctor without telling Mother, got it operated, and brought me back home. My mother was surprised; she did not think doctors would be so friendly or considerate.

I do not have many memories of my second brother. He died young. During summer vacations, my eldest brother and second brother visited my sister's in-laws' house in Onti Mamidi village. They wanted to enjoy the leisurely village atmosphere. My elder aunt Ramanamma (my father's eldest sister)came to see them from Venkata Nagaram (this village is ten miles away from Onti Mamidi).

She took my brothers to her village. There, her son Rama and my brothers went to swim in the village pond. Inadvertently they moved to a deeper spot while playing. Rama could swim but not to the extent to save drowning people, so he swam ashore and raised the alarm. One person rushed to the rescue; he saved my elder brother but, unfortunately, could not save my second brother.

This additional suffocating tragedy piled on my mother, who was already burdened with many tragedies, problems, and difficulties. My sister and brother-in-law also were very sad.

My one sweet childhood memory is admission to one small school across the street. My mother selected an auspicious time (sumuhurtam) and took me to Bhadragiri Ramamurty's school, which was close to our house on Kaspa Street. We had desks and benches. When we stepped out of the house, with me holding my slate and slate pencil, buffaloes were coming in the opposite direction. It was not a good omen, so we went back into the house. On next attempt, a group of women with water pots were coming towards us. Then my mother sent me to school since it was a good omen. I don't remember very well, but my eldest brother could have accompanied me to school on my joining day.

We could not enter the classroom unless we greeted (*namaskaram*) Headmaster Ramamurty garu. He was a Sathana vaishanava He would sit majestically attired in a spotless white dress and *panga namalu* (vertical stripes worn on forehead).

I remember only one incident distinctly. One teacher asked one question and kept lashing on the palms of students with a cane who could not answer correctly. He approached me. I said my answer and extended my palm.

'You answered correctly. Why did you stretch your hand?' he asked me.

There was a small compound behind school. We used to play there in recess.

I studied till fifth class in this school and joined in first form (sixth class) in Raja vari branch school opposite to this one. When I was in second form, management selected students who scored good marks in Telugu and planned to teach them Sanskrit. I did not show interest when the Sanskrit teacher asked me if I was interested. My one regret is not learning Sanskrit; I would have enjoyed Kalidasa's literature in Sanskrit.

I studied up to third form there and joined Maharaja vari high school for fourth form.

Even at that young age, I understood how deeply superstitions and undesirable practices were embedded in the middle-class families, even well-educated ones.

My grandfather's cousin passed BA and joined the Maharaja of Vizianagaram's estate. He joined as a clerk and rose to the level of Amin. He was renowned for his innocence and good nature.

Those who considered themselves to be smart had amassed wealth in estate jobs. They supplemented their earnings by many other means. But he was happy and contended with his salary.

Over a period, the management of the estate went into the custody of court of wards. One Sathyanadhan, IAS, was appointed as administrator. He called uncle to Vizianagaram to reprimand him since revenue administration was poor in his division. He was given appointment at 10 a.m. on a Monday.

Uncle was quite nervous; by nature he was jumpy. When he stepped out of the house at 10 a.m, he encountered a bad omen. He washed his feet, sat in his house, lit a cigar, and went out again after fifteen minutes. Again he encountered a bad omen. He kept postponing until he came across a good omen and by the time he went to meet IAS officer, it was past 11 a.m.

Sathyanadhan was enraged; he shouted at him for being late and retired him instantly. A person who was a graduate in those days and who worked in a responsible post for many years gave more importance to omens than to meet his superior officer at appointed time and lost his job.

My grandfather, Gurajada Apparao garu, had condemned the superstitions and such practices and led a movement. Even today, many people continue to be victims of superstitions.

Another undesirable practice is marriages within family, i.e. marriages between cousins and marriage of an uncle and a niece. The only reason is the greed or undesirable intention to keep properties within family.

My uncle married off his innocent daughter to his nephew, who had a wealth of all evil habits and vices. This nephew's sister was also married to a zamindar's son. Both marriages were performed at the same muhurtam, at a huge mansion or haveli. Zamindar's son was a womanizer.

After a few years, Zamindar died, and his son left his wife and blew up all his property and money for womanizing. His property vanished as fast as a lit camphor. The nephew's sister didn't go to her parents' house but stayed behind in city and led life by depending on the mercy of others who would lend rice, dhal, and spices. I used to pity her. Some unfortunate women are destined to live life in misery.

The nephew also melted away his wealth, married a second time, and landed at his wealthy sister's house in Rajahmundry. When I was studying BSc there, I would see him smoking cigarettes, joking and laughing in a carefree manner like a reincarnated Girisam (a famous character in my grandfather's epic *Kanyasulkam*).

In those days, middle-class families had the strongly rooted compulsive desire to marry off cousins. Brothers will view sister's daughter with affection; there is no scope for romantic feelings. But children's parents keep harping on about their marriage from their infancy, and I suppose this leads to a transformation of feelings among cousins. In Northern India, this marriage within family culture is not there. Only in south India has this culture taken deep roots.

My grandmother was not very well educated but my grandfather praised her for efficiently managing a large family with its many guests and relatives and looking after him very well. Anyone else in her place would have panicked and stunned into numbness when a widowed eldest daughter comes back with four young sons and a grown-up granddaughter. My grandfather passed away some time before. My uncle was not smart and stopped education while in the intermediate level.

He was neither employed nor was he interested in seeking employment; he spent money and whiled away time in leisure. I could understand from my aunt's nagging that he had the habit of womanizing. But he did not seem to have set up a second home.

My grandmother was quite judicious; she gave all her gold ornaments to her daughter-in-law and all her immovable properties inherited from her parents to her son and entered into an agreement. She put a condition that my uncle had to look after our family until my eldest brother completed graduation (BA).

My uncle and aunt honoured that commitment. My aunt deserves special appreciation. It is beyond imagination of present generations. It is not a minor achievement to look after an unfortunate sister-in-law (husband's sister) with her five children for thirteen years, spending their share of inheritance also.

My mother and her sister would get Rs 50 per year from their agricultural lands. Even those were given to uncle.

I sometimes felt that my grandmother had done injustice to her daughters because of her love for her only son. I realized her noble intentions only after I grew up. My mother was incapable of marrying off my sister and my uncle would not take any interest, so she wanted to fulfil the responsibility during her lifetime.

In a frantic haste, she fixed my sister's marriage with the eldest son of a wealthy family. This was a second marriage for my brother-in-law and he had a daughter of same age as my sister.

I was puzzled. My grandfather Gurajada Apparao Garu had fought lifelong for the eradication of the evil custom of child girl marriages to old men, and how my grandmother, who understood his principles, ideals, and ideologies had selected such an alliance for my sister, remains a mystery to me till now.

It is possible she might have thought that her son would not be happy with additional expenditure as he was already overburdened. When my father was alive, he fixed an alliance with Pasumarthi family, which fizzled out after his sudden death. In the social customs prevailing at that time, due to the sudden new tragic developments, it would be very difficult to find a suitable match after one got cancelled. So, my grandmother could have approved since the groom's family came forward with the proposal.

Though I was unhappy that my sister had to marry a man who already had a daughter of her age, my sister impressed everyone in her new household with her dignified behaviour and earned a very good name. Her husband was the eldest son and she shouldered her responsibilities as a senior daughter-in-law admirably.

His two younger brothers respected him and followed his advice. As long as he was working in his job, he left all the revenues of their combined property to his brothers. He was very dignified and was not at all arrogant and always was attired in khaddar clothes. He worked for a long time as Amin (tehsildar in revenue department) in Vizianagaram estate.

He did not accumulate wealth by illegal means, though many revenue inspectors employed in estate amassed wealth and acquired many properties. My brother-in-law was conservative in financial matters, except for food. My sister was blessed with four sons and three daughters. In her last stages, she was bedridden for ten years because of liver dysfunction. Her eldest son Ramam and his wife looked after all her needs and served her quite patiently and with love till she breathed her last.

I have to mention about our studies and education. The agreement with my uncle was that he was to provide us food but not our other expenses. When I was in high school, I was granted a ½ scholarship since Mr Jogi Raju, son-in-law of my grandmother's sister (he was a math teacher) recommended my case to Headmaster and got it sanctioned. Jogi Raju garu was a sincere follower of Gandhiji. He also always wore khaddar dress. His surname was Chadimella varu. All the houses opposite branch high school belonged to him and his brothers. Headmaster Ramadass liked me a lot since I used to score very high marks in math.

A full scholarship including expenditure for books was provided to my eldest brother for his BA. It was sanctioned by Dowager Maharani, sister of Vizianagaram Raja. She volunteered the help when my mother met her. I accompanied my mother on that occasion. So, my elder brother's education went off smoothly without any hitch.

He could not land a job after passing BA. All his efforts were futile. He could not get the job of even a clerk in Taluk office or district board. Finally he went to Sialkot (Punjab)as a tutor to a railway engineer's son.

During his unemployment phase, I passed SSLC with very good marks. My uncle advised my mother not to spend money on my education unnecessarily since my brother was jobless even after passing BA. He suggested that I learn typing and shorthand.

My mother's younger sister's son failed in SSLC, so she also seconded her brother's suggestion due to jealousy. But my mother stood firm, she told that I had blessings of Goddess Sarasvati and she would not back out in spending for my education, and what little money was left with her, she would spend for it.

Then my uncle refused to bear expenses for our food. He firmly told that their arrangement was to look us after until my elder brother passed BA and hence he would not bear our expenditure.

My aunt fought on my side; she refused to stop my education since I was quite good at studies. She said she would take responsibility for my education. My uncle reluctantly agreed since my aunt stood very firm.

My aunt was not my blood relative yet she showed great humanity, and in contrast, my own uncle and aunt (Mother's brother and sister) tried to disrupt my studies. Until now, I am still amazed by the extent of their jealousy and refusal to extend even a little assistance. My mother and younger brother shifted to my youngest sister. My brother in law welcomed and received them warmly.

I got ½ scholarship even during my intermediate. While studying in intermediate, I used to tutor high school students.

MR GURAJADA APPARAO

My father was the grandson of Sri Gurajada Venakta AppaRao. Gurajada AppaRao garu was a pioneer and architect of modern Telugu literature and a great social reformer.

Our Telugu society is notoriously fussy about caste, creed, communities, sects, and sub sects. Within the Brahmin community, *niyogulu*, *vaidikulu* ridicule each other. One community's people would find it very difficult to appreciate achievements of people belonging to other communities. Gurajada's greatest achievement is that he is revered by all, cutting across all lines and is put on a pedestal. I was amazed by the eulogies showered on him by writers as divergent as communists, religious leaders, politicians, scholars, and all and sundry.

What makes him so special? What did he achieve and why do people erect his statues and celebrate his anniversaries?

Once we visited my brother-in-law's house. A Kashmiri Brahmin young man was staying there as a guest. He did a diploma in drama and direction.

Somehow the topic of Gurajada cropped up. He was thrilled to know that we are his descendents. My daughters were embarrassed to hear him talk about Gurajada; he had such in-depth knowledge about *Kanyasulkam* (a famous play written by him) and about Gurajada, while their knowledge was nothing to write home about. It seems they had a full section about him and the play in their curriculum and he was fascinated by that great man's intellect.

Okay. Now to appreciate his monumental achievement, we have to view it in the present context.

Today's burning problems or issues are dowry harassments and deaths, ill-treatment of little girls and women, religious intolerance, and many others. We take out *dharnas*, *rasta rokos*, *bandhs*, candle marches, and protests. Did it make any difference? Have they stopped?

Now, suppose a person eradicates such evil from society, how would a country and its people react? Won't they worship that person like a reincarnation of Gandhiji?(Mahatma Gandhiji was a crusader of non violence movement, and achieved independence for India from Great Briton. Gandhiji was an inspiration for Martin Luther King and Nelson Mandela and many others). Is it really possible to change the mindset of people; is it really possible for one individual to eradicate an evil and barbaric custom from society?

In the nineteenth century there was a very cruel, barbaric custom which was accepted by society. Pre-teen young girls were married off to old men; a girl's parents would 'sell' the girl to highest bidder. That money was called *kanyasulkam*.

The girl had no voice or say and was too young to realize what was happening. Before she crossed her teens, she would be a widow.

Her head would be tonsured; she had to wear a coarse white saree throughout her life. She cannot sleep on a mattress, only on the floor. She is given only bland food of meagre quantity and made to slog like a slave. No gold ornaments, colourful dresses, fun, frolic, or festivities for her. Her life was doomed before it began. Remarriage was unthinkable and out of the question.

And it was accepted as normal.

Now, let us be prudent before showering abuses on the people of that era. Our great-grandchildren would be equally appalled and mortified when they see the pictures of children begging on the streets or pictures of thin old people begging on temple steps.

Gurajada was very upset and desperately wanted to put a stop to this barbaric custom. But how could he do it? India, even now, has a high illiteracy rate. More than a century back, there may have been very few people who could read and write.

Even if he wanted to address those literate people, there was another stumbling block. Colloquial Telugu (normal language people speak) was forbidden to be used in literature. It was considered a sacrilege and taboo. Only a few people could understand and enjoy *Granthic* Telugu. Gurajada was a frail man, not endowed with robust health, so hunger strikes, marches were not for him (In fact, he passed away when he was just fifty-three).

He was a minister and confidant of Vizianagaram Maharaja Ananda Gajapati Raju. Maharaja gave full support and encouragement when Gurajada expressed his desire to root out the evil practice.

Gurajada selected a medium of play, stage show to spread his message. Even illiterate people can enjoy a play if the characters speak common language, one which they speak at home. In those days only plays that were staged with complicated scholarly prose and poems were *Ramayana* and *Mahabharata*. So this was a revolutionary concept, opposed and fought tooth and nail by many scholars and pundits.

But Gurajada went ahead unflinching and wrote the play, *Kanyasulkam*.

It was extremely funny and became a tremendous hit. He selected such a tragic theme and the play doesn't have a single sad scene. Audience laughed their guts out but Gurajada left an indelible print on their souls. Everyone felt that the cruel custom should be stopped, and that custom *kanyasulkam* died a quick death. Many idealistic young men came forward and married young widows. Gurajada did not make his characters scream, shout, and give long winding lectures about how evil the custom was and why it should be abolished. None of the characters in the play 'transform', 'reform', or 'repent'.

Apart from achieving his goal, an unexpected by-product of *Kanyasulkam* was the revolution it brought in Telugu literature. If Gurajada did not rise like the sun on the horizon when he did, Telugu literature would have been languishing in darkness, shackled by scholars and pundits. The gates of the Telugu literature citadel burst open and tidal waves of enthusiastic poets and writers (anyone who could read and write could become one) flooded the Telugu literary scene, washing out scholars and pundits who were guarding the gates and who felt that the semi-literate, ignorant masses had no right to dabble in poetry and prose.

Gurajada was light years ahead of not only his contemporaries but even today's revolutionary thinkers, writers, and directors. Suppose you ask the best director of movies today to make a movie on the menace of, say, dowry, his movie would definitely have a handsome, idealistic, courageous hero and a beautiful angel without wings as a heroine, wouldn't it?

Now, guess who is the hero of *Kanyasulkam*? Girisam, an unscrupulous crook and liar who has the knack of changing opinions and versions to suit his needs. But you don't hate him; you love him with all his shortcomings because he makes you laugh.

His debtors are braying for his blood, so he imposes himself on his disciple, Venkatesam, and escapes to his village on the pretext of teaching him during the summer holidays. There he sees Venkatesam's young widowed sister, a victim of *kanyasulkam*. He tries to woo her by lecturing about how widow remarriages were approved in *Puranas*, citing Damayanti's case and how cruel *kanyasulkam* is, how it should be banished. At dinner, he fully agrees with her father that *kanyasulkam* is an excellent custom and vociferously supports it, much to the astonishment of Venkatesam.

When Venkatesam confronts him later, he coolly says, 'One can't become a politician unless he changes opinions.'

Now, heroine? Young widowed sister of Venkatesam? You are wrong. The heroine is Madhura vani, a prostitute. A very beautiful, kind-hearted, intelligent, and smart lady.

Anyone other than Gurajada would have made Girisam repent and reform and marry Venkatesam's widowed sister. But, when Girisam is kicked out, he leaves saying, 'Damn it, the story has turned upside down' (*Damn it, katha addam tirigindi*) at the end of the play.

I read once an eminent writer wanted to find a flaw in *Kanyasulkam*. He started reading it critically with a motive to find some deficiency, something overlooked by Gurajada. He said he got up one midnight excitedly as it struck him that Gurajada had forgotten to include a Muslim character. He read again and found Agnihotravadhanlu calling out to a Muslim character to give fodder to animals.

As a person also, Gurajada was quite humble, soft-spoken and could not hurt anyone. After Maharaja passed away, there was a vacuum as Maharaja did not have offspring and there were court cases and disputes. During that turbulent period, Gurajada was looking after an establishment and was almost an uncrowned king. But he remained a servant to his kingdom and could have amassed wealth easily if he so desired.

When men tried to bribe him, he could have thrown them into jail or shouted at them. Instead, he would fold hands, smile at them, and say, 'I am unable to digest even a fistful of rice, how I can I digest what you are giving? I am sorry I cannot accept.'

THE RELUCTANT CUPID

'Something is not right,' my mom said in a worried tone. I followed her gaze and saw Nalini, pacing agitatedly in the portico.

'What is wrong?' I asked her. 'Nalini is waiting for the postman, like every day.'

'Precisely. Why is she waiting so impatiently for the letters?' she asked in a puzzled tone.

Nalini is the daughter of my father's childhood friend. She was the only child. We were family friends. She is tall, very fair, and quite beautiful. She stopped getting education at the tenth standard. Her father was working in a remote village. He left her with us and he would come every weekend to look for suitable alliances for her.

My dad's friend was lucky. On his second visit, one boy came to see her with his parents and fell head over heels in love. In the next few days, the engagement would take place on an auspicious day, after elders of both sides agreed to certain terms and conditions.

The boy was tall and dark (not Mills & Boon type darkness) and was totally mesmerized by her beauty. So much so that daily he would land up at our home after office. I had to cancel all my plans with friends and stay back to entertain him by playing chess or caroms.

After a few days, I was irritated by this daily chore and wanted to go out with my friends. My mom insisted that I stay back for one reason: to deflect his attention from partial deafness of Nalini which she inherited from her mom's side.

I was very uncomfortable with this deception. But my mom belonged to the old school of thought that it is all right to tell a thousand lies to get a couple married, and it is not a crime. Later they would thank you.

Her plan worked. When I was present, he could only steal glances at Nalini, and my mom would be watchful and prod her when a reaction or reply was expected from her. I remember once Nalini gave him some suggestion about movement of a rook in chess.

He beamed ear to ear and said happily, 'Oh, You are guiding me like Satyabhama guided Sri Krishna.'

So when we were entering the final phase of fixing the match, this anxiety cropped up.

Just then the postman arrived and gave her a letter. Her face lit up like a thousand-watt bulb and she ran into the house.

'You see what I mean?' My mom asked me. Yes, I saw. Nalini was madly in love with another boy.

My mom made me draft a letter addressed to the postmaster requesting him to handover Nalini's letters to Mom and authorizing my mom to receive or collect letters on her behalf since she would be away for a few months.

My heart was in my mouth when Mom asked Nalini to sign that letter. Mom told her that when she went to her village, all her letters could be returned, hence it was better to give an authorization letter to the postmaster.

I need not have worried. Nalini signed it without batting an eyelid or even reading. I felt sad; God had given her immense beauty but forgot to insert few grey cells in the top storey. She was so gullible and innocent, anyone could take her for a ride and lead her as easily as you would a lamb, and nearly had done so.

Then we went to the post office and gave that letter to the postmaster. Had I given such letter, the postmaster would have handed me over to the police.

He not only accepted Mom's letter but told my mom to take a letter which had just come in.

We came out, Mom opened it, read, and blood drained from her face. She sat on a bench heavily.

'What happened?' I asked anxiously. She silently handed over the letter.

I refused to read. I told her I could not read others' letters. She could tell me the contents.

She hissed angrily, 'Do you want to see her killed? Read it.'

I reluctantly read and collapsed beside her. Our minds had become numb.

Her boyfriend was coming on Sunday morning and asked her to wait for him at the bus station. From there, they would elope. Sunday was only two days away.

After all these years, if you ask me if our subsequent actions were right, I am inclined to say yes, at least for one reason. It was apparent from the letter that her boyfriend was an illiterate youth, probably a rickshaw puller or a daily wage earner or a class IV employee like a peon.

Even if he genuinely loved her, did she deserve to lead a life in slums? If he didn't, she could end up in a brothel. If she were an intelligent and smart girl capable of making a judicious decision, yes, it could be left to her.

All is well in movies and novels where the heroine lives quite happily in poverty, slums, open drainage, stench, and mosquitoes, leaving palatial mansions, basking in the hero's love. One of my rich friends' sister eloped with an auto rickshaw driver and returned within a week. My friend had to compensate the driver heavily for his 'loss'.

I saw the *Rickshaw Karan* dubbed version in Telugu. MGR quotes Shakespeare while taking the heroine in his rickshaw and bowls the maiden over. Even in those days, I wondered what a masochist MGR was, a graduate enjoying driving a cycle rickshaw and living in a hut.

Mom recovered first from the shock and pulled me by the hand.

'We don't have a minute to waste. Take her to her village and explain everything to her uncle [Nalini's father's brother]. Don't hide anything. Tell him to keep her under twenty-four-hours surveillance. The village postmaster is their relative. Tell him to handover her letters to Uncle,' Mom told me as we were going home.

I told Mom that I would not take any part in later schemes; she had to work it out with Dad's friend and others. She agreed and kept her word. I did not know later developments.

'But how will you explain her absence at the engagement function?' I asked her.

'We will discuss that later,' she told me.

Mom told Nalini some story about her father sending word to send her to the village urgently. Nalini enquired about the nature of urgency; Mom said she didn't know.

During the journey I could not help staring at her, trying to fathom what thoughts were churning in the brain behind those beautiful eyes. How could she lead the poor fellow along garden path and decide to elope with her boyfriend at the same time? Did she really love him or was she confused?

When we reached village, it was 9 p.m.

Uncle's eyes widened in shock when he saw us. Later he confessed that his first thought was that I eloped with her since my parents did not approve.

I apprised him of the situation and the next day went back.

I do not recollect why I didn't attend Nalini's marriage. Her boyfriend continued to write letters for many months, and later I shifted to a hostel.

I was invited for dinner one evening six months after their marriage.

Of course, Nalini's husband had an axe, in fact, several axes, to grind. It is a miracle that he didn't hack me with them.

His first grouse was her father's atrocious behaviour and treatment. He was very unhappy about the way Groom's side were received and ill-treated.

'Can you imagine? He gave me dhotis with a black border and that too as short as towels,' he fumed.

I had to pinch myself hard to restrain from laughing. An image of Bridegroom wearing knee-length black-bordered dhoti and sitting on Mandap was flashing in my mind.

I nodded sympathetically.

Nalini's father was one eccentric guy. Jovial, funny, lovable, yes, but also eccentric.

Once in Nalini's dad's village, Uncle was holding his nine-month-old son and standing at the top of the stairs leading to the kitchen from backyard. I was walking towards him.

When I was about six feet away from him and he was standing at a height of five feet above ground, he suddenly said, 'Catch,' and threw his kid.

I grabbed the kid. I didn't stop shivering for a long time. When I shouted at him what madness made him do it, he just laughed and said, 'Nothing will happen. I know you will catch.'

He was literally thick-skinned. He would walk without footwear. Even in peak summer he would walk barefoot. One summer day, my mom was inspired to emulate him and was in bed for few days with badly burnt soles.

I liked him. He made the tastiest *gutti vankaya kura*, even surpassing my moms. When he was posted at a hill station, we went there and had a marvellous time, one of the happiest memories of childhood. He sent us, all kids, to one remote village to play in a waterfall.

Each kid was given a bullock cart loaded with rock salt in gunnysacks. We lay on our backs on the bags, enjoying the picturesque ride, basking in lukewarm winter sunshine, plucking tamarind and mangoes from overhead trees when we were passing underneath and eating with rock salt granules.

Still, I couldn't defend him. I sat there silently as his son-in-law shredded him.

Next grouse on agenda was Nalini's deafness.

'You and your mother conspired to hoodwink me. You had hidden the fact that she is deaf,' he accused me. I swallowed two glasses of water and protested.

'Not deaf. May be little hard of hearing,' I put in feebly.

He called her. She didn't turn back, though she was only few feet away. He looked at me angrily and shouted louder. No response.

Then he shouted at top of his voice. She turned and asked what he wanted.

'See?' he pointed out accusingly. I mumbled something, managed to complete dinner, and ran away.

Later, I had a heated argument with Mom, or rather, I burst out in anger but Mom just laughed.

'Take it easy. If we told the truth, she would never get married. Slowly he would learn to adjust. Her beauty would compensate. But why didn't you counterattack? He came almost daily and spent several hours,' she soothed me.

I met them after nearly thirty years.

When my parents were staying with me on second floor, they came to see them.

Nalini was still beautiful, but like an older version of heroines you see in movies (Suchitra Sen in *Aandhi*, Preity Zinta in *Veer-Zaara*). He was still tall, dark, and grumpier. They have three children, two girls and one boy, both girls were married and settled.

Nalini had become stone deaf but she could lip-read.

I didn't know whether to laugh or cry, when he repeated his thirty-year-old grievances in the same order, same sentences and with the same vigour and passion.

Nalini, who could lip-read, knew what he was saying, laughed, and said, 'I keep telling him to divorce me and I will go and live with my kids. But no, he can't live few minutes with me or without me.'

I went up and told my parents that they had come to see them.

My mom, bless her soul, laughed heartily.

'He must have given you your dose about black-bordered dhotis, her deafness, our complicity, and her dad's rudeness. I will brace up for my dose,' she said, laughing.

Nalini and her husband met my parents, got their blessings, and he repeated his ground-floor lecture verbatim. My parents nodded sympathetically.

Nalini told Mom to advise him to divorce her; she was fed up. But still she was laughing as she said that. I really salute her.

After they took leave, my dad said admiringly, 'My God. She is amazing. To live with this tirade day after day for several decades requires nerves of steel.'

My mom nodded. 'Yes. God is kind to her. If she weren't deaf, she would have gone mad.'

Tailpiece:

When I was telling Wife the story of Nalini after they left, my younger daughter was doing her homework.

At one point of story, Wife exclaimed, 'What? She wanted to marry a class IV guy?'

My daughter was also stunned. 'What? How can she marry a fourth-class boy? He would be so small. Is she mad? How is it possible? How did her parents allow?'

COURAGEOUS, ORTHODOX MOM

My mother was quite orthodox and conservative, like women of that generation, yet she was liberal.

She had no issues with my dad's agnostic attitude and never forced religious rituals on us. We were free to perform pooja or skip.

She followed her rigorous regimen, which would start very early in the morning. In fact, so early, we never got up before her (which is not saying much, considering how we loved to sleep).

On the night before, she would wash a saree and would spread it to dry on a long, horizontal wooden stick hung high on the ceiling. Every morning she would take a bath and wear that *madi* (uncontaminated, clean) saree. Until she completed her pooja rituals and cooking, she would not touch anyone and no one should touch her. Even when she was cooking, no one should touch utensils. If someone did, sanctity would be lost, she would take a bath again, and continue in a wet saree.

I used to be fascinated by the ease with which she would throw the wet saree expertly on the horizontal stick hung close to the ceiling and spread it with a long stick. The idea was that nobody should touch that saree even by accident or on purpose. You have to stand on a dining chair to reach it. When we had to dry our *madi* dhotis, I tried a few times; either dhotis would refuse to land when thrown or land in an awkward lump and refuse to move when prodded with a stick. Mother would laugh and show me how to do it in a few seconds.

She would get up early in the morning and complete all chores early to avoid inconvenience to others. It would be difficult to move about without touching her utensils. Later on, she relaxed all rules and had adjusted to the needs of the time but I could see her struggle to adapt.

Her pooja would take a long time, but she seemed to have a magic wand. With a two-burner stove, she would give us coffee, tea any number of times and breakfast effortlessly, at least seemingly. For a long time, we didn't have mixer and grinder, pressure cooker, fridge, or any of the modern appliances.

She had elephantiasis in one leg. It was quite bulky and must have been cumbersome. But not once did she complain of discomfort, pain or allow it to slow her down.

When my elder daughter was two years old, we went to Srisailam in a group. We had to start early. My wife set the alarm at 5 a.m., got up and went to kitchen to prepare poori, bhaji, pulihora, as was planned on previous night.

She was shocked to see Mom packing all the items. Mom got up, took a shower, performed pooja, and finished preparing all items. When we went to Srisailam, after darshan of Lord Shiva and visiting several temples, everyone was dead tired and collapsed after reaching the cottage.

'One more temple is close by, let us go.' My mom was trying to cajole and shake the young crowd.

'We can't move a step. It is enough for a day' was the general consensus.

'Can you climb that mountain?' I asked, incredulous. She got up very early, travelled, and walked as much as we all did.

'Yes. Come with me.' She was as enthusiastic as a child. Such was her energy.

Festivals were always celebrated with great vigour and joy. There were several *nomus*, *vrata*, *poojas* when house used to be cramped with ladies. She had to give *vaayanam* and go to their houses to receive. My parents used to travel in buses; they would think travel by auto rickshaw was a luxury they could not afford. It took great perseverance to change their outlook.

The amount of courage she showed at times of distress is unparalleled. I cannot think of anyone who is as courageous; my father would come closest.

When she was going into the operating theatre for a major surgery, she was the only one who was not nervous.

She smiled and told me, 'I will go and come back in a jiffy. Don't worry. I will be fine.' In many cases, surgeries get postponed as patients develop hypertension and here is a lady who is reassuring us and giving us confidence, which, in fact, should be the other way round.

Her subsequent recovery and fight to get up and walk will be or should be told as folklore. She refused to lie and vegetate. It must have caused her immense pain. She never showed it; she always smiled.

One doctor, who is a family friend, visited them when they were at my home. The doctor asked me since when did Mom have a catheter.

When I told him, he joined hands and exclaimed, 'My God. Do you know some people cannot bear to have it for even a few hours? It is quite painful. She has been suffering for so many years with a smile on her face. Her courage and will to fight are extraordinary. I have to seek blessings of such a great lady,' and he did touch her feet and Dad's feet and asked them to bless him.

She felt happy when guests visited us. Irrespective of whose side, Dad's or Mom's, any guest brought her joy. I cannot fathom how she was happy when her workload had increased. She was not just putting on an act either. I used to help her in kitchen. She would admonish me if I showed irritation.

'They visit us because they like us. It is our duty to keep them happy,' she would tell me.

She would welcome everyone, including our friends. Except for two, all my other friends are non-vegetarians. She would serve lunch or dinner, talk with them, and make them feel at home.

Her only condition was that I should remove their (non-vegetarian friends') plates after they had finished their food. She would not touch it.

I had no problem with that but I used to argue that this discrimination was not good. Everyone is the same, irrespective of caste, creed; colour of blood is the same.

'I have only this reservation. I am not showing any difference in treatment, I am treating all equally with you, am I not?' she would say. That was true. She treated all of them with the same affection.

'Still, it would be awkward if they turn up for lunch or dinner in my absence,' I would say.

'Don't worry. You will not lose face among your friends on this account,' she assured me.

One day, after Mother passed away, I was sitting with friends in one friend's home and we were talking about her. They were recollecting how generous and affectionate she was.

'She never showed it. Though she treated all of you equally, she would not remove your plates after you finished your food. I had many arguments with her. She said she cannot do that and I had to accept. It could be some guru ji (a teacher) may have told her dos and don'ts and this could be one of the don'ts,' I said.

They stared at me.

'What are you talking about? Many times, we went to your home in Tirupati when you were not there. Your parents received us well. We had food many times at your home with your father. She always cleared our plates,' they said.

It was my turn to stare.

'Impossible. My father or my sister must have cleared your plates,' I said after I recovered.

'No. Your mother cleared plates. Every time,' they said firmly.

And I broke down.

My Daughter's Musical Adventures

My younger daughter has a great voice, sings well but is infernally lazy. She didn't inherit her mom's capacity or zeal for hard work. Our younger Daughter would crawl back into her shell when we reprimanded her, and all our efforts were futile to pull her out. I hoped her friends would be able to drag her out since parental effort is viewed as nagging.

She is an enthusiastic starter and a great quitter. Though I also do start and quit, I feel bad about it. She has no such qualms. Though I exaggerate, I tell her that I could have bought a house with all the money she squandered on wild goose chases; she retorts that she would repay with interest once she starts earning.

She and her friend Mounika joined veena classes. She has a natural talent, her fingers move effortlessly, and the teacher was very impressed. After a couple of months, her interest waned and she quit. The veena is perched precariously in a corner and daily it has its heart in mouth when the servant maid pulls it out to sweep the surrounding area. It has survived miraculously and once every six months my daughter has pangs of conscience and guilt, so she pulls the veena out, dusts it, and strums for few hours (needless to say, after midnight).

One day, my wife ran into the veena teacher at the vegetable market and had no time to duck and escape. My wife need not have worried; the teacher monopolized conversation and left wife bruised and battered. The conversation proceeded like this.

Teacher: Hello. How are you?

Wife: Err... fine and how are you?

Teacher: Good. Your daughter is very irregular for classes.

Wife: Yes, you know, how schools are...

Teacher: Yes, poor girls must be tired, still they should have a hobby to unwind.

Wife: Yes...

Teacher: Don't think I am complaining. Your daughter plays veena very well, so I am disappointed by her irregularity.

Wife: But...

Teacher: I know, she is burdened with homework, exams. I understand, don't think for a second that I want her to neglect studies.

Wife: Yes, but—

Teacher: She can come on alternate days to class, she plays so well, you know.

Wife: I know...

Teacher: So you can understand my concern, can't you?

Wife: Yes...

So by the time Wife managed to extract herself from the tirade on the excuse that I was waiting, which, fortunately, was true, she was exhausted. She said she could not even speak a few words, the teacher performed all the tasks of prosecution, defence, and judgement.

Then my daughter searched the internet for a music school close to our home, pestered her mom, and paid a fee for six months, attended first lesson and then refused to go again.

My wife was upset, naturally. She literally pushed her to attend the classes.

After a few days, daughter told mom that she was reluctant to go since she was scared.

Wife was puzzled. 'Scared? Of what?' she asked.

My daughter reluctantly told her, 'Mom, it is a *bhutbangla*. My teacher and her family look deadly pale and are like Addams family characters. It is so dark inside, curtains are never drawn to let sunlight in. On few occasions power was gone and I almost screamed when a black cat walked on a piano and made such horrible horror movie sounds.'

Wife asked her, 'How many kids she has?'

Daughter told her, 'Two, boy and girl and I shiver when they smile, they have fangs like Count Dracula and I am scared they will pounce on me and bite my neck. Their mother plays piano and other instruments very well but she plays only scary tunes from horror movies,'

Wife asked her, 'What about other kids and students? They are not scared?'

Daughter retorted, ''How can I ask them without admitting that I am scared?'

Wife thought for a moment and asked her, 'How about teacher's husband? Does he look normal?'

Daughter answered, 'Yes, he looks normal. I saw him only on the first day. I am worried if they had eaten him. I had not seen him since that day.'

Wife didn't believe her; she thought it was one more ploy to skip going to the classes and accompanied her one evening to the class. Daughter wanted to return before dark but classes began at 7 p.m., so it was already dark when they reached the school.

But, as luck would have it, dark clouds loomed and it started to rain; the thunderstorm was ominous. Wife is also not very courageous, and both ladies went up the stairs nervously. Suddenly the power went off, plunging the building into darkness. Faint light from streetlights was guiding them.

On first floor there was a huge piano left in the portico. When they were passing it, the family black cat jumped on the piano keys, making a jarring sound causing them to leap since the sound coincided with thunder.

When they reached the second landing, the rainwater was pouring out on the steps, causing them to tread carefully. By the time they reached the third floor and knocked on the door of Music Teacher's flat, they were both quite jumpy.

She yelled, 'Come in,' and they entered.

They entered a huge, dark hall; not a ray of light could enter through heavy curtains. Wife says daughter was not exaggerating. The teacher was white like a sheet, plump and unsmiling; her red-lipsticked lips were enhancing her ghostly appearance. Two kids were playing piano. The windows and doors in the hall were covered with curtains and it was like a sealed tomb. A single flickering candle was playing tricks and terrifying them further.

To complete the effect, there was a huge dining table like in Hollywood horror movies, which can seat twenty people. As Wife and daughter sat nervously, teacher yelled, 'Tommy, come.'

Wife thought she was calling a pet, a dog or a cat. Right in front of them, a curtain parted and a ghost entered. It was her son; he emerged from a bedroom holding a candle below his face like the scary characters in ghost movies. Wife almost screamed, such was his hairstyle, arched, thick eyebrows and thin lips. His complexion was also chalk white.

Wife gathered courage and stammered that daughter would not be able to attend any more classes as we were shifting house. Teacher told her it was very unfortunate since her child has immense talent and money would not be refunded.

They thanked her and ran away from the place.

That was the end of daughter's music classes.

After a few days, younger daughter shook the elder one, who was fast asleep.

'Akka, wake up, wake up. Good news, great news,' she was shouting excitedly.

'What is it?' elder one asked groggily, trying to force open her eyes.

'Teacher's husband is Okay, he is alive. They didn't eat him after all. I am so happy and relieved. I saw him today driving a scooter,' she said happily.

MY DAUGHTER'S BIG, FAT TELUGU WEDDING

PART I

Pet cats have a habit of depositing unsavoury objects on the doormat and looking up at owner for appreciation and approval.

Similarly, like all fathers of beautiful daughters, I dreaded the day my daughter would deposit a male specimen and declare him as the prospective son-in-law. Since we have no control over Cupid or direction of his arrows, I used to pray that the specimen should at least be a vegetarian.

I may be old-fashioned, but I feel the most difficult hurdle in a marriage is the veg and non-veg divide and my feelings were biased by a chief officer I sailed with.

I once sailed in an Indian ship on a coastal run. It was a small ship and the chief officer was from the south. He was tall, dark, and heavily built.

One day when we were having lunch, his gaze fell on my plate.

'Ohhh, are you a vegetarian?' he asked.

I nodded.

'My wife is also a vegetarian,' he said, helping himself to a chicken leg.

'Oh, I see. Love marriage?' I asked politely.

'No. It was an arranged marriage. Her father is a very poor Brahmin and has four daughters and he could not even give them two square meals a day. Many days, they would stay

260

hungry. So they accepted my offer to marry his daughter. You know, she is very beautiful,' he said.

After a few minutes of silence, I asked him, 'Now she relishes non-vegetarian food?'

He laughed and said, 'My God, no. We could not make her eat but we finally managed to make her cook non-vegetarian food.'

I asked him, 'It must have been very tough for her.'

He said amused. 'Tough for her? No, it was tough for all of us. She would go on hunger strike and refuse to cook non-veg. We were adamant. She cried, begged, and pleaded and tried all stunts. We were unmoved. Finally, she relented and now makes very tasty dishes, fish, mutton, chicken…'

I resisted a mad impulse to grab him by collar and bash his face in his plate. My heart bled for that poor girl. I felt very sad.

'Do you make her kill the chicken also?' I asked him, after I recovered my composure.

'No. We kill the chicken and she plucks feathers and cooks,' he said.

So I wished for one major irritant to be removed.

My wife was not as shocked as I was, when my daughter told us that Akhil had proposed marriage.

Women are more intuitive and sensitive where love matters are concerned. My wife had a hunch that it was on the cards.

I did not expect it since I thought Amitabh Bachchan and Jaya Bhaduri were the last tall-and-short couple to fall in love. Akhil is very tall and hence I did not expect him to propose to my daughter, since though she is very beautiful, fair, smart, and intelligent, she lacked inches in height.

We asked Manisha what was her response.

She told us, 'I told him that I would tell my parents and that you are quite orthodox and unless you approve, things won't move forward.'

Our hearts swelled with justifiable pride; here was our daughter asking our approval rather than throwing an ultimatum.

'You tell us your genuine feelings. If you also really like him and want to marry him, we will move forward. If you don't and don't want to hurt him, we can say that horoscopes don't match,' I asked her.

She confessed that feelings were mutual.

There was no reason to say no, except that he was from the north and was not a Telugu Brahmin boy. We were mentally prepared for her to marry an NRI Telugu Brahmin boy and settle in the USA like her cousins. In fact, many offers were coming forth and we were dodging since she refused to get married until later.

Though I didn't express it at that time, I was deeply skeptical.

Akhil is good, in fact, too good to be true. He is a non-smoker, teetotaler, and generally 'Rama is a good boy' type.

I thought God stopped manufacturing such 'good boys' after the era of black-and-white movies ended.

In black-and-white movies, the hero is invariably handsome, kind-hearted, an epitome of all good virtues, saves damsels in distress from villains, respects elders, and is very studious and brilliant (always college first or university first).

In fact, in one movie, NTR runs and hugs his mom and says, 'Mom, your prayers are answered, I stood school first (or state first) in tenth class.' She sheds a few buckets of tears and takes him to the garlanded photo of his dad and gives a small emotional monologue.

I remember wondering why the director had to make NTR pass tenth class, instead of B.A or M.A (in those days, all heroes passed B.A or M.A).Though NTR wore half-pants and shaved and tried his best to pass off as a teenager, his hairy legs and stocky build reminded one of a bloated 'Amul baby.'

Alternatively, a retarded boy who passed tenth after dozens of attempts.

In fact, when I was in tenth class, I had such a classmate. His name was Potana. He was quite tall, maybe six feet, and wore half-pants. He was quite courageous to come to school at such age. Our teacher Sri Ramamurty garu used to say in exasperation when Potana was unable to catch up with the rest of the class, 'Why your parents have to name you after the great poet and scholar, Potana?'

After the B & W era ended, heroes in films became cheaters (it is projected as smartness), eve teasers, anti-social elements and made lecturers dance barefoot on broken glass (supposed to be comedy). All qualities that were hallmarks of villains in B & W movies have become coveted qualities of heroes of later movies. In fact, hard-working and studious young men with thick spectacles are portrayed as buffoons.

So Akhil was an enigma. I admit that I suspected he might be smoking and drinking on the sly, which would have been fine. My parents turned a blind eye to my occasional drinking and they did not confront me and I covered my tracks. All were happy.

But I was shocked and baffled to learn that he was indeed a teetotaler and a non-smoker and is indeed a 'Rama is a good boy.'

I confess I still had a few doubts and asked my daughter after marriage was over and we were alone for few minutes, 'He is so handsome like a Bollywood hero, many girls must have thrown themselves at him. Do you think he could restrain himself like Rishyashringa [a sage who is famous for his self-control]?'

Without batting an eyelid and pausing to think, she replied, 'Yes.'

I persisted "How and why?"

She counter questioned me, 'You were also very handsome, did girls throw themselves at you?'

I was taken aback.

'Come on, I was not so handsome and also—' I tried to tell her. She cut me short.

'You and he are intelligent but lack powers of observation or sharpness. You look straight ahead and are blind to peripheral vision. Mom can sense, hear, and observe what is happening in 360 degrees. Even if a girl throws herself, he will feel she slipped and fell and would politely get away from line of collision,' she replied.

I mulled over her reply. Then she continued.

'These minor things are inconsequential. I didn't tell you anything because you will get hyper but I told Mom about countless young men who hounded and pestered me for marriage since inter. days. I was really getting tired of thwarting them, some of them were very nice people. Anyway, I liked him because he has some of your traits,' she concluded.

'I hope those traits are passion for karela [bitter gourd], cricket, and WWE and not laziness, procrastination, and absent-mindedness.' I didn't utter aloud my thoughts.

My wife religiously buys karela every time she buys vegetables, stores them in fridge, and even more religiously throws them into dustbin after they ripen and become inedible. She says she can't force herself to cook karela, the shape reminds her of mice or rats. Her mother volunteers to cook karela for me.

Once I was watching WWE when I was alone at home. I kept the volume a little high and didn't hear my mother-in-law opening the front door. She sat behind my sofa.

I didn't know for how long she was watching; I jumped a foot when she exclaimed, 'Ohhh, that fellow seems to be already dead. Why no one is stopping the other fellow? He is jumping on him.'

I quietly changed over to Bhakti channel and retreated.

My sister attested to my lack of sharpness recently when she told that her five best friends in her college days were vying for my attention and one of them would have been her sister-in-law had I responded. I was shocked; I thought they were all disinterested and aloof and their feeble cupid arrows bounced off my thick skin. Only one girl I thought showed interest in me but she didn't make birds sing in my heart like in movies.

When I was in B.E, second year, India-England test match was scheduled in Kolkata and my dad was posted in Kolkata at that time. I asked my dad to arrange for a pass; in those days, the telephone department had a lot of clout and influence. He asked me to come to his office.

I went and sat in his chamber. He was signing some files, when suddenly ten to fifteen beautiful angels swarmed in (In those days, telephone operators were all girls). They flashed lovely smiles, and with voices dripping with honey, they requested Dad for something (could be increments or leave to see test match). Dad declined and the smiley angles of angels reduced gradually until lips became hard lines and honey stopped dripping and was replaced with harsh pungent acidic attacks as the arguments progressed. Dad refused to give in to pressure tactics, they went out shouting slogans, and if they were men, they would have gheraoed him.

Now I am sure if anyone else were in Dad's place, the angels would have got their demands and he would have got sucked into a quicksand trap.

My young heart protested; I thought Dad was being unreasonable. Such beautiful girls deserved to be granted whatever their demands were.

I asked him, 'Was it necessary to be so blunt and hurt them?'

My dad said, 'This is a daily affair, their requests are getting crazier each day,' and banged on the calling bell. He told an attendant to send Mr Sen.

A short, fair man entered and greeted Dad. Dad told him to arrange for a pass for the test match for me.

He said, 'Yes, sir,' and I followed Mr Sen. When I accompanied him to his desk, luckily I was seated when I asked him, 'How do you manage to get passes? Whom do you know?' Had I been standing, I would have reeled.

'I do umpiring. It is my hobby,' he told me. I was speechless.

'Oh, you do umpiring for Ranji Trophy matches?' I asked politely.

'Yes, test matches also. I am going to officiate for the England-India test. Your dad had granted leave,' he said so casually as if he told me where he was going on a vacation.

I was still in a daze when I returned to Dad's chamber with the pass.

'Dad, you didn't tell me he is the umpire,' I asked him.

'Yes, it is his hobby, that is why I asked him to arrange pass for you. You got it?' he asked coolly.

I was shocked. My dad was either unaware that Mr Sen was going to be the king on the field for five days and make superstars literally dance to his tunes or didn't know what it meant to be an umpire in a test match. When I told him that and that he should treat Mr Sen more like a celebrity than a subordinate, he gave an uncomprehending look.

He was more interested in tennis and football than cricket.

My third brother and I saw the test match on alternate days as I took only one pass. We were very fortunate; we had an excellent view from the VIP gallery next to the sight screen and identified some famous former cricketers like Subrata Guha. I was privileged to watch an excellent innings from Gundappa Viswanath.

His batting was poetry in motion and had such an elegance and fluidity, it was a treat to watch. I was spellbound even when he was playing defence, and his cover drives were classic. Tony Greg, who stood 6'6" tall, literally pulled his hair when he could not set field to contain Viswanath, who went on to score a fluid century, and India won the match. One memory of that match was Greg going down on knees and appealing to boisterous crowds to reduce the noise and the crowd responded by keeping silent.

Coming back to the track after unintended deviation…

Wife and I discussed. Naturally, we were concerned. North and south are literally poles apart. Anxiety of unknown is natural. We decided to approach his parents only after we consulted some astrologer about horoscopes. She gave his date of birth, time, and place.

When we were seated in front of a famous astrologer and presented our daughter's horoscope and boy's date of birth, etc., he asked about boy's gotra.

We called daughter and she asked him and then dropped the bombshell. His gotra is also the same as ours: Goutamasa!

PART II

By the time we got the details of groom's gotra, Astrologer had already fed the details we had given him in computer, took the print-outs, and was ready with the 'third umpire's' decision. By the beam on his face we knew his decision was in favour of the alliance.

'What is the matter?' he asked us when he saw the blank, stunned looks on our faces.

'Our gotras are same. Goutamasa,' I told him (Gotra is the lineage of sages. Marriages within the same gotra are avoided).

'Ohhh,' he said and was silent for a few minutes.

'Is that a big problem? Their horoscopes match very well,' he asked later.

'Not really. My brother's daughter was married to a boy of same gotra. My sister-in-law's brother did the kanyadan[giving away the bride]. But in north, they are very particular,' I told him.

'They are from north and you are from south. So the distance figuratively and literally is great. Try to convince them. They will be very happy,' he told us.

On the ride back home, we were lost in our own thoughts.

The north-south divide is more difficult to bridge than building a bridge across the River Godavari. Each is justified in his or her anxieties and worries. Our perceptions are coloured by media, movies, and newspapers.

Akhil's parents could be worried that I might resemble Mehmood in *Padosan*, wearing white dhoti, head tonsured, and sporting a plait and vibhuti stripes across forehead. For all they knew, I might be sniffing snuff and keep chewing paan and spitting all over and my wife might resemble Chachi 420 (a Bollywood remake of *Mrs Doubtfire*), along with karate skills, etc.

Like Akhil's mom said later that her son is a prince and one in a million (no dispute about that), they could be worried if his princess would pass muster. Like I was worried about pet cat bringing something and depositing it on doormat, they also could be justifiably worried. The general impression is that down south, people have deeper pigmentation.

When you read in papers and watch on TV that many people committed suicide when a movie star was ill or when a chief minister was jailed, there is bound to be uneasiness about general cerebral health of people down south. I used to wonder if ingredients or consumption of staple diet in large quantities had anything to do with this abnormal suicidal tendency, for this phenomenon was not observed in other parts of India when Amitabh had an accident and was critically ill or Raj Kapoor was sick or died or when Rajkumar was abducted by Veerappan or when he died.

As if it were not enough, during that period the headline news was female infanticide in the south. In our national anthem, states/areas are described as 'Dravida Utkala Vanga' and all south Indian states are clubbed into 'Dravida'. So for most northerners, south means 'Madrasi'. In south India, all four languages are as different as French and Latin. We are as lost as any northerner if we go to a different south Indian state.

Since Akhil had studied and worked in south, he understood the actual ground realities and assured us that there was not much difference in food habits or general pattern between his home and ours. I was under the impression that in the north, they eat only palak, paneer, rajma, and all the items in standard menu in Punjabi restaurants.

While on the subject of north Indian food, I have a large axe to grind. The virus of dhaba culture and Punjabi food has permeated to all nooks, corners of India, including remote villages, leaving 'normal' food-loving people like me high and dry. When I see the menu in any restaurant, all I see are paneer palak, paneer pasanda, paneer thika, and dal makhani, and other items. India is a blessed country with a huge variety of vegetables (bitter gourd, snake gourd, bottle gourd, yam, tendli, raw banana, brinjal, and many more). You will not find any item made from any of them on those menus.

My daughters are exasperated when we go out to dinner. I always order dosa or veg-fried rice and refuse helpings from their dishes. I endured long lectures about enjoying and relishing food, etc. but I tell them that though I love them, I can't shovel food that tastes like sand to me, with a happy face. So they learnt to leave me alone.

Once idli, dosa, and our dishes find a global market and become fashionable, KFCs and McDonald's will run for cover. My mom could make seven or eight varieties with brinjal, each tasting better than the other, and you could relish the same brinjal for a week.

When my wife complains of too much work in kitchen, I remind her that she should be grateful that she was not born in north India; she would be making hundreds of rotis and chapattis every day for male lions.

All Indian males are male lions, wherever they are from. Male lion is the laziest animal in the animal kingdom, after sloths. All day he sleeps under a tree shade and only gets up to have food while lady lion gets up before sunrise, goes for hunting, and leaves the food near him. She waits patiently for 'her master' to wake up and have his fill and then she and her cubs would eat.

My niece is in Singapore and she says that she prays to God that in next birth she should be born as a Singaporean lady. It seems there are no kitchens in Singapore; they all eat out all the time. My niece and hubby had a tough time finding an apartment which had a proper kitchen.

Though, I should apologize for digressing and going on a detour, I won't because I have to keep doing that after every few pages. If I stick to straight line, readers may fall asleep at the wheel.

I did not know that Akhil had been working for long here and understood Telugu, so our association did not have a flying start. When I was on leave and saw him for the first time when he visited our home, I became little impatient after a while and asked my daughter in a casual tone in Telugu, 'When is he leaving?'

He immediately got up and took leave, and my wife and daughter took me to the cleaners; like in the advertisement of a washing powder, they gave me 'sab se achcha dhulai.'

Uneasiness about something unknown is natural. Like his parents had apprehensions about us, we also had about them, I mean, not about his parents but about north Indians in general.

Those days, all newspapers and channels were obsessed with honour killings and khap panchayat judgments. It was somewhat understandable if parents or relatives are upset if their children planned to marry outside religion or caste. But parents killing their offspring for daring to love or marry people of same gotra was quite depressing and scary. Even scarier was the fact that they were given a hero's welcome with garlands and slogans by huge crowds when they came out of prison on bail.

On a few occasions, parents accepted but overzealous cousins and uncles took the law into their own hands. This phenomenon was not confined to villages and semi-literate people. There was a news item where an air hostess was killed by her folk in Delhi for the same reason.

I did not discuss with my wife but asked Akhil one day when we were alone.

'I fully understand that you and your family are very well educated and progressive and we might overcome the problem of your parents' objection to the gotra issue but I am worried about unknown X factor, your overzealous cousins or uncles...'I left my sentence midway and let him fill in the blanks.

He laughed and said, 'Uncle, you are unnecessarily getting worried, we are not from that state and my cousins and uncles are also like us, like-minded. I already talked to my mom and convinced her. But my dad is reluctant and I am trying to overcome his resistance...'

It took longer than we anticipated because of a few unfortunate events; Akhil's grandfather passed away and one entire year was lost since we are not supposed to even broach the topic of marriage, let alone perform any auspicious events within a year and then my father passed away.

Full credit to Akhil and Manisha for their relentless efforts in winning his parents over, Manisha talked to his mom on the phone and I think his mom must have been quite relieved and, in fact, joyous that she didn't have Deepika Padukone's accent in the movie *Chennai Express*. Half the battle was over.

This period gave us time to get to know Akhil better and for Akhil to know us. My younger daughter is the family Vidushak (king's courtier whose job is to make king and his sabha laugh with jokes and antics). She would make him laugh with her spontaneous repartees, mannerisms, and jokes. She could imitate our relatives and friends.

Akhil and my daughter had a colleague who is fun-loving and had high-pitched laughter which made people jump. One day Akhil, that friend, and my younger daughter were sitting in the hall and talking. My wife's brother is two dimensional and he just floated in the background like a blur. He was wearing a light-blue-coloured starched and ironed shirt.

She asked Daughter, 'Who is it?' Daughter replied, 'That blue *patang* [kite] is my uncle.' That girl laughed so much, my wife panicked and ran from the kitchen to the hall to see what the matter was. Akhil also laughed heartily.

Younger daughter's guitar featured in a few other articles. Akhil was the person to whom we palmed it off.

His father was still noncommittal; I think he was worried that I would resemble Mehmood in *Padosan* and my wife, Chachi 420. Then we came to a compromising solution. When his parents came to see him, I and Wife would visit them, say hello and come out without saying anything about alliance. That way, we would not be breaking any rules since it would be a casual visit.

It went off very well. Akhil's parents and we got along quite well; in fact, it seems his father was impressed by our simplicity. It turned out he was not anticipating Mehmood in *Padosan* but a suited, booted, pipe-puffing, arrogant, snobbish Amrish Puri.

PART III

We were greatly relieved after the major hurdle was crossed. Now we had to wait for the auspicious day and muhurat to officially visit Akhil's parents' town and finalize the dates, function details, and other formalities.

During the period from initial proposal to crossing the final hurdle of parental approval, many things changed. Akhil and Manisha resigned from their jobs, applied to prestigious European universities for higher studies, got admissions, and joined. In fact, Manisha got admission first. We were really touched by the fuss Akhil made and the tension he went through and the concern he showed when we sent her off at the airport.

I remember feeling guilty that my eyes were dry when tears were rolling down like a river from my younger daughter's eyes and Akhil and my wife were visibly depressed. I think I was quite confident of my elder daughter's capabilities and smartness and was not unduly perturbed. Even Manisha looked cool.

One excellent habit of Akhil that impressed us all is his respect for elders. Invariably he touches elders' feet to seek blessings. That trait we had in our home. Even if I wore a new vest, I had to touch feet and get blessings of all elder to me in the household and repeat the exercise for all festivals and other functions. So I had lot of bending and stretching exercises. Of course, my younger sister had one more set to do (since I was also elder to her).

I think it is a very good custom. When you touch their feet and seek blessings regularly, you cannot be disrespectful or arrogant towards elders. When they bless, they also have positive feelings. But my wife feels that there is no need for the show; if you have respect and regard within heart, it is good enough, so that practice is discontinued in our house.

Unlike in English, all Indian languages have two 'you's. One 'you' is formal and respectful 'you' and is used for all gurus, teachers, elders, and people to be venerated. Other 'you' is informal for youngsters, cousins, friends, and juniors. In my wife's household, they used second 'you' to address father, and she tried to follow that custom in our house, saying kids would become close to father and that kids and fathers would be like friends.

I differed with her, and when I see the scant regard and respect the kids show to 'friendly' fathers, I am not so sure if it is such a good practice. Anyway, during festival days and special occasions or when I am in the mood to bless them, I stand on the settee or bed and ask my kids to touch my feet and seek blessings so that they don't have to bend completely. Now, I observe Younger Daughter actually touching feet and seeking her mom's blessings on special occasions (exam days).

So, I was most impressed by Akhil's attitude.

Coming back to the story, once the major hurdle was crossed, I was in a great hurry to get them married at the earliest date and rushed to a pandit when the mandatory one-year period was over after my father's death ceremonies. The pandit made us wait for a few hours and called us in. We could not move an inch without deciding on a muhurat (auspicious day) for marriage.

Understandably, I was in a great hurry. If there was a muhurat in the next two weeks, I wanted to go for it.

And there was. In fact, the pandit told us that there were many muhurats for the next month.

'After one month?' I asked.

'No muhurat for next six months,' he said coolly.

We were shocked.

'How can it be possible? Please check once more,' my wife persisted.

It was long past lunchtime and the pandit was impatient and a little irritable since his 'master's voice' called him a couple of times for lunch.

'There is *Adhika maasam* and *Sunya maasam*[some inauspicious time periods] and there are many aspects,' he said.

I immediately called Manisha and told her the situation and asked her if they were ready for marriage in next month.

She said that it was impossible as they had exams and we reluctantly agreed for a muhurat in November, which was more than six months later. The experience was akin to the mixed feelings when a tough exam date is postponed. Part of your mind is happy that there is ample time to prepare and your subconscious mind reminds you that you would be as well or as ill prepared on that day as you are today and you might as wellopt for the ordeal to be over.

Anyway, in these matters you have no choice.

We talked to Akhil's parents and decided on a date to visit them to finalize things officially.

We were tensed up as can be understood since I had no prior experience, and since I was the youngest, I was always in the shadows. This project was quite a delicate one and had to be dealt with very carefully. One careless remark or comment could offend Akhil's parents and I am not a good conversationalist, and in Indian culture, men start the talk, no matter how ever-capable ladies may be.

So we booked our flight tickets and landed in Akhil's state capital and checked into a hotel. We almost missed our flight as the gate was changed and announcement was not audible to us from where we sat.

The next morning, we had a four-hour drive to his home town. We started early as we had to catch a return flight in the evening. Our tension started mounting as Akhil's father's mobile was switched off. Though my wife didn't voice her thoughts, she was also worried if Akhil's parents had second thoughts due to concerns expressed by 'well-wishers'.

Finally I called Manisha thirty minutes before we reached Akhil's town. We neither had the address nor an alternate phone number.

Five minutes before we reached there, Akhil's father called; he was in the night shift and he forgot to charge his mobile before going to sleep. We heaved sighs of relief.

He received us warmly, hugged me, and invited us into their home. What Akhil had been telling us was true; they were also like us in all respects.

We followed our customs and theirs, and engagement protocol was completed. Now, we came to the sensitive topic of the marriage ceremony. We wished to perform marriage ceremony as per our customs and were pleasantly surprised when they readily acquiesced (North and south Indian marriage protocols and procedures are different).

'But we will perform your rituals also, maybe we can club together,' I told him.

'For us, few rituals are very important.' Akhil's mother spoke.

'Groom's mother gifts five golden ornaments and Bride has to adorn them, Groom placing vermilion powder in the parting of the bride's hair [sindoor], Bride wearing a saree gifted by groom's mother, and ritual of couple walking around the sacred fire seven times [*saath phere*],' Akhil's parents said.

It was very easy to include those in the ceremonies. We were quite relieved.

'Anything else?' we asked.

They exchanged bewildered glances, and we were baffled when they said there was nothing else, no demands.

We could not believe our ears. Normally the groom's parents would demand, 'Oh, we don't expect anything, Just perform marriage in a grand manner befitting our status[indirectly hinting at a grandiose event], we expect 500 to 600 guests, you may have to provide good accommodation, silk sarees to our relatives.' The list would slowly keep increasing until you faint.

Here were Akhil's parents, who could think of nothing else they could ask of us.

We took their leave; Akhil's father hugged me and they gave us a warm send-off.

When we returned, we were quite happy, relieved, and relaxed. We knew they would love Manisha as a daughter they never had (They have two sons).

We thought we had six months' time to prepare and we could plan and execute all events carefully. But Pandit had further shocks in store for us.

'You should not start any marriage-related works until *Ashadham* month is over,' he told us sternly. *Ashadham* was a couple of months before November. We would hardly have two months' preparation time.

It meant we could not print wedding cards nor extend invitations until the inauspicious days were over.

We sighed a collective sigh of resignation and asked him if we could book marriage halls and decide on caterers since there would be a mad rush later. He acquiesced.

My wife, younger daughter and I went hunting. We were clear in minds that the venue had to be in the heart of the city, a five-star hotel. Akhil and Manisha would be coming two weeks before marriage and hectic travelling should be avoided. If landmark of venue is easy, it would save us a great deal of trouble explaining location to guests.

Our first stop was the best hotel in the city. It was simply magnificent, like in movies. But I vetoed against it since it was in cellar and you had do climb down forty-odd steps, no doubt, very beautiful, wide marble steps, still steps and you had to walk a long way through the hall if you were coming down by elevator.

Marriage hall was very spacious but buffet was arranged in corridor, which I did not like.

Then we went to a few other hotels and our fourth stop was the one I liked. It has such a beautiful ambience and tranquil soothing lighting that it immediately appealed to me. The marriage hall, which was quite spacious, could seat 400 to 500 guests (our estimate) and the dining section was spacious also, and in addition, the hotel was ready to give us four halls across the corridor for buffet.

I paid advance and booked the hall; I convinced my wife that we could always cancel later if we found a better venue.

The problem is my wife views my decisions with suspicion; she feels (rightly in a few occasions) that I want to complete things in a hurry because of my laziness. So over the next few months, she and our driver checked each and every marriage venue within 25-km radius.

I was also dragged when on leave; I obediently accompanied without complaining. Finally my wife conceded that our first choice was best.

During these six months, my wife shopped for sarees for daughter, her in-laws, and guests. My wife has an admirable hobby, shopping for sarees. She made a list of all ladies in our guest list and selected sarees that would suit them individually; she kept in mind their tastes, the colours and shades they already had.

I thought she was stretching beyond limits when I saw her spending a lot of time for selecting sarees for very old ladies. Most of them were widows and have lost interest in the colours and designs. What they wanted was easy-to-wear, soft sarees.

She replied, 'They are special. More than others. They need to understand we care for and love them.'

Akhil and Manisha arrived two weeks before and were on the run till the day of marriage; they had to complete shopping and get ready for the mega event.

For Akhil it was simpler. For Manisha, there were many activities, like deciding on make-up artist, saree draping, mehendi, and many more. Her younger sister stood by her like the Rock of Gibraltar and made us all proud.

We were amazed and touched by the enormous love and affection showered on Manisha by her friends from Germany and Turkey. They came all the way from their home countries for the event. They were very enthusiastic about our traditions, customs, and dress. They were all draped in beautiful sarees on the day of marriage. They were very enthusiastic about mehendi (herbal tattoo) and our food. We were worried if they would have special demands and how to cater to them. They were all very sweet and mingled as if they knew us for decades.

The actual event went off grandiosely. I fought with Manisha right from her childhood that I would not compromise on two aspects in her marriage. One was *poola jada* (long plait, colourfully decorated with flowers); second was the custom of carrying the bride in a bamboo woven basket (Bride would be seated in a basket, and her uncles carry her to the dais). She tried to wriggle out but I was firm.

She agreed and I think she enjoyed the ride though she was scared at that time since all uncles carrying were pencil thin and decorator pasted colourful paper on the basket and the grip was not firm.

Her flower-decorated plait gave nightmares to Younger Daughter, who had to untangle it to facilitate tying *mangalasutra* (a sacred thread, dipped in turmeric, tied by the groom around bride's neck).

Akhil had no objection to Telugu marriages except for bridegroom's dress. Bridegroom has to wear a thin white, transparent dhoti (a white cloth tied from waist down, usually worn by Mahatma Gandhi), and no vest or shirt is allowed (only an *uttariyam*, a rectangular piece of cloth). We found a ready-made thick dhoti and he put it on.

Marriage went off very well as per all the feedback I received later from relatives and friends. There was absolutely no tension or cause for anxiety from any quarter. Akhil' sparents, relatives, and friends were exceptionally easy-going and understanding.

Though there were lapses and omissions, we managed to cover them up because of enormous support from all. We made a mistake of depending heavily on outside agencies, an event manager. We did not wish to trouble my brothers, who were also ageing, or my wife's brothers. Hence we depended on an event manager to do the needful.

Fortunately my second sister-in-law came a week before marriage and guided us. On the day of the marriage, my sisters-in-law, my brothers, my wife's brothers, and my daughters' friends held the fort. We thank all for their support, blessings, and love.

Manisha had high fever and cold on the day of marriage and all guests mistook her watery eyes and consoled and gave her pep talks not to feel sad about leaving parents. She resisted the impulse to pull her hair and punch them, and managed to paste on a smile and nod.

Akhil was dignity personified; he was quite enthusiastic in all the rituals and sat through all long, winding ceremonies and smoke with a pleasant and smiling face and won everyone's admiration. Akhil's parents were impressed with the traditional marriage ceremonies, though some of the rituals were not in their customs.

Both were lovely, resplendent in wedding attire.

May God bless them with all joy, happiness, and bliss.

POTPOURRI

Random Thoughts

I had a temptation to call this section 'Drunken Monkey in a Banyan Tree,' the logic being the haphazard selection of themes of posts and swinging from one branch to another without rhyme or reason, but desisted to avoid embarrassment to my wife and kids. It is difficult for them to explain that I am not drunk on wine but on ecstasy and more difficult to justify my 'monkey' status.

Seriously, I am enjoying the freedom to write on any and every theme that catches my fancy. I might and have trodden on some toes but the owners of toes either have taken it sportingly and are grinning and bearing it or have not read so far.

AMNESIA: BOON OR BANE?

I have a vague suspicion that amnesia or forgetfulness is a contagious disease. If you keep an absentminded professor and a person with excellent memory under the same roof for some time, chances of the professor getting cured are remote but the person with a sharp memory will start forgetting things and names.

In school, my good friend Subbu suffered from amnesia but actually gave the impression that he was enjoying the effects of it. Some people are gifted to see the brighter side of even a handicap. If I land my foot on a banana peel, slide and fall, and make onlookers laugh merrily with my acrobatics, I will act as if it never happened and brush it under the carpet.

But if the same thing happened to Subbu, he would re-enact the scene to the delight of everyone. So he would elaborately describe his amnesia stories and have everyone splitting their sides.

Once he was waiting for a bus. Another friend who was passing by greeted him and they talked for some time.

'What are you doing? the friend asked.

Subbu was puzzled. 'What will anyone do in a bus stop? Waiting for a bus,' he replied.

'But why are you sitting on a bicycle and waiting for a bus?' asked the baffled friend.

Subbu looked down and sure enough, he was sitting on a bicycle.

There was a very cute baby girl in his neighbour's house. Her grandfather would be holding the baby and Subbu always played and joked with the girl and exchanged pleasantries with Grandfather.

One day Subbu said, 'Hi, Poorna, you look smashing in that green underwear. Give me a kiss, Poorna.' Grandfather glared at him and went off in a huff.

Subbu did not understand. After a couple of times, Grandfather started vanishing if he could spot Subbu at a hundred-yard distance. Subbu was baffled, until the girl's mother approached Subbu's aunt and pleaded with her to drill the message into his head that her (mother's) name was Poorna and the daughter's name was Aparna.

Though this story seems farfetched, he insists that it happened. However, this incident takes the cake. After he got married, he went with his wife to another city, where they boarded a crowded local bus. He suddenly recollected that he had some friends in one locality and got down from the bus two stops before their scheduled stop. For a few seconds, he says he was puzzled why a lady was following and struggling to catch up with him. Then it struck him that she was his wife! Poor lady, if she were not watchful and didn't see him alight, she would have been lost in a strange city.

I was sitting next to him in school for four years sharing the same bench. My suspicion is that the contagious nature of his forgetfulness infected me.

Amnesia is a bane; it makes you lose peace of mind, money, valuables, and sometimes relationships with friends and relatives. The worst is the fear that hangs like Damocles' sword above your head that you might forget or have forgotten some very valuable document or event.

Amnesia is a boon because you sleep peacefully, happily since you will soon forget that you lost something and don't fret and fume like others who worry about lost things.

To illustrate with a hypothetical situation, you and your wife go to a function and you spot a man who is looking at you furtively. You vaguely recollect that he did or said something unpleasant and that you should be angry with him. But why, you cannot fathom. After an initial hesitation, he comes and greets you. You start conversing with him and see wife look at you in surprise and shock. Then she throws angry looks and finally her eyes throw daggers which impinge upon your thick skin. You cut short the conversation and approach her.

'Why are you talking to him?' she hisses angrily.

'Who is he? I vaguely remember he said or did something nasty. But it is not polite to turn your back on someone,' you try to soothe her.

'Great. Go and hug him then. Don't you remember he...' She refreshes your memory with what he had done. When floodgates of memory open, you are deluged in fury and anger and want to strangle him. Then wife reins in.

'Don't be stupid. The time to strangle him was when he approached you. Not after enquiring about him, his family, his friends, and his dog and after discussing politics and yes, cricket,' she says firmly.

It is a very frustrating and tiring job to jog the memory of an absentminded person. It is like coaxing tomato ketchup to slide into your plate from bottle (I am not aware of present ketchups but in my childhood, ketchups used to come in glass bottles and they were very stubborn). You have half a mind to break it on a rock but have to tap it and shake it gently and eventually a spoonful would plop reluctantly on your plate.

My wife is also as absentminded as I am, if not more. She maintains that she developed absentmindedness after marriage, endorsing my theory of the contagious nature of it. But I don't agree. She has inherited it from her brother who holds a doctorate in amnesia.

I concede that she has a razor-sharp memory in one aspect which is common to all members of her sex (since they are from the same planet, Venus). It is the ability to recall any slight, snide or hurting remark or event with absolute pinpoint accuracy, with date, time, place, and who were present (including the design, colour, and type of sarees, i.e. Gadwal, Kanchi, Dharmavaram, etc. of ladies, if present). There are exceptions like my elder daughter, who might not forget but never recalls nor allows such things to bother her.

Barring that, we are made for each other. My kids are fed up of watching the same incident year after year without change of script, like being forced to see reruns of the same TV episode many times without a choice.

Every time I sign off and go home on leave, it is the same story. I reactivate accounts, which went into hibernation. Since passwords are forgotten, I open a briefcase and look for the relevant document or paper which mysteriously disappears.

I insist that I gave it to Wife; Wife stoutly denies and says that she remembers perfectly well that I had not given it, and if I had, it would have been safe. We turn the house upside down but it refuses to turn up. We get fed up and abandon the search, promising next time to be more careful.

After some time (can be days, weeks, or months) I might find it in a zipped concealed compartment of wife's old handbag (She buys a new handbag in the meantime).

'See, I gave it to you,' I point out to her.

She denies it. 'When I am busy in the kitchen like now, you may have wanted to give it to me and I may have told you to put it in my bag,' she says.

On some occasions, we find it right on top of other papers in the briefcase waiting to be picked up. How it managed to evade us thus far was always a mystery.

On other occasions both of us tell each other that we have to keep one particular document very safe and hide it safely, in fact, so safely that we can never find it. Both of us forget where we kept it. It might be unearthed during later excavations but not when we desperately need it.

We started writing things in a notebook and are mortally afraid of misplacing or losing it. So we preserve that red-coloured, dog-eared book like a precious ornament.

My wife still has the habit of placing examination hall tickets, air tickets, and important documents in the pooja room for Lord Ganesh and other deities to take cognizance of our petitions and move things as necessary to grant the desired outcome. On our first trip to Tirupati immediately after our marriage, she placed the train tickets for divine blessings in the pooja room. We boarded the train and realized that we hadn't taken back our tickets after they were blessed.

On another occasion, I changed my trousers at the last minute since my kids didn't like the one I was wearing and realized that I had left the train tickets (we had booked for our return journey also) in the discarded trousers after the train left the station. We had a tough time on our return journey as all the trains were full. We stayed in a hotel and had to come by taxi. My kids and wife were very understanding and supportive and bore the inconvenience in silence.

In college I was at the receiving end of several jokes, pranks, and digs by my friends. My absentmindedness was an unfailing source of amusement. Eashwar used to be the leader of the gang in cracking jokes about my amnesia. I had my sweet revenge one day.

Another friend Dinesh's brother-in-law had a medical shop near Saraswati Junction. We used to congregate there and spend time there until closing time. One day Eashwar also came, sat for a couple of hours, and left. As Dinesh was closing the shop, my eyes fell on a bicycle parked outside.

'Isn't this Eashwar's bicycle?' I asked him. Dinesh looked closely and confirmed it. We hid the bicycle in Eashwar's backyard.

Next day Eashwar came to college with a long face.

'Why are you looking so glum?' I asked him, warning Dinesh not to give the game away.

'I lost my bicycle. Can you recall if I came to Dinesh's medical shop on my bicycle yesterday?' he asked.

Both of us assured him that we were positive he came on foot. We kept him in suspense till the evening and then told him.

Finally, one question that must be troubling you; how do I manage to perform the duties of a chief engineer on ships with such a memory? My wife asked me the same question several times. Very simple, it is the Dr Jekyll and Mr Hyde principle.

Once I step on the gangway of a ship, I am a changed man. I become very organized, methodical, and efficient. Chief Engineer is entrusted with hundreds of millions of dollars' worth of ship, cargo, and machinery. Though the captain is overall in charge, fuel, lube oil, running and maintenance of machinery and spares requirements are entirely Chief Engineer's responsibility. One mistake or miscalculation by him can cause millions of dollars' loss to the ship owner and may risk lives of people on board.

I keep careful track of stock, plan for future requirements and store it all on computer, whiteboards in my cabin, and control room. I am very alert and active. I have always received appreciation for my efforts.

If you ask me why I can't replicate it in domestic matters, I have no answer except that at home you have the option of doing an activity 'tomorrow'.

Tailpiece: We are fortunate our children have followed the mathematical rule of two negatives resulting in positive when multiplied. Both are gifted with exceptional intelligence and memory power.

My elder daughter was seven years old when we were going to visit a zoo in Perth. When the bus was about to leave, the agent shouted his phone number and asked us to call him if we had any problem. None of us had a pen. The 2/E, David, boasted that he had a photographic memory for numbers and he would be able to recollect the agent's number even after several years. We went to the zoo, had a good time, and returned to the ship. We had no need to bother the agent.

Fast-forward fifteen years. Once David called me, he was sailing as chief engineer in passenger ships. My daughter asked me who it was. I told her.

'Ask David uncle if he remembers the Perth agent's number?' she asked me.

I asked David. He laughed and said who could remember a number after so many years.

My daughter took the phone from me, talked to him for a few minutes, enquired about his daughter and wife, and told him the agent's number. He was floored.

On another occasion, we performed Satyanarayana Vratam at a temple in Ashoknagar. Two slokas were painted on a wall. I thought of copying the same but forgot.

After joining ship, I called home and was telling my wife to go to the temple, write the slokas, and send it to me. My elder daughter, who was nearby, took the phone from her mother and asked me, 'Do you have a pen and paper? Write it down,' and she recited those complicated stanzas. She had accompanied us to the temple but sat through seemingly uninterested.

SIESTA CHRONICLES

I thought I was the torchbearer of Italians' siesta culture outside Italy until I visited my best friend many years back. I am reluctant to reveal the name of that friend since he is now a very big shot and a senior vice president in one of India's leading companies. He is very dynamic, energetic, a go-getter and the revelation of his love, no, infatuation with siesta in his younger days may embarrass him. He cannot tell his young staff to shun laziness and be active 24/7 like him.

When I visited him, I was surprised to find one side of the dining table turned towards a cot. My initial thought was that some dining chairs must be broken but that was not the case. All the six chairs were neatly arranged on three sides of dining table.

I asked his wife about the puzzle.

She laughed and said, 'Your friend cannot keep his eyes open for one second after the last morsel of *perugannam*[curd rice] passes his throat. He washes his hand in the plate and slides onto the bed. He is in deep slumber before his head touches the pillow. He pulled the dining table towards the cot for that reason.'

I always told my mother (before marriage) and wife (after marriage) that they could extract any amount of enthusiastic hard work, physical labour, or travelling from me from morning to midnight, provided they don't force me to have lunch. If they insist that I have lunch, then they should forget about my existence for the next two to three hours.

Poor ladies, their motherly nature prevents them from making me slog from morning to night without food (for some strange reason, mothers and wives feel that only a typical six-course Telugu lunch is food and anything else is not filling and makes one weak). So I get away with my lunch and siesta.

Once I finish lunch, brain logs out, shuts off computer, and instructs all organs (except heart and respiratory) to relax until further notice, which can be anything from thirty minutes to a few hours. It is not that it will refuse to work if you force it to, but the reluctance and lethargy will be too apparent to Mother and irritating also to Wife.

But science supports my theory. After you eat food, blood rushes to the stomach for assisting in digestion and the brain would not be quite active for some time. It is a natural phenomenon for one to be dull and to doze. One of my relatives, who was very vocal in his scathing criticism of my siesta, admitted that one day while driving after lunch he dozed off. When he woke up with a start, he was driving on the wrong side of the road. He pulled up to a side and snoozed for a while.

Director general of shipping, Government of India insists that we update and refresh our knowledge once in every five years, like overhauling of a car. So, we go to a training institute and spend two weeks once every five years, sleeping and nodding through lectures and collect our certificates. I regularly go to one institute.

That institute has a novel scheme; they start classes at 7.00 a.m. and complete them by 1.30 p.m. The changed timings came into effect after observing that all the people were dozing and some people actually snoring in classes after lunch. Their problem was that they were not dealing with kids but with chief engineers and masters whom they cannot very well ask to stand up on the bench. So they thought of changing the college timings. When I heard snores in class, I actually felt happy that I was not the only one afflicted with this syndrome.

I can very easily trace the origin of my siesta fever. My father put me in the best school in my childhood. Those days there were no LKG-UKG, so I must have joined in first standard. That school was every child's dream school. We were not forced to sit and listen to teachers. We could get up anytime (no need to get teacher's permission) and play on slides, see-saws, and swings. Teachers and ayahs would be on their toes, running behind us kids, like hens behind chicks. After lunch we were forced to sleep on small folding cots. If cots were full, a big mattress was arranged in the hall. They forced us to sleep for a few hours after lunch and then woke us up. We would play and go home. They didn't realize that they were injecting a virus named siesta into us.

As luck would have it, I joined shipping and became a chief engineer. I had my forty-five minutes to one hour siesta (power nap, I believe it is called) after lunch which would rejuvenate and keep me active till midnight. If for some reason I missed it, the dullness and feeling of deprivation continued till evening. I can't imagine myself sitting behind a desk for eight hours, especially after lunch.

I visited Italy many times. We went many times to Pozzallo, Pisa, and Rome. What they say is true. From 1 p.m. to 4 p.m. all streets are deserted; towns have that ghostly and eerie look. They have their wine, lunch, and siesta and have no feeling of guilt or face any digs.

My wife and her brothers are superwoman/supermen in this regard. They consider even a minute of shut-eye a crime and if they have their way they would make it a non-bailable offence. But there is no danger of such a law coming into force since even prime ministers doze off in parliament and we have many sympathizers in very high places.

I have this urge to make my wife and her brothers have a heavy lunch (with large helpings of curd) and make them attend a lecture by one of the lecturers with a lullaby-like voice and record the proceedings. It would be fun to watch their eyelids closing and heads dropping. It is one thing to actively run in the house, driving away sleep, and another to fight to stay awake in a lecture hall.

My most favourite episode in all of the *Mr Bean* series is his struggle to stay awake in a church. An unforgettable movie character is Keshto Mukherjee's role in the movie *Bombay to Goa*. In the entire movie he just sleeps. Once when all the passengers have to get down to push the bus, he goes to sleep while pushing and the bus starts. Someone remembers him, comes back, and wakes him up. On another occasion, a snake escapes from the container and sits on the backrest of the front seat. Everyone is in a panic. He opens his eyes, stares at the snake which is a few inches away from his face, is scared, and shouts, 'Snake, snake,' and goes back to sleep. You will find such people on bus and train journeys who can sleep while sitting.

But of late, I have become more responsible and am moving about after lunch (sometimes), to my wife's surprise and relief.

DREAMS OF A SOUND SLEEPER

I am a sound sleeper. When I say this, my elder daughter reminds me that they are well aware of it, since I don't let them sleep with my strange sound effects (snoring). I refuse to accept the charge (just like all the other snorers who are blissfully unaware of their affliction).

I hardly dream. I am always envious of my wife, who recounts her dreams daily. She vividly remembers all the details. I wish I could dream; in dreams you can do any and everything like a Superman, Spider-man, or Hanuman without being apologetic or needing to explain your actions to anyone. On rare occasions I dream but all the details of the dream evaporate by the time I brush my teeth and then there is only a vague, hazy feeling that I had dreamt about something. I started to keep a pen and paper next to the bed. On those rare occasions, I would jot down details of the dream as soon as I woke up. Thus a few dreams have survived extinction.

My sincere request to you is—laugh, smile, or frown at these dreams but please do not light your pipes and sit in a psychiatrist's chair to analyze my dreams and assess my psychological profile, and scare my wife.

One night, I went to sleep after reading a few chapters of *The Secret*, the book by Rhonda Byrne. I jotted down my dream in the morning.

I had gone to my second daughter's school to talk to her principal. I was sitting in the waiting area. A senior teacher was glaring at me. I felt uncomfortable and tried to ignore her.

Finally she beckoned me with her forefinger. I got up and approached her. 'Are you going to sit here for the whole day? Which is your class? Why are you not in uniform?' She kept bombarding me.

I looked behind me. I thought she was ticking off some student behind me. There was no one. 'Are you talking to me?' I asked her.

'Don't act smart. Of course, I am talking to you. Have you taken permission of your class teacher to loiter here? Why are you not in uniform?' she was shouting at the top of her voice.

'Madam, I am not a student. I came to talk to the principal about my daughter,' I retorted angrily. She was flustered and apologized profusely.

I felt very happy and on top of the world for a few minutes until I looked in the mirror while brushing my teeth and came into this real world with a thud. I may have wished for eternal youth after reading *The Secret*. Since I didn't specify age, this bizarre thing could have happened.

Few months later, I had another weird dream.

We (my wife and I) went to visit some friends. During the conversation, they told us that their neighbour was a singer of the old black-and-white movie era. We were really fond of some of her songs and asked our friends if they could introduce us to her.

They said no problem and took us to their house and left immediately. We were asked to knock and enter as the neighbours were friendly and there was no need for an introduction. We pressed the buzzer and a beaming old man opened the door and invited us in. We were surprised to see that the hall was filled with smiling uncles, aunts, grandparents, and a few teenagers.

They offered us some savouries and sweets that were kept on a low table. While my wife politely refused, I helped myself to a few savouries.

After talking about some general topics, I said, 'Can we meet her? We are great fans of hers.'

Again there were inscrutable smiles and every second my discomfort was growing. Something was not right here. Then the singer came, said 'Namaste,' and took her seat.

When my wife and I said her B&W movie songs were excellent and we were very fond of them, she blushed and said thanks. She was very fair, very short, and very plump. We talked about her songs for about ten minutes.

She got up, said it was nice meeting us, and went inside. Then the old man said he would be back in a minute and followed her. One by one, everyone went inside, leaving my wife and me alone in the hall.

'It is baffling. They are behaving strangely. Have you noticed?' I asked my wife.

She said it hadn't escaped her attention. I wondered what was happening.

'How can you be so dumb? *Pelli chupulu* [matchmaking ceremony] is in progress. You are the groom and she is the bride. All the relatives came for moral support and also to see the groom,' she said impatiently.

My jaw dropped.

'But they know you are my wife,' I protested after I recovered.

'How do they know? Did you introduce me to them? They are thinking I am your cousin or someone you brought along for moral support,' she said, venting her anger on me, rather unfairly, I thought. I panicked.

'Come on, I myself don't know them, how can I introduce you? Let us go, come fast, we can escape before they come out,' I got up and pulled her by the hand.

She refused to budge. 'I have no objection if you marry that *gangireddu* [a bull decorated gaudily for festive seasons],' she said with a hint of tragedy like Vanisree in *Dasara Bullodu* in the sacrifice scene.

Now I was almost incoherent in my panic. 'Don't be a fool. Come, let us leave. We don't have a second to lose.' I managed to pull her to a standing position when the old man returned with a long face.

We had no option but to resume our seats. I started gulping like a fish.

'I am very sorry. She thanks you for all the trouble you have taken but she says that she cannot forget Swami ji. So please forgive us.' He folded his hands.

I tried not to sigh audibly with relief.

'No problem at all. We respect her decision. But who is Swami ji?' I asked and my wife's looks burnt holes in my shirt.

He took us to a life-size photo of a Swami ji in the pooja room. Swami ji was smiling and blessing his followers. We folded our hands and paid our respects.

'She loved him in her youth. He chose the spiritual path, took *sanyas*, and joined this *math* and is now *peethadhipati*. She is unable to forget him,' the old man said and gave *aarti*. We took *teertham-prasadam* and came out.

I could not resist asking, 'Is it not possible for the *peethadhipati* to resign, come back, and lead a married life?'

He gave me a stony look.

'Just curious,' I mumbled and we stumbled out. We must have entered at a wrong time when they were expecting a prospective groom.

'Phew. That was close.' I let out a three-metre-long sigh.

The alarm clock obediently woke me up.

I think I read too many P. G. Wodehouse books where poor Bertram Wooster is always getting trapped into engagements with Roberta Wickham and other girls and Jeeves always rescues him. It was not gentlemanly to hurt a girl and so Jeeves manipulates things to save his master. Even in the dream, I was frantically looking for a way out from the problem without hurting the poor lady. Luckily, Swami ji saved me.

In another dream, I walked into an Australian airport holding two fully grown tigers on leashes. Within seconds, the check-in counter staff and people vanished. The airport lounges became deserted. I tied my tigers to a strong point. (I was leading them by the ordinary leash people use for dogs and not chains).

I went around looking for the airport manager. He had locked himself in his cabin; after my repeated assurances that I was alone, he opened the door. I told him I wanted to take my tigers home, so he had to arrange cages for their safe transportation.

Within minutes, customs and immigration authorities and the police turned up. Customs told me that their laws don't permit importing or exporting animals. I tried to argue that my tigers were my pets and not wild animals. They refused to budge.

When I came out, I was surprised to see snipers (zoo officials with sedative rifles).

I hugged my tigers, led them to their cages, and bid farewell and went home on my flight.

DREAMS, PART II

This is my younger daughter's dream. Before describing the dream, first I should write about the mini fight we had which could have produced the dream.

I was exasperated with her and told her that I would get her married one day after she turned eighteen and handover responsibilities of her college, breakfast, and control of Internet and FB to her husband and in-laws. I also told her that I and her mother would escape to some foreign country and lie low until we were sure that her hubby and in-laws would not shoot us at sight.

She retorted with her teenage ferocity that we loved Elder Daughter more and allowed her to indulge and get away with everything and that she was treated unfairly.

Then we went out and she closed her eyes for a short nap and dreamed.

Her mother and I were jubilant when we received a phone call that our missing children were traced. We went and brought home our lost-and-found daughters (2 nos).

They went missing at a village *mela* (village fair) like in old Hindi movies. Both were senior to my elder daughter and were married. My daughter says I heaved an audible sigh of relief. All were happily celebrating the reunion when my wife declared that now we should try to trace our other missing children also.

We went on that mission and after rigorous efforts, traced our other missing three daughters and brought them home. My daughters' joy knew no bounds as they hugged and welcomed their siblings. They were talking excitedly about the missing links. My younger daughter is positive that all kids did not go missing at one village *mela* but at different *melas* and at different times.

After the initial euphoria and excitement bubbled down and harsh realities dawned, it seems I was dazed and leaned on a wall for support, and to prevent me from falling as I was fainting, saying '*Ori Baboy*, seven girls? With two girls we are unable to cope up…'

Then the chime of a calling bell shattered her dream. She was laughing heartily as she recounted her dream when she opened the door.

HAMMER MASTERS' CLUB

It will forever remain a mystery as to who coined the term 'Bollywood'. The person who used that term first may not have realized its tremendous potential. Now, several thousands of people genuinely believe that they invented it.

In an identical manner, when I studied engineering in Andhra University the term *sutti kottadam* (hammering) was widely used and became an instantaneous hit. Like several thousands of people who studied there in that era, I also genuinely feel that I and my friends invented it. This became a household term after Jandhyala, the famous Telugu director, used it to good effect in his hilarious Telugu movie *Nalugu Sthambalataa*.

Sutti kottadam (hammering) can be loosely interpreted as boring others with non-stop talking. Those who indulge in hammering are called Hammer Masters.

There are essentially three types of Hammer Masters.

First type is the Reluctant Hammer Masters. They are sensitive, sympathetic, and do not wish to cause pain or anguish to others. But because of a quirk of fate or misplaced ambition to mould youngsters into model citizens and patriots, they land up in teaching profession. All of us have come across 'good' teachers and lecturers who bunk classes themselves or tell us that they don't have the mood to teach today and allow us to have fun in their periods. Outside classroom they are saints and prefer to be left alone.

Second type is Enthusiastic Hammer Masters. They don't hunt you down and hammer you, but if you prod them, they will not let you go easily. They are oblivious to your discomfort and pain and genuinely believe that you are enjoying chatting with them. You will also feel embarrassed to hurt them by showing your anguish. They don't let go of a chance to hammer others.

Third type is Hard-core, Sadistic Hammer Masters. They derive pleasure in others' pain. They are devoid of feelings like kindness, sympathy, or pity. All of us are victims at one time or other, either in classrooms, lecture halls, seminars or in train, bus, or air travel. The worst experience is to be trapped on a long-distance flight in a window seat, seated next to this type of Hammer Master. They are like some WWE superstars who keep thumping and jumping on unconscious, defeated rivals. They don't seem to notice if you fainted. Or even if they did, they will revive you by sprinkling water on your face and make you sip some fruit juice, and then start hammering again.

Hammer Masters come in all sizes and shapes. Like in Agatha Christie murder mysteries, the most innocent-looking and docile individuals can be utterly ruthless serial hammerers.

In my teenage days I read Dale Carnegie's *How to Win Friends and Influence People.* Like any do-it-yourself, self-help books, it gives you many tips to befriend others (Since I am nearing retirement age, I can afford to confess that I read that book to overcome shyness and befriend girls).

Before approaching girls, I wanted to practice his suggestions on elderly strangers in trains and buses. I smiled at them and initiated the conversation and that was all I could do. For the next several hours, my only contribution to the conversation was to open and close mouth like a fish out of water, gasping for air. They did not give me a chance to utter a word. I was badly bruised and battered.

I wanted to sue Dale Carnegie. In his Western world, Hammer Masters could be in short supply or were non-existent. How could he generalize and prescribe the same medicine to all? I sold that book in a second-hand book stall and have been happy and at peace ever since.

Now, when I board a train, I crawl onto my upper berth and bury my head in a book, pillow or listen to music and refuse to look at fellow passengers. As an additional precaution, I paste a frown or a scowl on face to ward off threat from Hammer Masters.

I leave winning friends and influencing people to my wife, who does a commendable job. She is the PRO of our family. But for her, we would have been like the Addams family.

During my college days, I used to hop in a train and go to my maternal grandfather's village if there were a few days' holidays or for festivals since my dad was posted in Kolkata and lot of time would be consumed in travel.

On one such occasion, the train was very crowded and I placed a newspaper near the entrance door of the compartment and sat on it. I was very tired since we played a cricket match on the previous day. A teenager sat next to me. Our legs were dangling out. I rested my feet on the second rung and moved them to top rung after some time and teenager moved his to the second rung.

Only God saved me, as in the next instant, the train zoomed past a small station and the platform grazed and removed skin from toe of my left foot and hit the teenager's foot and broke it. Other passengers pulled us in. I never saw blood in close quarters and I felt dizzy. One girl who claimed to be a medical student attended to that poor teenager and stemmed the flow of blood.

I got down at next station, which luckily was my scheduled stop, and limped to the station dispensary, where they dressed the wound.

I went to my grandfather's house and my grandparents, uncles, aunts, and cousins fussed over me. My uncle rushed and brought family doctor, who gave medicines and advised complete bed rest. My foot was already swollen and throbbing.

My uncle gave me a bedroom with a view of the street. My grandfather had a cot that was massive and huge. You had to get up on a stool or a chair to climb on it. It was made of heavy teak wood and had intricate, beautiful designs. The other end of the bed was touching the wall, which had a window overlooking the street.

It was luxury. I lay there enjoying all the attention, care, and love showered by all, until one Hammer Master uncle landed.

He was massive. He plopped next to me and clobbered me mercilessly. I lay there helpless, praying for an end to the ordeal. My one exit was blocked by window. I had to climb over him to get down from bed and I could not run very far with my injured foot. That was the most devastating experience. He was there for two days. I could empathize with concentration camp inmates.

I have fond memories of that window in Grandfather's bedroom. It was fixed in a one-foot-thick wall, so we could sit in that window ledge. It had vertical iron rods. My mom used to leave me there on the bed when she was busy; I could not get down from bed. I would sit in the window and watch people come and go and activity on the street.

Those days there was only one entry and exit point. Though I don't remember following incidents, my uncle keeps reminding me of these when we meet. My uncle who must have been a teenager wanted to go out alone and could never manage to avoid me. The moment I saw him going out, I would howl and scream, forcing him to take me along with him.

One day he decided to be strong and refused. Those days I was plump (not fat, mind you) and I pushed my hands and legs through the gap in the window rods as if I wanted to squeeze through and was stuck. He had to abandon his plans, come back, and assist my mom and others in extracting me. It must have been a traumatic experience to all, especially to my mom.

On another occasion, I demanded an explanation from my uncle why I could not accompany him. I would not take no for an answer. Finally he was fed up and hissed angrily, 'I am going to the prostitute, that's why I can't take you.'

I promptly ran to my mom. My grandfather had a huge house and let out some portions. All the ladies would congregate in the spacious hall and gossip after lunch. On that particular day there were many ladies. I did not whisper in Mom's ear but told her in a loud voice since I might have thought prostitute was a play or a movie, 'See, Mom. Uncle says he is going to prostitute and doesn't want to take me. Please tell him to take me also.'

They were all stunned. Many jaws became unhinged. There was pin-drop silence. My poor uncle was the youngest, with five sisters and two sisters-in-law. So all eight ladies (my grandmother led the assault) pounced on him.

In those days, mattresses were made of cotton, and after some time, cotton would become hard and form lumps in the bed. One particular Muslim clan called *Doodekula saheb* would remove the covers of mattresses and thrash the cotton lumps with a huge guitar-like instrument. The cotton would become fluffy again and the mattress would become soft and as good as new.

My uncle was thrashed in a similar fashion by all womenfolk. But he did not harbour a grudge but gave me all comforts during the trying period of swollen foot and assault by another uncle. He would pull him away on some pretext or other and give me some respite.

My wife has a soft corner for Hammer Masters since some of her cousins are exponents in Hammer Mastery (I hope she doesn't read this section).

My father-in-law was a gem of a man. I have not come across a more upright and honest person. To give an example, if you were to give him an open envelope and tell him, 'Sir, this envelope contains highly damaging information about you. I want to leave it in safe custody with you, I will collect later,' I will bet my last buck that he would never read it and will hand it over to you as it was given to him. He had many admirable qualities, including burning passion about cleanliness and tidiness.

But he was a Hammer Master. If he were to lose a pen on the bus while coming home from office and you were to ask him how he lost it, his answer would be something like this.

He would start the story at the time when he closed his files and was about to leave the office. Then his friends forced him to have coffee in canteen. So he was delayed and missed his regular bus. None of the other buses stopped and he had to run and jump into a moving bus. The conductor refused to give change even though he had and there was an argument and he would give graphic details of how fellow passengers supported him and conductor had to eat humble pie…

When you are hoping that the story would reach the point when he lost the pen, his daughter (my wife) would come and ask him what it was all about. You slump as he starts all over again and just when he is about to lose the pen, phone would ring, and by the time he completes the call, he loses track and starts all over.

And then her cousins carry hammers of intricate designs and awe-inspiring shapes.

Never commit a mistake of asking one of her cousins about directions to go to a place.

'You go straight to the signal, there take a left turn. Don't take right turn, then you will go to such-and-such place, nor should you go straight then you will land up at such-and-such place. Then you will come across a petrol pump, ignore it, if you don't, you will land up somewhere else, then you will come across a circle with six roads and…'By the time he finishes explaining, your head would be spinning.

If you are smart, when he asks if you followed what he said, you would say yes.

If you confess that you are confused and didn't understand, you will face another barrage.

Never commit the mistake of riding in a car driven by another of her cousins. If it is unavoidable, sit in the seat next to the driver's seat. He is a very passionate Hammer Master and gestures with both hands to emphasize points, leaving the steering wheel, and turns and looks into the faces of people sitting in the back seat when speaking. Since he has been driving like that for many years, there may be no cause for concern but it scares ordinary folk.

My wife attracts Hammer Masters like honey attracts ants. She has a friendly, cheerful countenance and Hammer Masters are like hammerhead sharks (sharks can smell and sense a small trail of blood several kilometres away). Hammer Masters travel great distances to torment my wife.

MURDERERS OF MELODY

I confess that I am a murderer of melodious tunes. It may be difficult to believe that I, a soft-spoken, gentle soul, am capable of committing such a brutal crime, but sadly, it is a fact.

We have to travel back several decades to get to the motive.

We (our generation) are a blessed lot. We have travelled in both bullock carts and flights. Our previous generation's folk had so much time, in fact, all the time in the world and did not know what to do with it. They would look at beautiful sunsets and landscapes until cows came back home, have early dinner, and go to sleep.

I remember the days in my childhood when during Devi Navratri, Ganesh, and other festivals, dramas in roadside pandals would be played the whole night and for several nights until the festival season ended. *Mahabharata* was the favourite show. Actors played Krishna, Arjuna, Duryodhana, etc. in shifts. They used to display names of actors, I, II, and III Krishnas, Arjunas, etc. So you can imagine the leisurely life of that generation.

Now, our next generation, they travel in BMWs, Lexus, etc. at breakneck speed and pass through breathtaking landscapes and sunsets but dare not look at them for fear of breaking their necks. Even if they stop the car and get down to enjoy the scenery, they cannot, because they will be seeing the deadlines, credit card bills, EMIs, flights to catch, etc.

Our generation, we enjoyed best of both worlds. We travelled on scooters with cool breeze ruffling the hair (of which we had plenty) and the pleasant lukewarm sunshine tingling our skins. We would stop scooter and enjoy the scenery as long as we wanted. We sat through whole nights watching *Mahabharata* enacted by three Krishnas, Arjunas, and Draupadis. We also watched *Avatar* in 3D in IMAX.

We were also lucky to be born when film music was at its melodious best. Rafi, Mukesh, Kishore, Ghantasala, Hemant, Lata, Asha, Susheela, Janaki, and many others enthralled and captivated us.

Lyricists would take months to write songs; music directors were also in no big hurry. Several evergreen classics were composed and created in that era.

In Telugu filmdom, there was a very famous lyricist and dialog writer. He would camp in star hotels in Ooty, Kodaikanal for several months at producer's expense, waiting for the mood to write. Producers would shed silent tears but waited patiently since he had the gift of writing super-duper hits. People used to say, 'That writer makes everyone weep. He makes audience weep by writing lyrics and dialogs that wring their hearts and makes producers weep by not writing' (*Atanu raasi prekshakulni, rayakunda producers ni edipistadu*).

My friend once met his brother-in-law (wife's brother) who claimed that entire credit for writer's achievements should go to his sister and not to his brother-in-law.

My friend asked why. He thought she inspired him and motivated him. She did, but in a different way.

He said, 'My sister is a *Gayyali Gampa* [shrew].' Compared to her, Suryakantam (a famous Telugu actor who specialized in such roles and was synonymous for a shrew) is an innocent baby. She made his life hell and so miserable that he wrote his best lyrics when she tormented him when she was at her shrewish best; he wrote several classics during those times. He used to escape to Ooty, Kodaikanal for months together for peace, not for 'mood'.

We could follow and understand each word and stanza, so we could hum the songs easily. There was no need to 'mutilate' and 'kill'.

Then the fast pace started. I can never understand a word of present Telugu songs. They are like Tamil or French to me. Hindi is better definitely but I am still lost. I like the tunes; I want to hum and sing but the lyrics are above my head. So what is the option left? I make my own lyrics and ram them into the tune. My elder daughter is a music lover, has faced the brunt.

When we were sailing, one Tamil second engineer had Tamil songs cassette. I recorded those songs. I was particularly fond of one song of Jesudas and Chitra (I think). I could not catch a single word, so I manufactured my own lyrics. The song is '*Maasi maasam naa laana ponnu kaanai kanaku dane*' (Correct one, not mine. If you wish, download only the song and not video; Rajnikant, Gautami, and others' acrobatics may make you squirm).

I used to sing with my own lyrics '*Paati pata maraka millai kadai kanda vaalam…*' My daughter had no idea that my lyrics were not original.

When she was in college, her best friend was a Tamil girl. I asked Elder Daughter to get lyrics of that song from that girl.

She came in the evening and started firing at me.

'How can you mutilate such beautiful song? Don't you have conscience?' she demanded.

I was puzzled. 'What happened?' I asked her.

'When I asked my friend, she told me there is no such song and not a single word in that gibberish was a Tamil one. Then I hummed the tune, she clutched her head and said, 'Ohhh… that is "Maasi maasam…"' She told me the lyrics and told all friends, and all had great fun at my expense. Seriously, even if you can't catch a single word, don't you think your manufactured lyrics should at least have similar sounds?

Where is "Maasi maasam…" and where is "Potty paata"?' she said furiously.

She made me repeat until I got lyrics right.

Then there was the song 'Tanha… tanha…' in *Rangeela*.

I used to sing *'Tanha… tanha…yahan kisi ki koi bhi kahin baat hai, kisi ka jaan lele… kisi par jaan de de'* and drive Elder Daughter up the wall.

'You are not content with killing songs? You want to kill people also? Where did you get the *"kisi ka jaan lele"* [kill someone]?'

'Lyricists will commit suicide if they could hear the way you mutilate their work,' she admonished me.

'Jaane kyon log pyaar karte hain' from *Dil Chahta Hai* became *'Jaane kyon log mujhe pyaar karte hain'*, prompting Elder Daughter to remark caustically that people would not love but hate me if they heard me mutilating that song.

Another song that I mercilessly killed was 'sarke jo sar se dheere, dheere… pagal hua re mein dheere, dheere… teri chunariyan meri dil legayi…'

I sang, 'Sarsoan ke sar se dheere, dheere…' driving daughter mad.

Once mind decides, ears will interpret sounds heard as decided by mind. So, Rafi's song *'Ek haseen sham ko dil mera kho gaya'* was heard by me as *'Ek haseen sham ko din mein raat ho gaya'*.

Elder Daughter was flabbergasted. 'Dad, I salute you. You have no reservations. I thought you killed only songs of our generation. You didn't spare Rafi also. How can day become night in the evening?' My protests that day begins to become night in evening did not cut ice with her.

In our college days we 'killed' in a different and novel way.

We had one lecturer, Balaji, who was quite strict (or stingy) while correcting papers. I remember once he started giving 1/8 mark but stopped after realizing final addition was becoming tedious. We, not being greedy for gold medals or any such nonsense, did not really fight with him for marks.

Our friend, one Pavan, used to fight tooth and nail for every 1/4 mark. Balaji and Pavan used to fight like gladiators as if their lives depended on that 1/4 mark. Pavan would argue that he deserved to get 1 mark and Balaji would refuse to budge from 1/4 mark he awarded for that question. We used to watch the fun and have bets on who would win. If Balaji was feeling weak, Pavan would get his 1 mark or sometimes Pavan would get tired and accept defeat and 1/4 mark. On few occasions, a draw would result, Balaji would award 1/2 or 3/4 mark.

My friends and I composed a song (Individuals cannot take credit for group effort, but I think Eashwar should be given full credit for this innovation).

Those days M. Balamuralikrishna sang '*Paluke Bangaaramayera…*', which was a hit.

Our song's lyrics were (to be sung in above song's tune):

> *Marke Bangaaramaayera…O Balaji rava…*
> *Marke Bangaaramayera…*
> *Subjectemo bodhapadadu, bodha padina*
> *gurtundadu, Gurtunna raayalemu,*
> *Raasina mari markuliyavu…Marke*
> *Bangaarammayera…*

Translated into English,

> Has mark become as precious as gold? O
> Balaji raava...
> We can't understand the subject, even if we
> understand, we can't remember
> Even if we remember, we can't write and
> even if we write, you don't award marks

Has mark become precious as gold? O
Balajiraava...)

Bobby was a super hit movie. So we adopted one song for
our plea to lecturers.

We had grading system A,B,C,D, and F. If you land up
getting 'F', you have to repeat the subject. The song was '*Na
chahoon sona, chandi, na mangoon hira, moti... ee mere kis
kaam ke...*'

Our song was

> *Maaku 'A' grade vaddu, maaku 'B' grade
> vaddu, okka 'C' grade chaloooo.
> 'D' grade aina emi paravaaledu, 'F' grade
> matram chaste ivvaddu, Malli repeat
> cheyyalem...*

Loosely translated in English,

> We don't want 'A' grade, we don't want 'B'
> grade, we are happy with 'C' grade,
> We don't mind even 'D' grade, but please
> never give 'F' grade, we can't repeat the
> subject

Theory of Machines (TM)was one subject that gave
us nightmares, with complicated cam design profiles and
convoluted problems. Our song on the day of exam was copied
from 'Yaad nahin ab kuch...' from the film *Julie*.

Our song was,

> *Yaad nahin ab kuch, bhool gaya sab kuch...
> oho...aha...lekin ek baat na bhooli, Teeee
> Mmmm ...aaaaaaaa...I hate you...*

Loosely translated in English,

> Don't remember anything, forgot
> everything ... oho...aha... but I can't forget
> one thing... Teee Mmmmm... aaaaaaaa ...I
> hate you...

These songs we sang at our farewell party to thunderous applause. All lecturers took it sportingly.

In defence of Melody Murderers, the only thing that can be said in their favour is that they are die-hard music lovers and a handicap of not understanding or catching lyrics will not stop them.

A few years back, one video song, 'Asaha re...', was quite popular and my daughters could effortlessly sing the entire Spanish or Portuguese lyrics of that song and if you held a gun to my head and asked me to learn, I could not have.

So that is the difference.

Tailpiece: Elder Daughter wonders, with so many thousands of songs to choose from why I hum only a few songs like 'Teri zulfon se...', 'Jo tum ko ho pasand...' and 'Maasi maasam...'

I think it is hereditary. My dad used to have two, three pet poems which he would sing relentlessly. One was from *Mahabharata*: Arjuna asks Krishna how he could fight Bhishma, who a veteran of many battles, whereas he was a young novice.

'Aatadaneka yuddhamula ariyu terina vruddha moorthi, yeno tarununda...'

Another was *'Janda pai kapi raaju...'* Third was *'Oho, vinu Mister...'* from *Chivaraku Migiledi.*

I also used to wonder, with so many songs of Ghantasala, P. B. Srinivas, etc. to choose from, why he kept singing those same songs.

A few more of my 'killings':

I am like a bull in a china shop. Even if the bull wants to tread carefully, it cannot help dislodging and breaking few artefacts because of its size and big horns.

I realized this when I was humming *'Aasaan nahin yahan Aashiq ho jana, palkon ko kaanten pe sajaanaa...'* a hit song from *Aashiqui 2*. I heard this song many times and wanted to impress my elder daughter with my prowess in singing melodies without actually murdering them.

She clutched her forehead and implored me not to murder that song.

I was righteously indignant and told her haughtily that I was singing lyrics correctly.

Then she said, 'Just think for a moment. *Palkon* means eyelids and *kaante* means thorns. How can you put eyelids on thorns? Are you going to peel them off and place them on thorns?'

I thought for several moments. Only explanation was that that lyricist had many drinks to get into the mood.

I told her, 'Not necessarily. One can lie down and place eyelids on thorns.'

She explained patiently, 'The lyric is *palkon pe kaanton ko sajaanaa...* and not *palkon ko kaante pe bichana*. What the lyricist wants to say is that to be a passionate lover is not easy, it involves decorating thorns on eyelids... etc.'

My eldest sister-in-law sang a beautiful song on the eve of their engagement.

It was *'Padamule chalu Ramaa...ni pada dhulule padivelu...'*

I mutilated that song by singing in English, 'Words are enough, Ramaa...your feet dust is ten thousand...'

Instead of laughing and encouraging me in my pursuit of demolition of melodies, parents and elders should have reined me in. Maybe they are also guilty of omission, if not commission.

THAT EXQUISITE 'TWO MINUTES MORE' SLEEP

You may have had blameless, dreamless, and peaceful sleep for eight to ten hours but if you have not experienced the exquisite pleasure of 'two minutes more' sleep, then you are missing something. On a cold winter morning, to leave the warmth of bed and blanket is a tough task for anyone but impossible for those afflicted with 'two minutes more sleep' virus.

I used to yearn for 'ten more minutes' sleep, my elder daughter wants to sleep for 'five more minutes', and my younger one for 'two more minutes', which gets extended by many times. More than half of my wife's energy is drained in waking them up many times at regular intervals.

Finally when they are late, the blame is put not on their 'five minutes' and 'two minutes' syndrome but on Mother, who did not 'put in sufficient effort' in waking them up and she should have tried 'harder'. Wife is rightly exasperated and moans why both girls should inherit my laziness and not her workaholic nature or her active lifestyle.

The day is not far off when you can decide how your kid should look and what qualities the kid should possess. You can opt for one uncle's height, one aunt's silky, shining thick hair, one cousin's sense of humour, and another's intelligence and press Enter and bingo, your dream kid would arrive.

But, we had no such option to choose and gratefully accepted the gifts God had bestowed on us. At times like

317

above, you can't blame my wife if she feels that God could have been a little more considerate, and instead of giving both daughters Mom's beauty and Dad's laziness, he could have given Dad's beauty (or lack of it) and Mom's active lifestyle to one kid.

When my dad was transferred from a small town to city, we stayed in first floor of one house. That was pre–Dr Kurien and 'white revolution' era. Every day, you had to go to milk booth at 4 a.m., carrying a two-litre can and a card. You place your can in the queue and wait for milk van to arrive. Two men would carry fifty-litre aluminium cans from the van into the booth. Then, the man in the booth would dispense milk with 1-litre and ½-litre measures.

We were five male members in the family. My turn would come every fifth day. You can imagine how traumatic it was for my mother to wake me up and push me out of the house with a can and card at 3.45 a.m. I would fight tooth and nail and try to find excuses to escape the duty. It was not fair to punish a child like this. Why can't sister bring milk? Ladies queue is so short (which was true). I was having pain in leg, etc. and finally would set out grumbling, when Mom would volunteer to come with me. I had the decency not to allow her to stand in queue at that hour. Though I was not awake when she woke up others, I don't think they gave her any trouble. She had to get up every day to wake up others but never grumbled once. On occasions when I was adamant, my third brother would go in my place. He was very decent about it and never complained.

As luck would have it, on many occasions when it was my duty, the milk van would be late and my dad would come and take over at 7 a.m.

During Telangana Agitation, we lost one academic year. We were totally idle. It amazes me when I think back how we could sleep like in office hours. My father would leave for office at 9.30 a.m., we would have sumptuous lunch and put thick bed sheets over the windows to make the room dark, and go to sleep. We would sleep from 10.30 a.m. to 4.45 p.m. (office hours). We get up, have whatever snacks Mom made (we had very healthy appetites and consumed by tons), played indoor cricket (in bedroom with a rubber ball and small bat), and then hit the road.

My eldest brother is a master storyteller; he would start narrating Sir Arthur Conan Doyle's Sherlock Holmes stories (*The Sign of Four, The Hound of the Baskervilles,* and other books.) as we walked for about three hours. Our route was from Kachiguda, Himayat nagar, Liberty, entire length of Tank Bund, and then back. He had a knack for stopping the story at the peak of suspense. We had to wait impatiently for next day to know what happened next. We would be tired. We would listen to *Binaca Geetmala,* Vividh Bharati and hit the sack by 10.30 p.m.

After a few days I had an idea: why should I not read the books myself? I owe a lot to my eldest brother; he introduced me to the wonderful world of literature. Before I completed tenth standard, I had read many books by P.G. Wodehouse, Conan Doyle, and James Hadley Chase.

I have one cousin; I have not seen a more determined, valiant, and courageous sleeper than he. He would refuse to accept defeat and wake up.

I went to my aunt's place once. We slept on the terrace. Sun is the worst enemy of 'two minutes more' sleepers sleeping on the terrace. He would relentlessly poke you in the eyes with needle-like rays, roast exposed parts of your skin, and heat up the blanket like an oven, forcing you to wake up.

I gave up and got up after a token fight and was shocked to see my cousin sleeping it off. I was curious and wished to see how long he would resist. I was privileged to see a most fearsome battle between my cousin and Sun.

First my cousin got up and slept in the shade of parapet wall of terrace. Sun steadily climbed up in the sky and shadow became shorter and shorter and finally parapet wall offered no protection. Then he shifted to the shadow underneath a folding cot. He kept shifting his position to remain in the shadow of the cot and Sun was in danger of losing the battle.

Luck was on Sun's side. Had there been cloud cover, he would have lost. The sky was clear without a wisp of cloud, so Sun heated up the terrace floor, which became so hot you could make an omelette. My cousin finally got up, but not without a fight. Sun God would have granted him any boon had he offered *namaskar* and requested a boon.

In my college days, I was with my eldest brother and sister-in-law for the first two years. Like every 'two minute more' sleeper, I sincerely wanted to get up and jog or study from next day. My sister-in-law has a very beautiful voice and she specialized in singing lullabies. I would ask her to wake me up at 6 a.m. She would be singing and going about her chores, unaware that she was pushing me deeper into slumber with her lullabies.

She would wake me up, I forced open my eyelids weighing a ton and see that time is 5.58 a.m. I tell her she woke me up a few minutes before so next wake-up call should be at 6.10. She wakes me up at 6.12, which is not acceptable. It has to be in round figures. Finally, when I gather all willpower and push myself from bed, it is 7.00 a.m. After several days of repetition of this exercise, she asked me, 'Why do you sleep in increments? Why don't you wake up at 7.00 a.m., at least you will get one more hour of good sleep?'

She didn't understand. If I started the waking up process at 7.00 a.m., I would get up 8.00 a.m.

But unlike my daughters, I always felt guilty and did not accuse her of not putting in sufficient effort in waking me up, if I was late or missed something.

Then I shifted to hostel. My best friend Dinesh was my roommate. I had an alarm timepiece. I don't know where it was manufactured or what technology was used, but that little fellow would create such a racket to give heart attacks to weak-hearted people. You have to silence the sound within a few seconds or else there would be chaos as people would scramble and rush out of hostel in panic, thinking that a fire engine had entered the hostel to put out fire.

I was still determined to get up at 6 a.m. and study hard. But the routine didn't change; I kept setting the alarm to the next ten minutes. Dinesh was going mad; he would scold me for disturbing his sleep.

One day, I groggily extended my hand to tap on the head of the alarm timepiece. I could not find it; my hand was pawing air. The alarm timepiece was now screaming shrilly. I scrambled out of bed and frantically searched. I could not locate it. I started turning everything upside down to find it, and the sound was so jarring.

Dinesh extracted a promise from me that I would give up my effort to get up at 6 a.m. and pulled it from where he hid it and gave it to me.

Once, one of our friends was morose and dull after returning from home. He would not say anything but we could make out that he was worried and distressed about something. Next day he didn't turn up for breakfast; we knocked on his door. There was no answer. Then we banged on his door; there was only silence. We were very worried. We decided to break open the door. Then I had a bright idea. I brought my alarm timepiece, set time, and kept it near keyhole.

It worked like magic. He was up and awake and scrambled to open the door, shouting, 'Wait, wait ... I am coming. Shut the damn thing off.' He said he was very tired and slept soundly.

Sometimes, I feel only my daughters and I are afflicted with this malady. I cannot find anyone else on the horizon: my parents, brothers, wife's parents, her brothers, my nieces and friends. I cannot imagine any of them lazing around, or maybe everyone suffers like us but hides it, and we have no means of knowing.

I wonder what would an active person who never stays in bed a minute more than necessary do in a hypothetical situation. Suppose that person is dreaming, in dream he is a Superman, wearing that tight dress with 'S' and underwear on top of pant ...or a Cat woman and is rescuing children and teachers from a school building which is going up in flames. Everyone is rescued, except an old woman who is screaming for help. This super person is flying to rescue her, then alarm buzzes.

Will the active person coolly get up, go, and brush teeth and consign that old lady to flames? Will that person's conscience forgive him? Or will that person try to go back to sleep, revive the dream, and save the old lady?

TALE OF TWO MEN

There is a saying in Telugu '*Peratlo mokka intlo vaidyaniki paniki raadu*' (A medicinal plant in your garden is useless in curing members of the household). In a larger context, it implies that Amartya Sen, Manmohan Singh, and other eminent economists' suggestions and advice will be disregarded by members of their households as they might view them as senile old men.

When I was in school, our Telugu teacher Rangachari garu used to tell us a story about Swami Vivekananda. He was asked after his famous Chicago speech if he wanted to send his message to his countrymen why he had chosen Chicago as a platform and not India. He replied that when his countrymen's eyes and ears were focused on the West, the only option for him to be heard was to go to the West and send message from there to be heard.

My kids are the best but when I start advising them about any topic, they don't actually roll their eyes and say, 'Oh, not again. When will you stop lecturing us?' However, their resigned expressions and slumped shoulders tell it all. I don't blame them; some people have a technique of hypnotizing audience with inspiring clichés and I am not one of them.

So I have chosen blog as the media to reach out not only to my kids but many other youngsters, for I feel many can benefit from this story. Other grown-ups may read it only for entertainment value, for they could have fallen into the same pits that I did or they could have been quite judicious and invested wisely; in either case, there is not much that they do not know already.

The story is about two men of the same age group from diverse backgrounds. 'A' comes from an upper-middle-class family, son of a Central Government officer. Though they were not rich, he had no difficulty in completing education, landing a well-paid job, and reaching top post in his department quickly. He was handsomely paid.

'B' comes from a family of meagre means, could not complete education, and joined as a salesperson for a real estate owner. He would travel in buses and walk great distances and would sell plots of Mr. Murthy, the landlord. He didn't switch loyalties, worked for him for more than three decades. He got married and had two children. His dad gave him neither properties nor debts.

Now, after three decades, both reached retirement age. Anyone would bet on 'A' to be financially better placed than 'B'. But if such is the case, there is no point in writing the story, is there?

Story of A

There is no need to beat around the bush. I am 'A' and one Mr Naveen is 'B'.

I know I am sitting on a gold mine. If I can write a don't-do-it-yourself book (on similar lines as do-it-yourself type magical books) on financial mismanagement and squandering opportunities, it would be a best seller. Here is the list of my gems of mismanagement.

Share Markets

When Harshad Mehta was at peak and stock market business was booming, I attended a class on stock market investment strategies by a leading stockbroker of my city, one Mr H.B. He was brilliant. He said no one can ever lose in stock market, provided they followed a few simple steps. First was to have a balanced approach, sell a share if it reaches 20 per cent margin on either side (i.e. + or -) and never feel bad if it soars high after you sold it. Second, don't marry share certificates, they are pieces of paper; don't feel sentimental or emotional about letting go. Third was, never put all eggs in one basket. Fourth was, identify and invest in emerging blue chips.

During the class, one semi-literate youth stood up and asked him if he should hold on to the shares of Dr Reddy's labs, which had just sprung on the horizon. Mr H.B. told him that he did not foresee Reddy labs emerging as a blue chip and he had better sell it and buy some xxxxx shares. I hope that youth did not follow his advice.

I met Mr H.B. later and told him of my predicament. I was working in ships and would be away for six to eight months at a time, hence cannot follow and take action in buying and selling shares. I requested him to invest in emerging blue chips (in which he would invest himself) on my behalf and my wife would give cheques.

He did invest in about eight shares which he felt were emerging blue chips, since their fundamentals were strong, promoters were highly qualified, well experienced, and dynamic, and markets were booming. And he put eggs in different baskets, and not even one egg survived. Without exception, all had become rotten; even *Raddiwala* refused to take the share certificates to wrap peanuts.

I still remember I made out a cheque to buy Satyam Computers shares as he said it had an excellent potential. Later he had second thoughts and suggested we invest in Midwest Iron as there is never a shortage in demand for steel and bought those shares instead. I missed Satyam bus and 'Dr Reddy lab' bus and several others. Market expert Mr H.B. had failed miserably in identifying the emerging blue chips. He consoled me later by saying that he lost millions by investing in shares that he prescribed to me.

I shied away from investing in shares after I burnt hands ...until they were healed.

Onboard ship, the conversation at mealtime was invariably about stocks and shares, and everyone would boast how they made a killing and how their investment adviser was a genius, etc. They were all as smart or as dumb as I was. They invested money with those advisers on friends', brothers' or brother-in-law's recommendation and were as ignorant about market strategies or potentials as I was ...and were minting money.

So, I located one Mr. Swami, who appeared to be philanthropic, was aiding poor Brahmin students and widows and was running a charitable organization. He was running a financial consultancy service as a side business. I felt my money would be safe with him.

He told me, 'You know where Mr H.B. went wrong? He did not diversify your funds. He invested everything in risky ventures. I would invest half your money in mutual funds, your money is safe. I will play with rest half. You will be surprised how your money multiplies.'

I, of course, overruled my wife and gave him money and went to abroad for two years to work as chief engineer in a power plant. During that period, 9/11 happened, markets collapsed everywhere, and Mr. Swami apologized and handed over certificates worthy of rejection by *raddiwalas*. It was not total loss like last time. I could salvage a little from mutual funds. The big bus I missed this time was Reliance. He purchased Reliance shares when I went abroad but after Reliance converted the shares to Petroleum, Mr. Swami felt that Reliance was cheating the public and sold them and purchased some Saravana Industry shares which sank without a ripple.

I consider my wife's scathing criticism as mild compared to the gravity of the blunder. I promised her that I would not venture again unless she also approved.

Again, there was a huge gap before the next misadventure. This time it was a family friend whom we knew for several decades. In fact, he tried to brainwash both of us. We resisted tooth and nail.

He would tell us, 'You know where Mr. Swami went wrong? You cannot afford to leave computer for a minute. You have to watch like a hawk the movement and take prompt action. I am twenty-four hours on the job. I will teach you also. It is so simple, even a small kid can do it.'

We refused to take the bait, until I met one Mr. V.V., a chief engineer who relieved me in a ship. He told me he was making awesome amount of money from share trading. Those days Internet in ships was not available to crew and officers. So, I asked him how he was trading.

He told me that his friend recommended one financial adviser whom he trusted blindly and reaped a harvest. So, again I had the itch.

My wife, of course, threatened to walk out of the house if I again dabbled in it. When our family friend visited and tried again to lure us (I should give him credit for his perseverance, he didn't give up for several years). I told him that I had no objection if he could convince my wife.

He gave an inspiring sales talk, about how he would personally guarantee safety of our investment and how he would be on the job 24/7 and how our money would grow manifold. It didn't cut any ice with Wife. She reluctantly agreed, more because she was embarrassed saying no to family friend so many times.

This time our money vanished faster than a lit camphor. On previous occasions, it took several years before our advisers announced with regret the demise of our investments. It amazes me how our family friend managed to bring it down to zero within two months. When I later tried to contact him (he was suddenly unavailable), he was not even apologetic. He told me that he had not pocketed the money. I should have known and should have been prepared for the risks involved in trading. When I tried to remind him of his promise to stand guarantee for our investment, he said he would refund our money 'as and when he received money from some other quarter' (meaning, never). Only conclusion I could arrive at for his bizarre behaviour was that he must have bet with someone that he could fleece money from me and make it vanish in record time, and get away with it.

My wife was justifiably angry and upset and has not forgiven me to this day.

REAL ESTATE

I started my tryst with real estate in splendid style, like Vinod Kambli who hit two double centuries back to back on debut, and fizzled out. I constructed an independent house even before I turned twenty-eight (Those days, people would think of a house only after retirement). Moreover, that was the only thing I was destined to do. I did not even construct a second floor, let alone build another house.

There are a hundred reasons for my disaster in real estate investments. There is a saying in Telugu, *Karnudi parajayaniki veyyi kanaralunnayi.* (There are a thousand reasons for Karna's failure).

Likewise, there are many reasons for my debacles on this front. I don't blame anyone but myself. But to be impartial and to narrate the events dispassionately, I have to narrate the sequence.

I was like a king or queen cornered on a chessboard. I could not move a step in any direction.

My first handicap was the notion that all people from my generation were afflicted with, that you should not buy land or a flat unless you wished to live there. When I was first promoted as a chief engineer, my first captain was one

Capt. Nair from my city. He was an ex–Indian Navy captain. He purchased six plots in a remote area and would daily urge me to buy one or two as a future investment. I said I was not interested since I had no plans of living there. We had the same mistaken notion until prices everywhere shot up sky-high.

My second handicap was my profession. For several months I had to leave wife and children, so the houses I had taken on rent had to be quite close to the schools and close to my in-law's house. We naturally got so used to that locality, we could not think of living anywhere else. Land prices there were always out of our reach. Wife had reservations about living in flats and we kept shifting houses in that locality till now.

My third handicap was lack of friends and advisers. If I were employed in a shore job, I would have had several colleagues and friends whom I would have observed or followed. All my friends were from Delhi, Mumbai, Kerala, and Punjab and even Sri Lanka.

Fourth handicap was my well-wishers. There are two types of well-wishers. First type, they advise you, argue, fight with you but finally leave you to make a decision as you felt right. Second type thinks that they are duty bound to protect you from making suicidal moves in investment. They may even handcuff you to restrain you, all well intended, of course. I had one such well wisher, Mr W.W.

Within a year of getting married, I had an urge to buy a flat and located one close to our home. Construction had not begun yet, but builder's features were impressive. Mr W.W. checked, found it was a good buy. Later, builder backed out from providing swimming pool and W.W. saw red. He forbade me from buying the flat; today, builder backed out on swimming pool, tomorrow he will not give something else, so he should not be trusted, he reasoned.

Still I wanted to buy the flat. Then W.W. threatened that the builder may not have had necessary sanctions or approvals and I may end up landing in the soup. I naturally hesitated and let it go. Had I taken that flat, I might not have been shuttling in rented houses till retirement. My college friend, a chief engineer himself in ships, had taken a flat there and stayed there for several decades.

During this period, I went to Dinesh's city to attend some function. My return train was at 7 p.m. I visited my best friend Dinesh and he offered to drop me at station. When we were about to start, he asked me to see a fourth-floor apartment under construction nearby. He knew the builder and we could negotiate if I liked. I refused to see since I had no intention of staying in that city.

Still, since he insisted, I reluctantly followed him. I immediately liked the flat. It had five-foot balconies on entire length and breadth of flat. It had two side roads and there was excellent ventilation. To top it all, the view of majestic hills was breathtaking. I paid advance and booked it—and faced the onslaught by everyone, led by W.W. and wife. What was the necessity to buy a flat in that city when we were not going to stay there and who would look after it? I mildly said Dinesh promised to look after. As luck would have it, Dinesh was transferred to my city and I had a very tough time managing it.

I think I am like Paramanandayya Sishyulu. They do all foolish things, which later turn out to be blessings in disguise and they avert major disasters by their seemingly foolish acts. Tenants were hard to find and I had to spend a good deal of my leave finding tenants and looking after repairs and had to silently suffer the digs by one and all.

I realized the value of moral stories taught to us in school, after I grew up. During schooling, you mug up and answer questions to gain marks and never appreciate the profound meaning.

For instance, there was a story of a Brahmin leading a goat to sell it at a market. Four thieves plan to steal it and work out a plan. First one meets Brahmin and asks him where he was taking his dog. Brahmin shouts at him, is he blind, can't he tell a goat from a dog? Man shrugs and goes away. When same thing repeats again and again, Brahmin is convinced that he was hallucinating and leading a dog, and leaves it and goes. Thieves make merry.

Same thing happened to me about that city flat. Everyone except Dinesh advised me to sell the flat, as I was not getting much rent, much of my leave was wasted in repairs and finding tenants.

The final thief who pushed me into selling the flat was one retired bank officer whom I approached in that city for an alliance for my niece. He received me very well, apologized since his son was already engaged. When he asked me why I had come there, I told him about my flat.

He exclaimed, 'Oh, you too? There are hundreds of flats lying vacant. Why did you purchase flat here? Do you know, many people thought that steel plant personnel would prefer to stay near plant and built and purchased hundreds of flats there? All of them are vacant. Everyone prefers to stay in city and travel to the plant. Poor chaps, major portion of their salaries are going for EMIs. There is no future for flats here.'

I asked him what I should do.

He said, 'Sell for a good price and forget about it.'

I sold it but cannot forget about it since the prices have skyrocketed after Telangana state separated. Now it would cost a fortune to buy it.

As luck would have it, I dumped that money in a project recommended by W.W. and needless to say, it was a total washout.

I still remember my elder daughter asking me, 'Dad, why did you sell it? Such a beautiful flat?' and W.W. responding, 'Your dad will buy four flats like that or better, in a year. Just watch.'

He felt very bad after the debacle and promised to reimburse the cost of the flat 'when he received his funds'.

I believe him; he is not like the family friend who sank my money without remorse. Only problem is W.W. is yet to take off. His career is like a plane running up runway, losing nerve at time of takeoff, and returning to hangar.

About that time, computers were beginning to pickup, and Windows, DOS, were taught in coaching classes and computer literacy was much sought after. I joined one class at Liberty Talkies second floor. I wanted to be computer literate before going to UAE as chief engineer of power plant.

I got friendly with the owner. There were not many students so we used to discuss several things.

One day he told me, 'Do you know, I think our city is going to develop and expand in a big way, I have purchased several plots in outskirts for 50k to 60k. I suggest you also buy a few plots.'

I took his advice and took my wife (then I started involving her in all my decisions) and booked a plot in one place, close to a movie studios on instalment basis, and left for the foreign country where I got a shore job.

I paid eighteen instalments, and when I returned to India on annual leave, I was shocked when that real estate developer told me that the project ran into troubles as proposed ring road could cut through our plots. I stopped payment and said I would pay everything once it was sorted out. The manager used to plead with me to pay instalments to avoid being labelled defaulter.

I refused and two, three years passed. One day, one of our relatives casually asked me if I saw outskirt areas recently. I said no and asked him why.

'You will not believe, you feel as if you are transported to US or West, such magnificent development has occurred in such a short time. I really envy the people who had foresight of buying land when it was dirt cheap,' he said sadly.

We immediately went and tried to locate our land in a concrete jungle.

Manager was very happy when I told him I was willing to pay the entire outstanding amount. He told me outer ring road was passing more than a kilometre away from our plots. Hence there was no worry.

Unfortunately I had to join a ship urgently and I told my wife to give a cheque to him. My wife was reluctant to go to office and sent Mr W.W. with the cheque.

Mr W.W. returned an hour later and fired at my wife, 'When will your husband stop doing such silly and idiotic things? I asked Mr R.B. to show municipal sanctions, approvals. He did not. I threatened him I will drag him to court for cheating public and I did not give him cheque, here is the cheque.'

When I returned after my contract, Manager not only refused to receive payment, I was declared defaulter. To make me more miserable, people were approaching to buy the land from me for a huge amount; their only condition was that the passbook entries were to be up to date and that I should not be a defaulter.

I had no option but to take back the amount I paid the developers without interest.

Mr W.W. is not a bad man. He just suffers from a massive ego that he alone is a smart man and rest all are dumb and stupid and he has no patience in dealing with stupid people, so he goes alone on his ego trip.

After that debacle, we did what we should have done earlier. We stopped discussing with him about anything, and seeking opinion or advice. It is not the fault of a tiger cub if it scratches and bites you if you try to cuddle it. You should learn to admire it from a distance. Similarly, it was not Mr W.W.'s fault if he was instrumental in all our debacles. We should not have sought his help or advice.

But unlike the share fiasco, all is not lost. Some eggs are still in good shape. One house is still intact and is my insurance for marriage expenses of my daughters. There are some plots which went into hibernation after local unrest. In entire India, real estate boomed everywhere else, except in my city. Maybe I made a mistake in putting all my eggs in one basket; I should have invested in other states where I had good friends.

GOLD

I mentioned somewhere about our forgetfulness. I hesitated in buying gold, since it requires lot of care and effort in preserving it. The small gold bangles which my in-laws presented to my daughter on her first birthday did not last even few hours. Someone pulled them off from her tiny hands.

My wife and kids belong to a rare category; they have no fascination or desire for gold. Unlike many wives, my wife never pestered me about gold ornaments. So we did not acquire anything substantial.

STORY OF B

As I mentioned earlier, B had very limited resources and was finding it difficult to make both ends meet. Every day he would travel extensively in buses and on foot, to sell plots of Mr Murthy or collection of funds. Most of his clientele was from middle and lower middle class, who would purchase lands on monthly installment schemes and he had to make several trips on collection drive.

His children were quite good in studies, so he had to provide for their education.

But he is deeply religious. He spends several hours in pooja and visiting temples and attending religious discourses. He is very kind-hearted and philanthropic, in the sense he would take aged people every year on Kashi, Prayaga, Badrinath, and Kedarnath trips. I was curious and asked him several times if he didn't have anxious moments if and when some of the aged people had health issues, since it is a physically demanding pilgrimage.

He would laugh and tell me that God was great and would look after His devotees and anyway, he would take many precautions like taking a cook and utensils along and they were provided homely food most of the time.

And his wife was a lady with great fascination and desire for golden ornaments. Daily she would pester him for bangles, necklaces, etc. and daily he would pray to God to fulfill her desire to such an extent that she herself would say, 'Enough, no more.' He also would tell her to be patient and give him time.

For the last thirty years, he would deposit Rs 100, 200, or 500, whichever and whenever he could spare in gold schemes. When a sufficient amount accumulated, he would buy a bangle or a chain.

At the end of thirty years he had accumulated several kilograms of gold, so much that his wife did indeed plead with him to buy no more; it was enough. With the present gold price, if he were to sell even partially and retire, he could lead a very happy, comfortable life.

Is there a lesson? There is.

Please do not dissect, analyze, and judge my actions and inactions since nothing can be gained. I may have missed out living in mansions but I don't regret much. There is more joy in sharing and watching TV together, fighting for control of remote. Sometimes I sacrifice cricket (anyway, whenever I watch, India play horribly and lose miserably), and at other times, kids volunteer to sacrifice their shows. It is a better alternative to having your own home theatre in your room and watching programs alone.

But one advice I would give. Had I read the book *Rich Dad, Poor Dad* in my younger days, I would not have committed so many blunders.

Ponder and make decisions wisely. Good luck!

MOHAMAATITIS

Unlike hepatitis, mohamaatitis (caused by a virus called *mohamaatam*)is not a virulent, contagious, or dangerous disease. It causes the patient some inconvenience, embarrassment, and sometimes, indigestion. There is no known cure.

I tried searching a suitable English word for *mohamaatam*. Shyness, hesitancy, etc. come close but do not accurately describe it.

My wife's distant cousin is afraid of darkness, ghosts, cannot sleep alone and is afraid of heights and is scared of going on rides, let alone riding in a giant wheel. But he is a *nirmohammaati* (one who doesn't suffer from *mohamaatam* malady). I am not afraid of darkness, ghosts and enjoy riding in daredevil rides, but have been a victim and am a *mohamaati..* (There is no such word; it is my invention. I am lazy to type *mohamatastudu*).

You may find that firebrand orators like Kejriwal or Modi are *mohamaatis* if you invite them to lunch or dinner, hesitating to ask for a chapatti or second helping and politely declining even if you push them. So it is really a complex phenomenon. Tigers would become lambs when seated before a dining table in an alien environment other than home or when forced to accept hospitality of others.

I think we *mohamaatis* emit a fragrance or send signals like a tracking device. We can't hide even in a crowd. If a thousand guests are present and you sit for lunch and hope the crowd will camouflage you, you will find the host stopping in front of you, calling his nephews, nieces, aunts, and uncles and declaring in a loud voice, 'See, this fellow is a *mohamaati*. He will not ask for anything. So ensure he eats well.'

You try to shrink and cringe as several eyes focus on you, as if looking at an interesting and endangered species. Then starts the grueling task of thwarting enthusiastic relatives who are bent on seeing you burst open like Lord Ganesha in that story where Chandra, Moon God, is cursed by Goddess Parvati, Ganesha's mother, since Chandra, unfortunately, could not control laughter when he saw the spectacle.

They refuse to heed to your pleadings for mercy and keep dumping items on your plate, under the mistaken impression that you are feeling shy to ask for second and third helpings. Only way you can make them stop is to cover your plate with your back by being prostate, which you are reluctant to do.

You feel anger surging against elders who drilled into your head that you should not waste or throw away any food item, since farmer uncle had toiled day and night in rain and hot sun to produce the rice, vegetables, etc. and he would be hurt.

We, *mohamaatis* of the universe, are eternally grateful to the genius who invented the buffet system. He or she must have suffered untold miseries and must have felt 'Enough is enough,' and invented buffet to escape.

There is an interesting story about a *mohamaati* son-in-law. This story was told by my aunt in my childhood.

One *mohamaati* son-in-law visited his wife's parents during a festive season. He liked Gongura chutney immensely but hesitated to ask for second helping and declined when they offered while serving, because of *mohamaatam*. In the night he could not sleep, he could not forget the taste and had an irresistible craving. He got up quietly and tiptoed into kitchen and searched everywhere. He was disappointed to see it was consumed. But he could find some left in the *rubburolu* (original manual wet grinding equipment of villages). He put his head inside and licked the chutney, and his head was stuck inside.

He had to stay the whole night in that ignominious position, and imagine his embarrassment next day when his mother-in-law found him in that condition.

When I was married, I had a tough time when invited for lunch or dinner. Those days they did not have dining table. We had to sit on the ground.

My father-in-law had a few idiosyncrasies. He wanted piping hot rice and dishes. My mother-in-law would be alert and serve a small quantity of rice and dal or sabji. The rice would be so steaming hot, vapours would be swirling. He had a technique of mixing rice and other items and eating without burning his fingers or scalding his mouth, tongue, and throat. I suppose it is the same technique used by people who walk on coal fires. They walk fast without giving chance for fire to burn.

Once he finishes that small quantity, Mother-in-law would again serve a small quantity of hot rice and another item. His theory was that plate should not be clustered with many items.

I was always in a tight spot. I tried mixing hot rice and burnt my fingers and scalded my tongue and mouth when I tried to eat that hot food. So, I would wait till it cooled down to tolerable temperature. Father-in-law, meanwhile, would finish his first course and would be waiting patiently for me to catch up with him. When I managed to finish the first course, mother-in-law would again serve a small quantity of piping hot rice. By the time I completed my meal, it felt as if I was sitting there for a year. My father-in-law also was intrigued.

After a few such instances, I shunned *mohamaatam* and told my wife that the solution was to serve me food at tolerable temperature and large quantity at a time and piping hot in small quantities to Father-in-law as he desired. My mother-in-law must have heaved a sigh of relief. Though my father-in-law must have felt that I was an unrefined tribal not to appreciate steaming hot food, he did not voice his thoughts. My mother-in-law had to do several bending, stretching exercises everyday in serving food to her large family. She remains thin like a reed even now.

When I visit in-laws or relatives where my wife has full access to kitchen and when sometimes they forget or overlook to offer coffee or tea, I developed a code word to pass on message to Wife that I desire a cup of coffee.

Background story is, one very brilliant football champion in a college was a big zero in academics. The champion won many trophies for college. Principal wanted to help him.

So he told him that he would ask him to write spelling of one word he would dictate, he would pass him if even one letter in the spelling was correct. Champion was quite happy; it could not get any easier than this.

Principal asked him to write spelling of 'coffee'; champion wrote 'kaphy'.

I used to spell to wife K-A-P-H-Y. She would bring. Some smart people deciphered it, so now a days I just say, 'K-A.'

I am quite fond of coconut chutney served with idli, dosa, etc. My elder daughter inherited my liking (I don't know why my kids have not inherited many admirable qualities of wife, except beauty). We like chutney so much; we consume huge quantity of chutney equal to the size of idlis. Normally one small cup is sufficient for others.

Now, it would be embarrassing to keep asking for refills of chutney. So I had a code word, 'Gabriel' (sounds close to *kobbari*, Telugu word for coconut). I would whisper to wife, 'Gabriel,' and she would serve me more coconut chutney. I think my eldest brother coined that term first.

Until a few months back, my elder daughter was under the impression that 'Gabriel' was another name for coconut and used to wonder why some people named themselves after coconut. She was flabbergasted when she learnt the story behind 'Gabriel'.

Younger daughter laughed and laughed, since she had a chance to ridicule her 'smart' sister.

She was very upset and said she would have been hugely embarrassed by such ignorance.

The process of unlearning is more difficult than learning.

Tailpiece:

One day my elder daughter was working on her computer. I and Wife were finalizing list of friends and relatives to whom we had to send invitation cards for a function

I was writing addresses on envelopes.

'What is the real name of Sutti Velu?' I asked Wife.

My wife flared up. 'You and your nicknames, even I am forgetting their real names...' and she told me.

As I was writing his name on envelope, Elder Daughter jumped a foot in the air.

'What? It is not his real name?' she asked, worried.

Younger Daughter burst out laughing. 'Come on, will anyone have such name?'

Elder Daughter clutched her head in hands. 'My God, what have I done?' she moaned.

We asked her what happened.

It seems when we attended the marriage of a cousin, she came across him. They talked for a long time on several topics. He was quite pleased.

'Do you know who I am?' he asked her.

'Yes. You are the father of so-and-so,' she told him.

He was not satisfied; he kept prodding her. She told him that he was the husband of so-and-so.

'No, do you know my name?' he asked her.

'Of course, I know. It is Sutti Velu,' she told him innocently.

She said she didn't understand why his mood was suddenly off.

'I know who is the culprit, I will hang that fellow.' He left, muttering angrily.

Wife recollected him thrashing her cousin later, and at that time, she wondered why.

'So you were the culprit? Not my poor cousin?' Wife accused me.

I shifted uncomfortably. 'Maybe. I don't remember. Maybe it was a collective effort. Can you blame us? Doesn't he remind you of that actor and doesn't he hammer like him?' I said apologetically.

Though she agreed, Wife didn't reconcile easily.

My daughters pleaded with me to come out openly and educate them about all nicknames, pseudonyms, and whatever wrong information I fed them from childhood.

I remained silent. Where to begin?

IS IT IMPOSSIBLE
TO FORGIVE?

All of us are hurt, invariably, at one time or other, by colleagues, friends, relatives, or bosses. Some memories fade, others remain fresh like raw wounds, refusing to be healed by passage of time. Sometimes, it would seem impossible to forgive a person and you are not inclined to do so even if that person apologizes and seeks forgiveness. Our trials, tribulations seem unbearably heavy and persons responsible for that, utterly detestable and loathsome.

When I was a chief engineer in a ship that frequently visited South Africa, I used to enjoy watching several good programs on TV in my cabin. One day, I was surfing channels. Normally, I skip talk shows. I prefer to watch news, English movies, and sports. On one channel one beautiful lady was interviewing a dark, African young woman. I was about to change the channel, when one word made me pause. It was 'Rwanda'.

As all of us know, that tiny, impoverished African nation that was witness to a most gruesome genocide. The number of people killed was on par with Bosnia and Nazi Holocaust. Its geographical obscurity and unimportant status had diminished the actual horror in the eyes of civilized world. Two tribes, Tutsi and Hutu, suddenly went into a frenzy and killing spree; tens of thousands of people perished in that madness. They were too poor to afford machine guns, AK-47s, or grenades.

So they massacred with hatchets, sickles, sticks and stones, or whatever they could find.

That young black woman was from Rwanda, sole survivor of her family. She managed to escape and seek asylum. It was a very difficult interview and full marks to the host of the show. She spoke slowly, in measured tones, always sympathetic and understanding.

It was very well made. They reconstructed scenes to make the show gripping and riveting.

Rwandan girl was speaking slowly and narrating her story. When I started watching, she was describing how she was hiding terror struck in the bathroom as she listened to the screams and sounds of mayhem.

'Could you see anything from where you were hiding?' host asked.

'No. I shut my eyes and was struggling to stifle my cries,' she said.

'Did you see the killers?' host asked.

'There were several, brandishing hatchets, axes, and knives. Before I closed the bathroom door, I had one look at one of the men. His clothes, hair were all drenched in blood. He was wielding a hatchet. He didn't see me,' she said.

Then they reconstructed the scene. Girl crouching behind a plastic drum, screams and shouts slowly coming to a stop and then silence.

'Let us leave now.' Man in charge gave a command.

The man the girl had seen wanted to check the bathroom and in fact starts opening the door when he is pulled up by the man in charge to leave.

A few more seconds, and the girl would have been killed.

Both ladies were silent for a few minutes.

'Every night I have nightmares, I see him in dream, scream, and wake up,' said the young black woman.

'What will be your reaction if you come across him?' the lady asked.

Young black woman thought for a while and said, 'Nothing.'

'Nothing? Don't you want to see him tried for murder and see him hang?' lady asked.

Young woman shrugged. 'What is the use and what is the purpose? If we start hanging then you have to kill one third of the number already murdered. It was a momentary madness and even my tribe people also murdered. There would be no end to the cycle of violence,' she said.

'Would you like to meet him? If so, why?' lady asked.

'Yes. I would like to meet him. Only for one reason. Once I see that he is an ordinary person and not a devil or a monster, the demons tormenting me may be exorcised and I may be able to get peaceful sleep,' young woman said wistfully.

After a few minutes, the interviewing lady got up and said, 'Please meet that man. He is in the studio.'

A door opened and a tall black man walked in. Young woman sprang to her feet and started screaming. That tall black man was weeping like a small kid, kept saying, 'Please... forgive me... I am sorry...'

As he approached her, she also started weeping bitterly and as they hugged, weeping, credits scrolled onscreen and the program ended without any message.

It disturbed me for few days. I kept thinking what are our hurt egos, pride, troubles, and tribulations worth? Do we have any right to be unhappy or angry when there is so much misery and suffering?

These philosophical thoughts run their course like viral fever and I was back to where I was in due course.

But I firmly believe that you can never change a person's thinking or behaviour by lecturing or sermonizing. Each person has a built-in mechanism to resist any external efforts to do that. Any change is possible only if that person's mind allows it of its own accord.

My father-in-law had a terrible temper. But he was quite enthusiastic about learning new and exciting things. So I encouraged and accompanied him to undergo reiki meditation and Sudershan Kriya (Art of Living) courses. After a few months there was a sea change; he complained that he was unable to generate anger even when my fathier-in-law felt he was justified in venting out anger.

I had the privilege to attend Art of Living advanced course at Bangalore under Sri Sri Ravi Shankerji's guidance.

He said that by forgiving a person who caused you harm, you are not doing that person a favour but you are doing yourself a favour. His theory was that once you have forgiven a person, all negative baggage will be removed and you would be happier and healthier. It can be achieved only by saints and yogis, I thought. He said the purpose of meditation and Sudershan Kriya was to make one elevate to that plane.

My unique experience in Bangalore is worth mentioning since it includes my elder daughter also.

All kids love to bunk school. I think it is really tiresome sitting in the same seat for several hours. My daughters are notorious for their shoddy attendance. Teachers and lecturers suspect that we encourage them to bunk and stay at home. They never realized that we left no stone unturned; bribes, threats, and pleadings and shouts—nothing worked. They were stubborn.

My elder daughter would have preferred even solitary confinement to school. So she said would accompany me to Bangalore and would play when I attended the course. My wife was in the family way and was very reluctant to send her with me. I don't fret and fuss like her. I ask the kids a few times to have food; for instance, if they refuse, I shrug and leave them. My wife would keep preparing or ordering different items until they have food to her satisfaction. Hence, she was skeptical and reluctant. But my elder daughter is very stubborn. I suspect some exams must have been round the corner and she wanted an excuse to skip. She was just a little over six years of age.

A/C sleeper coach buses had just started. So, I and my elder daughter set off to Bangalore in A/C bus. I didn't reserve my seat for the course but my teachers told me that I could gatecrash.

When we reached Sri Sri Ravi Shankerji's ashram next day, I was told that there were no seats, the entire course was booked by a Reiki practitioners group from Mumbai. We were disappointed and dejected. I thought I would request the person in charge before heading back home.

After an hour, hordes and hordes of people landed, quashing any hopes that I had.

I approached one Shyamalaji, their guru and asked her, 'I came from another city with my young daughter, I am very keen to do this course. I see the course is overbooked. But can you please accommodate me?'

She was dark, beautiful, and huge. I think plump people are friendlier, happier, and kindlier. Thin people are irritable whenever their stomachs are empty.

She gave one look at me and daughter and laughed loudly. 'You came because Sri Sri ji wanted you to come. Squeeze in. You can always find some place to sit in the hall.'

I thanked her and paid the fee. Now the problem was I and daughter could not stay in same room. I was allotted a bed in one cottage with other males. Daughter had to stay with several other kids in another cottage. She was the youngest and others were all teenagers and had their own groups.

In the night I could not sleep; I went to kids' cottage to check on my daughter. She was sleeping on a cot adjacent to an open window. Bangalore can become really cold at night. She didn't cover herself with a blanket and was shivering and her teeth were chattering. I covered her with blanket and kicked up a row I refused to leave her in their custody and slept beside her.

She was happy about absconding school but didn't expect the boredom would be so overwhelming. All other kids had their own groups. She would be asleep when I went to attend classes; when she woke up no one would be around, she skipped breakfast. I would see her at lunchtime only. She missed her mother and was homesick.

After two days she declared war. She wanted to go home. In our course, we had to keep silence for two days. We were not allowed to talk; we had to communicate only with gestures. Guruji wanted us to experience the joy and beauty of silence. I could not convince her to be patient for a few more days.

So I went and met the organizer.

I wrote on a piece of paper. 'I have to go back to drop daughter at home. She is refusing to stay even for few hours.'

She told me that I cannot leave without Guruji's permission. I did not attend class; I asked her to take me to Guruji.

After waiting for about thirty minutes, that lady took me and Daughter inside.

Guruji was clad in spotless white dhoti. He was radiant and his smile was magnetic.

When I was about to talk, he stopped me. 'You cannot break silence.'

I told him, 'Guruji, I am forced to discontinue the course. So it doesn't matter if I talk.'

He smiled at me. 'Why do you want to discontinue?' he asked me; there was no anger.

'My daughter is homesick. She never left her mother. She is refusing to stay,' I told him.

He called her and made her sit in his lap and told me to go and attend class.

'But…' I wanted to tell him.

'Don't worry. She will be fine and will stay happily,' he told me. I reluctantly left.

What transpired and how he convinced her, I don't know. Maybe my daughter will share with us when she writes her own blog. But that was a magnificent gift my daughter was bestowed with. His disciples do not allow anyone to touch his feet while seeking blessings.

That lady who took us to meet him told Daughter later, 'You don't know how lucky you are. You sat in his lap and he showered his blessings and love. People consider themselves lucky if they can see him from close quarters.'

On the last day, when the course had come to an end, Guruji called all the kids to come on stage, hugged and blessed them. It was amazing to see him laugh and play with kids with such innocence and carefree manner. Suddenly he stopped and asked, 'Where is my young friend?' He called out my daughter's name and she went onstage and joined the group. That was one memorable experience.

We, people who sail on ships, have to battle many enemies: rough seas, pirates, and many others. When you are battling angry, violent seas, you can become demoralized, exhausted, and quite pessimistic. If pirates manage to capture the ship, the fate of the crew is no less bad than that of prisoners of war or people in concentration camps. Anyone who dares to talk to captors is shot dead. You can only speak if they ask you something. You have to survive on a biscuit or a bread slice and a glass of water. The survivors' stories shocked the civilized world.

But rough seas and piracy attacks are seasonal or territorial. Once you pass out of the piracy-prone zones or stormy seas, you can relax. But the one enemy that will not leave him until he gets down from the ship is loneliness. That is his worst enemy. He is away from family and friends, and any tense or anxious event at home, like an illness of a family member or a financial debacle, can make him feel miserable. Now, ships have only eighteen to twenty-one people of different nationalities onboard, irrespective of the size of the ship. No one has the patience or time to listen to others' woes.

To survive in ships, you must like your own company and solitude. Even before I read *The Secret* by Rhonda Byrne, I mastered the art of diverting mind from dangerous, negative thoughts. I had my own share of worries: health issues of wife, parents, in-laws, and sometimes kids, financial crunches and a few irritating fights with relatives. Once the mind starts to think about how miserable you are, it keeps reminding you of many aspects to make you more miserable and sad. This geometric progression continues until you lose your sleep, health, and well-being.

Only way out is to forcibly divert it to think of pleasant and happy moments and events. I keep a complete set of Asterix comic books in PDF format on my desktop in engine control room and one book of *Three Men in a Boat* by Jerome K. Jerome. The moment my mind warms up to remind me how and why I should be sad, miserable, and unhappy, I open any Asterix book or any chapter of *Three Men in a Boat* and start reading. Within seconds the clouds will lift.

When I found that on certain occasions this ploy was not working and though eyes were reading, the mind was refusing to let go of negative thoughts, I started writing my blog. I found this to be fail-safe, since mind has to leave everything and go back, search, and retrieve memories from archives, and those pleasant memories will definitely keep my mind happy and free from negative thoughts.

KARNA

The terms, forgiveness and generosity are synonymous with Karna, the legendary hero of the epic *Mahabharata*. *Mahabharata* has many characters, each equally fabulous, with unique strengths and weaknesses, and several volumes can be written about each character.

In fact, several full-length movies have been made on Karna's story and many books written.

I will briefly write his story since it is appropriate here.

Once, one great sage visited a king. King deployed his own daughter instead of servants to look after him. Sage was quite pleased with her devotion and hard work and granted her a boon.

Any god to whom she prays would appear before her and grant her wishes.

Next morning, Princess was curious to find out if the boon really worked. She prayed to Surya, the sun god, since her gaze fell on the rising sun.

He appeared in full glory and splendour. He was so handsome a thought entered Princess's mind unbidden, 'How I wish I had a son like him.'

And next instant there was a beautiful male baby in her lap and Surya vanished. After the initial joy and euphoria at being blessed with such a gorgeous baby, Princess was gripped by panic and fear. How could she explain the baby to her parents and others?

So she placed the baby in a bamboo basket and let it drift in the river. Downstream, a charioteer who was bathing in the river found the basket and the baby. He had no children so he and his wife accepted the blessing from God and brought him up.

The baby was born with armour like a second skin. They knew he was not an ordinary mortal. They named him Karna.

Karna excelled in all martial arts, weapons. He was prolific in archery. Prince of that Kaurava kingdom noticed him and they became best friends, irrespective of the class divide.

During an archery competition, when Karna is forbidden to participate since he is not from royal lineage, Kaurava prince immediately makes him a ruler of a province; such was their friendship.

Meanwhile, the mother of Karna got married and had three sons, and second wife of king had two sons. The sons were called Pandavas.

Kauravas and Pandavas are cousins and Kauravas grab Pandavas' empire by deceit and refuse to give them back their kingdom after all obligations are fulfilled by Pandavas and a fierce war ensues.

Karna's mother recognizes him when she sees him in the archery contest.

Among all the Pandavas, Arjun was the one most feared by Kauravas because of his archery skills. So Kaurava prince banked heavily on Karna to defeat him.

Like Karna was a gift from Surya, the sun god, Arjun was a gift from Indra, king of gods. Indra wants to protect his god son and plans to deprive Karna of his natural armour.

Karna is so famous for his generosity and donations, even today his name is invoked when referring to very generous, philanthropic, and kind-hearted persons.

Any needy person could approach Karna and beg or request anything, anytime and Karna would never say no. In fact, once one friend asks him why he was donating with left hand sometimes since it is not considered appropriate, Karna replies that he is worried that in the split second it takes to shift from left to right hand, his mind might change and he might refuse to donate.

Once, one poor Brahmin comes to his house and requests for firewood he needed for his daughter's marriage. Because of heavy rains, not a single dry wooden piece was available to cook food for the guests. Karna gets the wooden beams of his house cut and gives to him.

There are many such stories about his generosity.

So Indra plans to don the attire of a poor Brahmin and beg him for his armour. Surya gets wind of this and rushes and warns Karna, his son.

But Karna obliges Indra; he slices his armour plates, gives them to Indra, and tells him, 'Why did you take the trouble to disguise? Even if you asked as Indra, in your own form, I would have given to you.'

One day before the battle, Karna's mother comes to his tent and reveals that she is his mother. He is astonished to know that he is the eldest brother of the Pandavas and he was going to fight his own brothers.

Karna's mother urges him to come back and be coroneted as king. Since Kaurava prince is his friend, matters could be solved amicably and his friend would give back kingdom happily.

Karna refuses; he tells her she abandoned him but his friend gave him love, prestige, honour, and respect. So he would die for him and his loyalty was to his friend.

Finally he tells her that he would spare all her sons, except Arjun. Either he would live or Arjun would; either way she would have five sons. His forgiveness is the ultimate.

In the fierce Kurukshetra battle, he gets many chances to kill his brothers but he lets them go, on the day when he finally confronts Arjun.

Karna is very unfortunate; he is cursed by so many sages and gods, for no fault of his. All curses combine on that eventful day, resulting in his death.

Karna requests one sage to accept him as disciple and teach powerful mantras to invoke in archery. Sage tells him he would teach him only if he is a Brahmin. Karna lies to him. Sage accepts him and teaches him.

One afternoon, Sage is sleeping with his head in Karna's lap. Indra senses that his son Arjun will stand no chance if Karna invokes the mantra the sage had taught. So he transforms himself into a bee and bites Karna's thigh. Karna bears the pain stoically and does not move; he doesn't want to disturb his guru's sleep.

The bee keeps drilling into Karna's thigh and his clothes start getting drenched in blood. Sage's sleep is disturbed because of wetness. He gets up and is shocked to see Karna's condition.

Sage is outraged. 'You cannot be a Brahmin. You lied to me. No Brahmin can tolerate such excruciating pain.'

Karna confesses and Sage gives him a curse: Karna would forget the mantra when he needs it most, and Karna cannot recollect when he wanted to use it against Arjun.

On another occasion, one small girl is weeping by the side of the road. Karna stops his chariot and asks her what is the matter. Little girl says she was bringing cooking oil, the container fell, and oil had soaked in sand and her mother would scold her.

Karna squeezed sand with his hands and extracts oil back into girl's container. Mother Earth gets angry and gives a curse. His chariot's wheel would get stuck when he requires it most.

When Karna is engaged with Arjun in warfare, earth caves in and his chariot's wheel gets stuck. Arjun strikes him with his arrows as Karna tries to lift the wheel up with both hands.

As Karna is in death throes, Arjuna gloats. Krishna admonished him that Karna was a great warrior and a very generous person and needs to be respected.

To demonstrate, Krishna and Arjun approach Karna in the disguise of poor Brahmins and ask him to donate. Karna asks them what a dying man can give and then recollects he has a golden tooth; he takes a stone and breaks it and gives to them.

He realizes it has blood on it and gathers strength and shoots an arrow into earth, and when water jets out, he washes the tooth and gives it to them.

Karna is an epitome of forgiveness, hence I added his story.

FLASH IN THE PAN

I have recorded somewhere in my earlier posts how navigating officers and engineers are like cats and dogs and suffer each other's presence like a necessary nuisance. But I was privileged to have excellent friendship with all the captains I sailed with. I retained my integrity, dignity and never compromised on several operational issues and had heated arguments with them on many occasions, but at the end of the day, we would open couple of beers, relax, and be friends again.

In Asterix comics, the first sentence is 'Romans occupied all Gaul? All? One small village of indomitable Gauls still holds out.' Similarly I was reminded of my friendship with all captains. All? No, I had very bitter, acrimonious fights with a couple of them. I would have bashed up one of them, had my second engineer not restrained me. I lost my cool to the point of being tempted to bash up the perpetrator on only two or three occasions. I actually was involved in a fist-fight only once, during my college days.

Once our ship was berthed, an Italian port which was not completely shielded from sea, and we were forbidden to undertake any major maintenance on main engines, since in case of rough seas, we required engines to take corrective action. One of the main engine units was due for major overhaul and Captain was daily insisting that I immobilize the engine and overhaul clandestinely, without informing port authorities.

I refused to compromise safety of the ship and personnel. He argued that he was monitoring weather forecasts and he would take responsibility. Still I refused to break the law of the land. If any shore person observed or crew member leaked out the information, I would straightaway be imprisoned. Captain can always get away, claiming that he was not aware.

Captain started taunting me several times saying that I was unprofessional and a shirker of responsibilities. Finally, I got fed up, talked to the superintendent of the company, warned him of the dangers and made my stand clear and overhauled the engine on a weekend. In Europe, it is almost impossible to make people work on weekend, hence we took a calculated risk.

His tirade and taunts didn't end. I completely ignored and avoided him. But he would seize any opportunity, like in elevator or at dinner table, to taunt and provoke me. I was about to sign off in the next few days and wanted to avoid a confrontation.

One day he barged into engine control room and started shouting. It was my domain. I asked him to shut up and leave, and if he didn't, I would bash him up. He didn't stop and I lost my cool. I advanced to hit him; my second engineer had to physically restrain me. Captain panicked and left.

After I cooled down, Sri Lankan second engineer told me, 'Maybe I should have allowed you to bash him up. He richly deserved it.'

One day before I signed off, he called me to his cabin. He showed me an appraisal report; he had shredded me to pieces, he commented that I was incompetent, rude, abusive, lacking any skill or knowledge. Anyone reading his appraisal report would wonder how I could have served as a chief engineer for so long. He expected me to fall at his feet and beg for mercy and to plead with him to consider my kids' future.

I was prepared for this. In the space for officer's comments, I wrote 'I totally disagree with Master's observations. In fact, the report should be viewed as a self-assessment. Attached please see my report' and I signed and asked him to send his appraisal report with my report attached. I took a copy of both reports, asked him to acknowledge and sign in my copy.

'You don't trust me to send your report? Master of the ship?' he asked angrily.

'No, I don't trust you to attach my report after reading it,' I told him point-blank and left. I went to recreation room and was watching a movie.

Within twenty minutes, he came running down. His face was ashen.

'Come to my cabin,' he asked me. I went.

'What is this? Do you know I know MD and all top brass personally? I can ruin your career,' he shouted at me.

'Then, by all means do so. If company decides to sack me after reading your appraisal report and my report, then they don't deserve to have me in their ranks,' I told him coolly. I had mentally geared myself not to bash him up, irrespective of any provocation.

'If you withdraw your report, I will make another appraisal report. A good one.' He tried to coax me.

'No. This report and attachment will go as they are,' I told him firmly.

He was fair like a European. His face was flushed red with anger.

'I will destroy your career,' he shouted.

'You can't do a damn thing. Try your best,' I told him and left.

He was very nervous and was like a cat on a hot tin roof. He kept pacing up and down the alleyway, and when I was about to fall asleep, someone knocked on the door. It was Chief Officer; he tried to persuade me to take a lenient view and try to forgive and forget. I politely told him that it had reached a point of no return.

I went home next day. A month later, I received a phone call from office. Superintendent talked for great length. I expected his call much sooner. It seems Captain didn't send reports in mail from that port but waited for Superintendent's visit at next port and told his version first, and then handed over the reports.

It had no advantage. He continued to have fights with Chief Officer and other officers and was signed off at next port when all officers refused to sail with him. He later joined as a chief officer in a container ship. I was given a prestigious assignment.

Tailpiece: That chief officer had sailed with Aishwarya Rai and her parents. Her father was chief engineer of that ship. He said that Aishwarya was a cute little girl and they all went to Mr Rai's house for dinner when ship went to Mumbai.

I also had the honour and privilege to meet the great man. He is so humble, down to earth. He kept addressing me as 'sir'.

CAN ONE PERSON
CHANGE SYSTEM?

Captains and other deck officers have one handicap: they are not educated, I mean, academically. They join as cadets after tenth class or intermediate and they have no college education.

But knowledge and education need not necessarily go together. I have sailed with some masters who were extremely intelligent and very well-read with profound all-round knowledge and some graduate engineers who were deplorably dumb.

I had the privilege to sail with Capt. Prakash. He is a cousin brother of Hemant Karkare, the gallant police officer who was martyred in 26/11. He is a thorough gentleman, soft-spoken and extremely knowledgeable about any subject under, over, and beyond sun.

Once we were talking about filthy cities. I told him Surat was the filthiest city I had seen so far, the streets and pavements filled with heaps of rotten garbage and people living there as if it was normal. I said that even God can do nothing to salvage that city.

He was silent for a few seconds and asked, 'Which year did you visit Surat?'

I told him it was 1993.

He got up, brought a magazine and gave it to me, *India Today*, I think.

The cover story was about Surat. How it became the cleanest city and the transformation was so amazing that teams from Singapore and other places were coming to study.

'You can read later, I will give you the gist. One Mr Swami, an honest IAS officer, was shunted and transferred all over the place, as he would step on toes of all local high and mighty. Yet he maintained his honesty and integrity. When he was posted to Surat, Chief Minister called him to discuss about cosmetic upgrading of the city. Swami asked Chief Minister for an assurance that he would not be transferred for two years irrespective of political or social pressures. Chief Minister gave his promise.

'The bottleneck at railway station was the root cause of congestion of traffic and accumulation of filth. This was due to one old construction of one local strongman cum politician. No one dared touch a brick, let alone demolish. Swami got all legal documents, permissions from court clandestinely and started demolition on Friday night. The politician could do nothing as Chief Minister was backing Swami. Once that building was removed, suddenly traffic woes eased up and public loved him so much, they gave him full support.

'They respected and revered him so much that they mended their littering habits voluntarily. Correspondent related one incident where one small schoolboy threw chocolate wrapper on pavement, his sister nagged him and made him pick it up and put in dustbin. "Swami uncle will be upset. Do you want to see him sad?" was what his little sister was telling him, not "Swami uncle will be angry, he will punish you," etc.

Someone should get a brainwave, which has an emotional button to motivate the public to shed its reluctance to change and lethargy.

Then Capt. Prakash told about another retired police officer.

In Mumbai (all Mumbaikars will know) there is a very posh locality with all skyscraper buildings, beautiful wide roads, except for one particular stretch of a few hundred yards. That stretch of road is used as a public lavatory for slum-dweller kids. The stench is so overpowering, people in cars with powerful A/C s have to hold their breath until they pass that stretch of road. No one could do anything about it for political reasons. Everyone accepted and learnt to live with it.

One honest retired police officer was allotted a plot nearby. He constructed a house there. Daily in the morning he would arrive with a broom and containers and sweep all the feces and dispose them. He neither ranted nor raved at people; he would patiently wait for the slum kids to finish their business. People laughed at him, ridiculed and heckled him. Undeterred, he went about his task.

After a few days, a few local boys came and started helping him. Slowly the area started to become cleaner. Some local politician's conscience must have been pricked (though unlikely) or maybe for political mileage, latrines were constructed and kids and their parents were trained to use them.

Then this retired officer started planting trees; now he had many enthusiastic followers. Within no time, that stretch had become talk of the town for its lush vibrant greenery and beauty.

Capt. Prakash is from Pune. He said he remembered, as a child, a barren hill. A few senior citizens would go up the hill for a walk and exercise. Once, they planted a few saplings on top of the hill, and every day, each would carry a bottle of water and would water the plant with remaining water in their bottles and would go down. He and a few other young boys started following their routine.

Now he says that hill is covered with thick, lush greenery and has huge trees. Those senior citizens remain unsung, unremembered heroes.

He recounted another interesting incident. He is senior to me by a couple of years. Those days, newspapers used to allot considerable space for letters to the editor.

He said he read a letter from a foreigner in that section.

This foreigner was from the USA. He was diagnosed with a serious heart ailment, and those days, open-heart surgeries were not so common and there was a long waiting list. His turn would come after six months. One of his friends told him about some ashrams in India and advised him to go there and spend six months and come back for treatment instead of twiddling thumbs.

He came to India and joined one ashram. The guruji told him that there would be no medication; he had to follow what other swamis were doing: get up with them, accompany them to meditation, lunch, gardening, prayers, and supper. He had to sleep when they slept. He was there for six months.

It was time for him to go. He went to Guruji and told him, 'I am very disappointed. I thought you would give me herbal medicines to cure me. I was neither diagnosed nor treated. All you made me do is eat, pray, work in garden, meditate, and sleep. Now it is time for me to go. I think I wasted my time.'

Guruji smiled at him and asked him, 'Do you see that flag on that hill?'

Guruji told him, 'Run as fast as you can, touch the flag post, and come back.'

He ran up the hill, touched the flag post, and came back.

He asked Guruji, 'Now what?'

Guruji smiled, 'Now nothing. You go home.'

He was very upset and angry, He felt that he had been duped and cheated. He went back to the USA and went to hospital on appointed day for his surgery.

Doctors were shocked. His heart was better than ever, much better than even of people younger to him.

He wrote in that letter to the editor that we Indians did not realize or appreciate our wealth of wisdom or potential of our methods of healing. Instead of getting fascinated and aping the West, we should look inward for solutions.

I am very grateful to Capt. Prakash for not only just enriching my life with inspiring anecdotes but also standing by me in real emergency situations (Please see 'Flooding of Engine Room' and 'Pollution in Fos on Christmas Eve' in 'Close Encounters' folder). He did not lose temper or cool and handled the situations coolly.

Mahatma Gandhi, Nelson Mandela, Gurajada AppaRao, and several others transformed lives of many.

TRAUMATIC SCHOOLING

(These are entirely my personal thoughts. I have no intention to be critical of ambitious parents).

I am not a great fan of Indian schooling. I do not think anyone is, except countries like the US, which import talented and skilled people from India and they may be attributing the abundance of talent to schools. They fail to realize that these people shine not because of schooling, but in spite of it.

I will give a few examples.

When I was in school, there was a lesson about Japan, informing us about how this country is prone to earthquakes and how they live in wooden houses. A few years back, when we visited a relative's house, I was casually flipping through pages of a sixth-class textbook, and there it was, the same lesson, not a word changed!

We are still teaching our children that Japanese live in wooden shacks when they have built skyscrapers with electronically controlled counterweights to prevent collapse of building even at 7 Richter scale earthquake. Yes, kids write exams and get grades but update their knowledge through TV or the Net or books.

My daughter once mugged up a few answers to some questions of a Hindi lesson and asked me to correct her when she recited. I was reading the question and answers and I had a very big jolt.

'What nonsense is this? What are they teaching you? Bring me the textbook,' I asked her, horrified.

I was shocked beyond belief when I completed reading the lesson.

I am a great fan of suspense, horror stories, and movies. The scarier the movie, the better. Horror movies literally keep you on the edge of the seat; there are no ground rules that hero or heroine will be spared. In college days, I was an avid reader of Alfred Hitchcock and horror story series.

So, it is not easy to shock or scare me but that lesson in my daughter's textbook made me lose sleep for few days. Why and how such a story landed up in a children's schoolbook speaks volumes about the total apathy of our education system.

The story goes like this. One chief engineer and his family are living in a bungalow. One gardener, wife, and children live in an outhouse. Chief Engineer and his family are snobbish and high-brow. One day the family dog has a litter of six puppies. Chief Engineer's family doesn't want nuisance of puppies and asks Gardener to dispose of them. So Gardener drowns these yelping puppies in boiling water as his daughter is watching.

Daughter asks him, 'Will you do the same to your kids also if you don't want them?'

Maybe there is a moral or a powerful truth. But is the story suitable for tender minds? Why and how did so many teachers, principals, and authorities not shiver with horror at necessity of teaching such a macabre story?

I wonder if the parents and kids of other countries are subjected to same stress and trauma like their Indian counterparts. Do first-grade kids' moms commit suicide fearing their children might fail? Do teenagers end lives when they fail or fail to score expected marks or even fear failure before results are announced?

Schools and the crazy expectation to excel drive parents, lecturers, and of course, students to nervous breakdowns. Every parent wants child to be state first-rank holder if not college first. In this rat race, one precious commodity that gets lost is childhood fun.

My parents had a much laid-back attitude to education and schooling. My dad never appeared to even see progress report. He would give a cursory glance and sign. Not once did he admonish or demand why I scored lower marks or why my rank dipped. If I approached him with a problem, he would help. When he was transferred to Hyderabad from Rajahmundry, I panicked as Hindi subject had text and non-detailed books, poems, etc., whereas in Rajahmundry school they had not even started teaching alphabets. He would teach me for an hour after he came back from office.

My dad seemed to be happy so long as there were no complaints from school or demands to meet the headmaster. My mom was happy if her kids had healthy appetites and consumed food to her satisfaction and were happy, healthy, laughing, and generally having a good time. While some may argue that this passive indifference is not good for a child's education, at least it didn't make us neurotic, nervous, and successful wrecks.

I remember once one Mr Amos sir (my fourth-grade class teacher) told my dad that he should reward me for my hard work and good grades to motivate me further. My dad was stumped; it never occurred to him that he was expected to reward kids for studying.

'You have a point there. Can you suggest a suitable gift?' Dad asked Amos sir.

Those days you could not walk into a mall and pick up a gift from shelf. Amos sir thought for a while and said, 'Anything. He will appreciate the gesture. An umbrella would be a good idea.'

My dad also lacked imagination (like me—I can never decide on a suitable gift. Once I purchased a necklace with stones embedded for wife in Dubai since the shop owner insisted that this was the latest craze and design. Wife exchanged it in Hyderabad; it was too dull, she said). He bought an umbrella and gave it to me as a gift. Even he was embarrassed to see the umbrella was almost as tall as I was. Those days the folding-type, compact umbrellas were unheard of. I, of course, never used it.

I replicated my parents' laid-back attitude regarding my children's education. I never hounded or harassed them about grades, marks, or ranks. That they slept off happily and didn't use their energies to pursue any hobbies is another matter.

I always was envious of beautiful girls. If I have a choice, I will opt to be born as a beautiful girl any day. A beautiful girl can get married to a handsome, rich boy and lead a leisurely, happy life. When you finish manicuring nails and don't know what to do with heavily weighing time, you can pursue any hobby or passion or do social work. There is no need to meet deadlines, work like a donkey...leave it all to hubby. My daughters are beautiful but it never occurred to me that they could have different thoughts, career passions and goals.

I thought I would get them married after graduation. Now, I realize that all beautiful girls need not think like me; they can be passionate about career, goals and growth. I cannot understand why anyone loves to slog unnecessarily but I have to accept. Had I known about this, maybe I would have hounded them for grades and ranks.

In retrospect, everything went according to plan. Elder Daughter enjoyed laid-back college education, graduated with very good grades, and would have married a rich, handsome US boy if she were not selected in campus selection for Deloitte. Then the career bug bit her, she suddenly realized her immense potential, intelligence, and passion to achieve higher goals. Her razor-sharp brain is making her indispensable wherever she goes. I hope she will guide younger one properly and younger one is sensible enough to be guided.

I insisted on personality growth. I encouraged them to participate in all social activities. They don't have stage fear, are confident and I am sure it will ensure that they achieve their dreams and goals.

Once our ship was at Malayisa anchorage. I was getting all local channels on TV in cabin. I was surfing channels and I was about to skip a talk show on a Tamil channel (Vasantha, I think) when two things made me pause. There were subtitles in English and I read 'Sending Rahul to school was a daily nightmare for us.' Mother was telling an interviewer, one Suma, a smart lady.

I had similar problem with younger daughter. So I was glued to the TV for next hour or so.

A middle-aged couple and a twelve-year-old boy were being interviewed. All three were smiling ear to ear. They were typical upper-middle-class Tamil couple, Boy was plump with glasses. I was puzzled, why were they so happy if kid's schooling is creating hell?

'Did you talk to class teacher and friends?' Suma asked.

'Hundreds of times. They say everything is fine. He will take little more time to adjust,' Dad said.

'What did Rahul tell you? There must have been reasons? Did you ask him?' Suma asked.

'Thousands of times. He clams up. Defiantly he will say he doesn't like that school,' Mom said.

'Why didn't you change school?' Suma asked.

'This is the best school. Very close to home. Travel time is less. What guarantee is there that he would happily go to the other school?' asked Dad.

'Then what happened?' Suma asked.

'We were desperate. Except on Saturday nights we could never sleep properly, the tension of next day's school kept us all edgy. Then one of my friends suggested this "coffee club". I went there and met Mr Sivan and explained to him. He said not to worry, Rahul will be Okay within a month. He is Sivan,' Dad said and gestured to another man sitting quietly.

Sivan said, 'Vanakkam.'

'Did you expect results?' Suma asked.

'Frankly, no. Rahul is very shy, never talks to strangers. We had no hopes at all,' said both Mom and Dad.

Suma turned to face audience and said, 'Now we will talk to Mr Sivan and ask him how he succeeded where everyone else failed,' and turned to Sivan.

'Mr Sivan, what was Rahul's problem? Why teachers, parents could not identify and solve? How could you solve?' she asked him.

'Rahul's problem was he had no friends. He is plump, bespectacled and some of his classmates made fun of him and he went into shell. Even if someone wanted to be friends with him, he was suspicious and would not respond. Then he started having fist fights and it had a cascading effect. He had no control,' Sivan said.

'He could have talked to parents? Teachers?' Suma asked.

'What response can he expect? You must have done or said something wrong. Go and apologize to the other kid, etc. He had no friends so no one would speak on his behalf. He became defiant. It had a snowballing effect,' Sivan said.

'He is shy and doesn't trust anyone. Why did he open up to you?' Suma asked.

'He didn't. He would not even give monosyllabic answer. I even gave my mobile number to him and asked him to call me anytime day or night for anything. He never called,' Sivan said.

'Then how did you break his citadel?' Suma asked.

Sivan laughed.

'Even mightiest fort will have a weak spot. I sensed he was interested in football. So one day I collected football memorabilia and magazines which are not easily available and went to meet him during lunch break. All kids were playing. I called him over and handed over the magazines and books of football. His face lit up. All his classmates crowded around us. Not just Rahul, everyone in his class was crazy about football.

'They were very excited to see so many magazines about their favourite stars and teams. When there was a sizeable crowd, I told Rahul, "Rahul, if you require anything just call me on mobile anytime day or night. If you have doubts in any subject, give me a call. All your teachers are my best friends. Okay?' And I left,' said Sivan.

'Then what happened?' Suma asked.

'Like you put on a switch, suddenly Rahul was popular. Rahul was not alone, he had a very good friend who will take care of him. That friend is a very good friend of their teachers. In addition, he has excellent collection of football magazines. Help and assistance poured from all classmates. His friendship was valued. His detractors became his best friends. Children are not like grown-ups, they forgive and forget easily,' Sivan said.

'When did he finally open up to you?' Suma asked.

'Not suddenly. First day he called, said thank you. Next day he told a sentence or two about an exam. Slowly by the end of a week, he was freely talking about football games, pranks they played, he started talking for even an hour sometimes,' Sivan said.

'We can't thank him enough. Now Rahul doesn't want to skip even a day, even when we ask him to if there is some urgent work,' Rahul's mom said, beaming.

Sivan was modest. 'I did nothing. Entire driving was done by Rahul, I just showed him the path,' Sivan said.

'One last question. Would it have helped if Rahul had an elder sibling? Brother or sister?' Suma asked.

'No. Kids distrust everyone in family. They are the "establishment." It has to be an outsider. They will not open up to teachers, parents, siblings, and friends,' Sivan said.

Tailpiece: I am gratified that none other than A. P. J. Abdul Kalam has endorsed my view.

A. P. J. Abdul Kalam encapsulates my views best. He said, 'Sometimes it's better to bunk a class and enjoy with friends, because today when I look back, marks never make me laugh, but memories do.'

I confess we have many memories to make us laugh; marks make us wince.

HENPECKED HUSBANDS

This term was coined before women's liberation movement and would have incurred wrath of easily irritable feminine population had it been coined now. While husband-pecked hens outnumber henpecked husbands any day, that activity doesn't tickle funny bone but falls under 'domestic violence' category (Please read 'The Reluctant Cupid' for an account of a husband-pecked hen).

While Socrates is the most prominent henpecked husband of ancient times, in India Lord Sri Krishna was one of the first (With due apologies to the religious-minded, my impression was based on a movie in which NTR acted as Lord Krishna and Jamuna as Satyabhama).

In my school days, there was a lesson in non-detailed textbook. Chandika, a shrew and a pecking hen of highest calibre, harasses husband to desperation. Whenever he tells her to do anything, she purposely does exactly the opposite. If he wants her to welcome guests, she would chase them away with a broom. If he wants his favourite dish to be made and brings vegetables, she would burn it to cinders.

One of his bright friends gives him a brilliant idea, to tell her exactly opposite of what he wants to be done. It worked like magic. He would tell her that his friends or guests were coming to visit. They were to be insulted, humiliated, and thrown out after showering choicest abuses. She would welcome them and treat them like royalty. He would tell her he wanted his favourite dish to be burnt like coal and she would make a very tasty dish. He was very happy but he had to remember constantly that he had to tell the opposite. The story culminates when he forgets for an instant and asks her to pay respect to *pindas* (offerings to departed souls of parents, grandparents) during yearly ceremonies of his parents. She promptly takes them and dumps them in garbage pile.

In another story, an irritable wife has a habit of breaking earthen pots on husband's head if she gets irritated by anything, even if he is in no way responsible for her irritation. Then she would pester him to buy new pots for next requirement.

Bapu, the greatest cartoonist of our times, has immortalized henpecked husbands and pecking hens in his cartoons. If he were born in the Western world, he would have been worshipped; such is his expertise and fluidity of expression with a few strokes of his brush.

Invariably, pecking hen is an obese, scowling lady (*pakkinti laavu paati pinni garu*). Husband is wafer-thin, bespectacled, and mild (more like R.K.Laxman's common man).

In one cartoon, husband is having lunch and hen is serving him. In first frame, he is making crunching sounds (*kara… kara… kara*) while eating. In second frame, hen admonishes him, 'What are you doing? It is not papad, it is papad dough mix (*Appadam kaadu, appadaala pindi*). In third frame he makes 'kasa… kasa… kasa' sounds as if he is eating a soft paste-like substance.

In another cartoon, hen is cutting vegetables and Lord Emsworth, husband, is reading newspaper.

Hen says, 'I forgot to tell you. Vishali came yesterday.'

He asks, 'Who is Vishali?' He is immersed in paper.

Hen says, 'Don't you remember? They gave her to Ramarao.'

He says, 'Ohh, that Vishali? Okay. What is her husband doing?'

Hen says, 'Oh my, I forgot to ask Vishali.'

He asks, 'Who is Vishali?'

She dumps all vegetables, cut and uncut, on his head and leaves.

In yet another cartoon, she asks him several times to come into kitchen and take coffee and tiffin. He is immersed in his newspaper and doesn't respond. She comes and pushes two vadas (they are like doughnuts, with a hole)on his nose and bangs coffee cup on his head and leaves.

Hen opens the door and bangs rolling pin on the head of Manager, whom Husband invites and brings home for dinner. She profusely apologizes for mistaking him to be her husband, and Husband justifies her action as she is 'slightly short-tempered' and not to mind.

In Telugu movies, Suryakantam (in Hindi, Lalita Pawar) left an indelible mark as husband-pecking hen, shrew, or a heartless mother-in-law. She is one of the most natural and gifted actors; she was so successful in her roles, for entire generations no girl was named Suryakantam (In north India, it seems male kids were not named Pran, since Pran played evil, villainous roles to such perfection that his name became synonymous with evil). In the last reel of the movie, either she has a change of heart or her docile, meek husband slaps her and suddenly becomes bold and authoritative, to the claps and whistles of audience.

She must have inspired Bapu.

Now, the crucial question, am I a henpecked husband?

During one of our parties in ship, one captain declared that all husbands are henpecked.

'What is the big deal? I am henpecked, all husbands are henpecked, even if they deny,' he said after downing one too many. His wife was embarrassed and tried to change the topic to movies. But once sozzled, men can be stubborn and mulish.

'Dear, don't try to divert the topic. Ma'am, did you never peck your husband?' he asked my wife.

All eyes turned to my wife; she blushed and said, 'Occasionally, when he does something that deserves pecking.'

I think she hit the nail on the head. Smart husbands know danger areas where mines lay in marital combat field and tread carefully. Not-so-smart husbands trample on all mines and get pecked incessantly and become immune after some time.

One of my wife's cousins always boasted that he was undisputed king in his house and wife was absolutely scared of him and would not dare oppose him, and had to eat humble pie as once his wife took him to cleaners in a large gathering. I and Wife were present and were amazed at her ferocious attack and his meek surrender.

So I will take with a scoop of salt any husband's claim that he has never been pecked. There may be exceptions.

Coming to my case, my wife is very patient and understanding. Any other lady in her place would have used rolling pin or broom like they show in cartoons.

You can appreciate my point if you are a fan of P.G.Wodehouse or at least have read few of his Jeeves and Blandings Castle books. I think I read too many of his books and enjoyed so much that I have imbibed many idiosyncrasies of Lord Emsworth and Bertram Wooster.

You cannot make Lord Emsworth listen to anything you say, unless it has something to do with gardening or pigs, two things he is passionate about. He is fanatical about a prize pig of his, Empress of Blandings, and his rose garden. He is always worried that Empress is not eating sufficiently, if she was well, or about the status of his rose garden. He has several sisters; Lady Constance is his chief tormentor, always nagging him to dress well, attend to functions, entertain guests, etc. It requires superhuman effort to make him understand what he is expected to do.

My wife is exasperated and irritated when I ask her what it was all about after she explains patiently at length, especially in a crowded restaurant or when TV volume is high or when we are talking in a group. I have a single-track mind; I can listen to and respond to one person at a time, unlike my wife, who has amazing skills in following several conversations or events at the same time. She can listen and follow what people are discussing at different tables in a restaurant and talk to you at the same time (That is a gift very few possess, like scholars of *Ashtaavadhaanam, Shataavadhaanam*). It is like an Olympic sprinter irritated with a lazy and lethargic runner unable to keep up with him or her.

Sometimes when I am working on my blog post, she talks and I keep on saying 'Yes, yes,' half or quarter listening and when she realizes nothing registered in my mind, she blows her top. Who wouldn't?

What Bertram Wooster and I have in common is our inability to say no. We don't want to hurt others. Bertram gets engaged to Madeline Bassett, Roberta Wickham, and many other girls. Those girls want to get even with their fiancés and use him as a ploy. He cannot say no since he is chivalrous and Jeeves saves him every time. My inability to say no to others (of course, there are no proposing girls) has led to a few peckings.

CHANGING OPINIONS—
IS IT BAD?

The other day I was watching Kiran Bedi's interview during her disastrous foray into politics. She was asked why she changed her stand on so many issues, including entering dirty cesspool of politics.

She asked, 'Is it a crime to evolve? With passage of time, your perceptions change.'

I think our obsession to view sticking to one's principles and ideals rigidly, irrespective of hardships and pains, as an admirable, courageous trait, has its roots in Raja Harishchandra's epic tale. This story has been drilled into us from childhood in textbooks, movies, and plays.

For young readers, I will briefly narrate the story, since they may not have this story in their curriculum.

Raja Harishchandra was a great noble and generous king. He had an amazing reputation for never having told a lie. Sage Viswamitra is jealous and takes a pledge to make the king utter a lie. King refuses to tell a lie and loses kingdom, gets separated from wife and son. He becomes poor and broke; he finally finds a living as a caretaker of cemetery (shmasaan). He arranges wooden pyres and cremates dead bodies.

His wife, the queen, has also become destitute, and while son is collecting wood sticks for fire in the forest, a snake bites him and he dies. Raja's wife cries bitterly and carries the body to Shmasaan for final rites. They don't recognize each other, since Raja had grown shaggy beard and long tresses of unkempt hair. Queen also is in torn, wasted clothes and is covered with mud, slime.

Raja refuses to cremate the body unless she pays for the firewood. She pleads with him to have pity on her since she doesn't have any money or valuables.

Then Raja asks, 'Why don't you sell your mangalasutra and pay for the firewood?'

Queen is stunned since mangalasutras of very pious and devoted wives of that era were visible only to husbands. She reveals her identity and they hug each other and weep bitterly.

Viswamitra relents, accepts his defeat, and all gods and angels shower flowers on the couple and Lohita comes back to life.

Like all the kids from that era, I also had immense respect and regard for persons who stuck to their principles through all hardships and contempt for those who changed opinions and principles as and when convenient to them, until a few years back.

In *Kanyasulkam*, the revolutionary play of the late nineteenth century, written by Sri Gurajada AppaRao, Girisam exemplifies the chameleon which changes colours to blend with environment as necessary. He lectures and educates his disciple Venkatesam about an evil custom, *kanyasulkam*, and the barbarous system of child girls' marriage to old men. At dinnertime, he heartily supports Venkatesam's father's views and argues in favour of *kanyasulkam* and child girl marriages. Venkatesam is baffled and when he confronts, Girisam coolly says, 'One can't become a politician unless one changes opinions.'

In our college we had one professor who was an ardent atheist. His articles were published in *Illustrated Weekly of India* also. He scoffed at gods, god-men, and rituals. He would tell us that any good magician would be able to perform all the tricks of god-men. In fact, roadside magicians were better than god-men since they have to perform all their tricks in open areas and streets with no shields available like in halls. He had two daughters; younger one was polio afflicted. Many people told him that it was a curse from God. He laughed at them.

His elder daughter fell in love with a chemical engineer who graduated from our college and joined a manufacturing unit in our city. They were from different castes and boy's parents opposed. Professor told the boy that he would perform the marriage only if the boy agreed to marry his daughter at a most inauspicious muhurat. He agreed, maybe because of love or maybe he was also an atheist. After six months of marriage, boy had a terrible accident: an acid pipeline burst and he was drenched. He was rushed to King George hospital. He battled for a few days and succumbed to the injuries. To make it more tragic, his wife was pregnant.

During those days, we visited the hospital and met the professor. Though he was sad, he was still defiant.

'Everyone wants to convince me that it happened because of the inauspicious muhurat of marriage. It is just a freak accident,' he said firmly.

I was quite impressed by his firm beliefs and principles.

I scorned people who changed their stands on issues. Now, I would apologize to them if I meet them again, for I realized rather late that changing opinions does not necessarily mean that people are fickle-minded.

I have a distant cousin sister who was a staunch critic of one baba. She said she couldn't understand how famous scientists and scholars could be so gullible to follow him. I met her again after a few years. I was surprised to find that she would wake up early in the morning and join the satsangs and participate in processions in streets, chanting his bhajans. I asked her about her transformation, she smiled and said that she realized her folly and she found peace and tranquility after she became a devotee.

Of course, my regard for her was rather diminished by her change of stance.

Later on, I realized that it is necessary to have a spiritual and psychological anchor to prevent one from drifting into depression, sorrow, and helplessness. This could be belief in God, religion, or even a god-man or an object. In my childhood, the combined families were the norm and each house would resemble a village, with grandparents, parents, uncles, aunts, and cousins staying under one roof. It had many disadvantages but a few advantages also, like there was no place to be alone and you developed a rapport with someone or other to share your joys and sorrows.

In Western society, they lacked this kind of bonding and camaraderie. They seem to have no emotional, warm bond and tend to become lone souls as life moves on. Everyone is polite, decent, and well behaved but they normally build up barriers. When they get married, they are not sure how long the present one would last and what sort of alimony would be slapped on him. They may not share the bond with their kids that we find natural and normal.

I met one European who said he hardly visits his father who stays in the next street. I was surprised and asked him if they had any fights, he said no, he just doesn't visit and his father also doesn't mind his indifference. I met an Australian taxi driver who said he was married three times and swore never to marry again; more than half his earnings were going towards alimony.

No one has patience, interest, or time to listen to others' woes, troubles, or tribulations. So they go to psychiatrists, pay by the hour and pour out their troubles. Slowly, India is catching up with the West.

In India, the role of psychiatrists is fulfilled by god-men, in a way, and sometimes, effectively.

I've known my friend's wife since her college days. She is a staunch devotee of Sathya Sai Baba. She neither preaches nor lectures about his miracles or greatness. She simply worships him. It must have been traumatic for her, since many people are not only critical of him but they talk derogatorily, insultingly. She just ignores them and continues on her path. Sathya Sai Baba has done what several governments could never hope to do: he built a super specialty hospital for the poor people, the best of its kind. He brought water to the parched villages of Rayalaseema. It is unfortunate that he lived in an era of cynicism.

I watched my friend's journey through life with interest. He had not scaled great heights, nor plumbed to depths. It went on smoothly: he retired as a senior government officer; both his kids are well settled, happily married, and blessed with cute children. His is a life that any normal person would dream of having, happy, contented and it has been smooth sailing.

I knew the secret of their success. In fact, I knew of it even during my college days.

It was this. His wife, when faced with a problem, illness, or doubt, would write to Sri Sathya Sai Baba on a postcard, inform him of it and pray to him to solve the problem or grant a solution, and post it to Puttaparthi. She would then forget about it or worry about the problem; she was confident he would solve the problem and experienced the joy that she would feel after her wishes have been granted, and invariably, without fail, all her wishes have been fulfilled.

Once they came across a building under construction and were just walking through. They liked the layout of the flat and they met the builder. After talking to him, on an impulse, they booked the flat, giving him a cheque for 5,000 rupees. They had no savings; there was no way they could raise money, even after taking out a housing loan. It was just miraculous how the money flowed as and when required.

Superstition? Coincidence?

Now read what a few eminent people said.

Rhonda Byrne, author of *The Secret* says that you are Ali Baba and the genie is the universe, waiting to grant your every wish. What is required is for you to send your wish, believe that it is sanctioned, and you have already received it. Feel happy and grateful, and your wish will be fulfilled.

She recounts an incident where a plane crashes and pilot survives but is so badly injured and paralyzed that only his eyelids, brain, and ears are functional. He listens to all doctors proclaiming that he would never be able to walk again. He is determined to leave the hospital before Christmas, walking out. And he does, much to the astonishment of doctors. He just followed what she professes.

Dr Murphy wrote a book, *Power of Subconscious Mind*. His theory is that your subconscious mind is an amazingly powerful car and your conscious, reasoning mind is the driver. Car engine or mechanism has neither control nor interferes where driver wants to go. It is the driver who decides whether to drive on a highway or on a rocky, hilly terrain and break the car to pieces.

Dr Murphy says just before going to sleep or just before waking up, your conscious mind is not quite active and doesn't resist suggestions. If you instruct your subconscious mind about what you want, it will move heaven and earth to make your desires come true. If your conscious mind truly believes and instructs subconscious mind to achieve something, it will.

He recites an incident: an old man in Australia is diagnosed with a debilitating disease and doctors had given up hope. His son who returned from a trip to Europe, Rome, and Vatican City, gave his father a small rotting wooden piece and told him that that wooden piece was from the cross on which Jesus Christ was crucified. He came across a priest in Vatican City who showed him and the son pleaded and begged the priest to give him a small portion to cure his dad. Initially, Priest refused but Son did not give up and kept on pleading. Finally, Priest relented and gave him a small portion and told Son to make his father hold it in his palm or wear it around neck so that it was in constant contact with his body.

Then followed a miraculous cure baffling the medical fraternity. After his father passed away at ripe old age, Son revealed that the wooden piece was not from a cross but he picked it from a garden and he fabricated the story.

So I learnt to keep an open mind and resist impulse to ridicule, scoff, and laugh at seemingly outlandish claims or fanatic beliefs.

We always preferred Zandu balm or Vicks over Grandmother's treatment of turmeric and jaggery paste. Now science reveals that our grandmothers were quite wise, as turmeric has the most potent antiseptic and many other healing qualities.

So long as each person follows what he or she believes without lecturing, sermonizing, or attempting to convert others to his or her path (like my friend's wife), then it is quite fine, I believe.

New experiences and information cause people to change their opinions and it should not be held against them. So long as you practice your principles without being too rigid or obsessive and are flexible, it is good.

EPILOGUE

Finally, we have completed the voyage and the ship reached port. The gangway is secured, and time has come to disembark. I hope you have enjoyed the sailing, excitement, and adventures ...and wait, I am also leaving with you.

Yes, I have decided to hang up my coveralls, working shoes ...and retire.

A career in shipping and sailing is not everyone's cup of tea, like any career; it has flips and positives. On the flip side, you miss out on family, friends, festivals, birthdays, anniversaries when you are sailing. You are away from mother earth for months together, and for many, it is a scary thought that beneath the steel hull, there is nothing but hundreds of meters of water. You are on your own to fight your battles and survive since you would be thousands of miles away from land, and no one can come to help or rescue you.

Sea has many *avatars* and moods. She can be like a caring, doting, lullaby-singing mother... or an insanely furious woman with devastating rage and fury...or a seductive, sensuous lover. Only a person who loves sea and sailing can understand her in all her forms and admire her.

On the positive side, there is never a dull moment; life is an exciting, continuous adventure. You enjoy fresh, clean air and enjoy beautiful sunrise and sunsets, and nature in her right elements, you don't go to the same office, face same pollution and traffic, sit at the same table, go through the same routine, hate the same boss. Every time you join a ship, colleagues, equipment, routes can be different. You will visit new countries and new cultures. When you are at home, you enjoy quality time for several months with family and friends. You can plan wonderful holidays and be with wife and kids 24*7 until you leave. (after a few months, you tend to get on their nerves, and when they start wondering when you would go, it is time to join ship).

So, what are my plans after retirement? I look forward to pursuing my hobbies of painting and writing.

India is a country with thousands of years of civilization and countless exciting, mythological, fantastic epic stories. The problem is that I thought these stories might not be palatable to readers of other countries and cultures, western, in particular since all these stories defy logic and scientific explanations. For instance, Lord Hanuman jumping across the ocean from India to Sri Lanka in search of Sita, or Lord Krishna lifting a mountain with his little finger to give shelter to his folk and cattle to protect them from the fury of Lord Indra or flying chariots (*pushpak vimana*).

Now, I see there is change and acceptance. Harry Potter, Indiana Jones, Lara Croft, Steven Spielberg, and science-defying ideas, concepts are firing people's imagination, and are a huge success.

So, my goal is to write such exciting stories from India's rich heritage.

The best story I heard was told by my aunt when I was six or seven years old. We were lying on our backs on the terrace, watching full moon and stars. I can still recall her soft, soothing voice.

A poor village woman wanted her son to be educated and forced him to go to school. The small boy refused since he has to cross a thick jungle to go to the only school in that area. His mother told him, 'Don't be afraid. Shout 'Bala Krishna, Bala Krishna, brother, please escort me,' and he will escort you.'

The boy reluctantly set off, and before entering the jungle, he shouted as his mom told him. Immediately Lord Krishna appeared as a small boy, of the same age as he, and escorted him, he told him many stories, and they became good friends.

Mom was relieved that her son was going happily to school every day. It became a routine. Lord Krishna would regale the boy with all his adventures.

After a few months, Guru's birthday was approaching. It was a tradition in those days for students to present gifts to the teacher. There was no compulsion or demand; each student would select a gift which he could afford. His classmates were from wealthy, affluent families, and they were planning to present Guru with expensive clothes and items.

The boy was depressed and unhappy and pestered his mom to spare money for any gift so that he would not go empty-handed that day. Poor Lady cried and cried about her poverty and helplessness, and told the boy to ask his friend Bala Krishna for help.

The day arrived, and Bala Krishna noticed that his friend was morose and dejected. He asked him the reason.

'Brother, today is my Guru's birthday. All students are excitedly planning and discussing the expensive gifts, and mocking my poverty. I do not mind digs about my poverty, but I am sad that I am unable to present a gift to my Guru. Mom told me to ask you, but you have been so kind and affectionate, how can I ever do that?' the boy told him sadly.

Lord Krishan laughed, and gave him a small earthen pot and told him to dispose of it in the river after the celebration was over. It was covered, and the boy wondered what it contained. He was overjoyed that he was not going empty-handed.

The Guru's birthday was celebrated grandly; all students presented him with expensive gifts which he accepted with a beaming face. When the boy approached with the small earthen pot, he scowled and looked with disdain at the boy's present and told him curtly to give it to his wife in the kitchen.

The boy went to the kitchen, and gave Guru's wife the earthen pot and told her not to destroy the pot, as he had to dispose of it in the river. She was a kind-hearted woman, and she thanked him for a thoughtful gift. When she opened, she saw it contained curd, and a lovely fragrance filled the room.

When lunch was served, Guru's wife emptied contents of the pot into a container and was shocked to see it was full again... and was full as soon as it was emptied. Since Guru was busy with the guests, she did not inform him.

The curd was so tasty, in fact, out of this world, that all the guests ate nothing but curd and rice. No one touched any other item. Guru was shocked when he sat for lunch, he found that the taste of curd was usual and wondered why people were going crazy and devouring the curd by buckets. He wondered how his wife procured such vast quantities of curd and asked her, and she showed him the pot.

He waited until the boy started for home and followed him. The boy went to the river and gently put the pot in the water, remained until the pot disappeared in the current and turned back and was startled to see the Guru.

'Who gave you the gift?' he asked sternly.

The boy remained silent with bowed head. Guru shouted at him, for insolence and even accused him of theft.

Finally, the boy broke down and told him that Lord Bala Krishna gave him that gift.

'You are lying. Show me your friend', Guru challenged the boy, and the boy took him to the jungle where he used to meet Bala Krishna. He called him several times, but his friend did not appear.

Guru was in a fit of rage, 'I will teach you never to lie again,' and he raised a hand to slap the boy.

'You insolent fool, I gave him the gift.' a voice boomed in the forest.

Guru was startled, and looked around and found no one. He realized that it was Lord Krishna and prostrated on the ground with folded hands.

'My lord, I am your ardent devotee, I spend many hours in prayers, reciting your hymns, you never appeared even in my dreams. You do not appear even before sages who worship and meditate for decades or even hundreds of years. Why did you shower love and gifts on this poor boy?' he asked Lord Krishna.

'Your arrogance and selfishness prevented you from receiving my boons; you gladly accepted all expensive gifts but refused even to touch the gift from God. God seeks only purity of heart and unshakeable faith in Him, and now you mend your ways and lead a pious life,' God's voice sternly told Guru.

Crestfallen, Guru stumbled out of the jungle.

The end

GLOSSARY

A

ANR - A famous Telugu movie hero of the 20th century. Akkineni Nageswara Rao.

Aishwarya Rai - Indian actress, model, winner of 1994 Miss World pageant.

Antakshari - A spoken parlor game played in India. Each contestant sings the first verse of a song that begins with the consonant on which previous contestant's song selection ended.

Agarbatti - A joss stick.

Aatma lingam -The Hindu Gods attained immortality and invincibility by worshipping Aatma lingam. Demon King Ravana desired immortality and asked for it when Lord Shiva granted him a boon.

Ayurveda - A 5000-year-old system of natural healing with origins in Vedic culture in India.

Amin - An arbitrator and assessor who collects revenues.

Amul baby - Amul is a famous dairy product in India and has chubby kids in its advertisements.

B

Bhajan - Group singing of devotional songs and hymns.

Bodhi tree - The tree under which Buddha attained enlightenment.

Boundary - A cricket term. When a batsman hits the ball along the ground, and the ball crosses the boundary ropes, the batsman gets four runs.

Badaa Saab - In Indian ships, the chief engineer is called thus.

Baksheesh - A small amount of money given as a tip.

Bollywood - Hindi cinema. Combination of Bombay and Hollywood.

BHP - Brake Horse Power.

BT - Bow Thruster, The propeller fitted in forward of the ship assists in manoeuvring.

Budugu - A naughty boy character, Telugu 'Dennis The Menace.'

C

CO_2 - Carbon-di-Oxide, used as a fire fighting medium in some ships.

C/O - Chief officer.

CDC - Continuous Discharge Certificate, seaman's document issued by the government shipping department

Cable - A unit of length used to measure nautical distances or depths, about $1/10^{th}$ of a nautical mile.

D

Door Darshan - State-owned TV station of India.

Dabbawalas -Lunchbox delivery and return system in Mumbai, India. Semi-literate people managed an amazingly complex network efficiently and featured in BBC also.

Dry dock - A structured area where repairs and maintenance of merchant ships are carried out.

Dosa - Somewhat similar to a crepe in appearance, favorite south Indian breakfast dish, made with fermented rice batter.

DPA - Designated Person Ashore. Shipping companies designate an officer to liaise with each ship.

Darshan - Auspicious sight of a deity or a holy person.

Dhaba - A road-side food stall.

E

ECR - Engine control room.

E/O - Electrical officer.

E/R -The Engine room.

F

FOSMA -Foreign Owner and Ship-Manager's Association

G

Gaali gopuram - A monumental tower on a hill visible up to 40 km in Tirupati town.

Ghoonghat - Head covering worn by Hindu married women.

Gangway - Narrow passage used to board or disembark a ship.

Gandhi - Indian leader of the Indian independence movement against British colonial rule. Employing nonviolent civil disobedience, he achieved freedom for India. Richard Attenborough made a film on him.

Gutti vankaya -A delicacy dish made with eggplant.

Guru - A Hindu spiritual teacher.

Gherao - A protest in which workers prevent managers from leaving until their demands are met.

Gotra - A Hindu clan tracing its paternal lineage from a common ancestor, usually a sage or a saint.

H

HFO - Heavy Fuel Oil - used in ships.

I

Idli, Idly - A type of rice savory cake, popular south Indian breakfast dish.

J

Jhoola bag - A sling bag for the shoulder to carry food, and water.

K

Karna - A character from the epic 'Maha Bharata', renowned for his valor, charity, and loyalty to a friend.

Kanya Sulkam - An evil practice in certain parts of southern India in the 1800s, small girls married off to old men for money. A play by that name by Gurajada Appa Rao eradicated this evil custom.

Kirtan - A devotional song, in which a group repeats lines sung by a leader.

Kanyaa Daan - Giving away the Bride.

L

Lungi - Traditional wrap-around garment worn by men in south India.

M

MOT II Class - Ministry of transport examination. For an engineer to work in ships as a second engineer, he or she has to pass the MOT II Class exam.

MOT I Class - Ministry of transport examination. For an engineer to work in ships as a chief engineer, he or she has to pass the MOT I Class exam.

Mrs. Indira Gandhi - Former Prime minister of India, she was assassinated by her bodyguards.

Mohamaatam, Mohamaatitis - No such word exists. Like 'Hepatitis', this word is coined to indicate a malady few people suffer from, inability to say 'no' when served food. (Mohamaatam- a Telugu word).

Maha Shivaratri -A Hindu festival celebrated annually in honor of Lord Shiva, marks the day of the marriage of Shiva.

Mirchi Bajji - Spicy Indian snack.

MMD - Mercantile Marine Department.

MOT - Ministry of transport.

Mokkubadi - Telugu word, meaning 'solemn vow,' a personal commitment to do something in return for something or somebody for seeking a favor. A solemn vow is a serious promise and has serious consequences for breaking it, mostly related to the religious matter.

Muhurtam - An auspicious moment, a selected good time for doing something.

Mandap - A temporary platform set up for marriages and functions.

N

Nagin - A snake which can take human form when it wants.

Nomu- An act of undertaking a vow (Telugu word.)

Namaste - In Hindi, 'I bow to you,' with respect.

NTR - A Telugu movie Superstar of the 20th century.

NRI - Nonresident Indian, one who works or settles in another country.

Nautical Mile - A unit used in measuring the distance at sea, equal to 1,852 meters or 2,025 yards.

O

OBO -Oil- Bulk-Ore carrier ship. OBOs are designed to carry
all three types.

P

Paan - Paan is a preparation of betel leaf and areca nut and is
chewed for its stimulant effect.
Paisa - Indian 'cent'. Paise is plural.
Pandal - A temporary shed or shelter for public meetings.
PSC - Port State Control.
Pooja - Act of worship.
Puranas - Sanskrit sacred writings on Hindu mythology.
Pandit - A Hindu scholar, learned in Hindu philosophy and
religion, a practicing priest.
Padmaasan - A sitting position in yoga, lotus position, in which
legs are crossed with each foot resting on the opposite
thigh.

Q

R

Rupee - Indian currency, like Dollar.
Rani Laxmi Bai - the queen of the princely state of Jhansi and
one of the leading figures of the Indian rebellion of 1857
and a symbol of resistance to British Raj.
R/O - Radio Officer.
Rudder - A flat piece provided near the stern of a ship or boat
for steering.
Rajnikanth - A Tamil movie superstar.
Rishya shringa - A sage who had never seen a woman in his
life. His father's severe penance was disturbed by Urvashi,
a beautiful damsel from heavens, sent by Indra, king of

heavens. Urvashi left after Rishya shringa was born. His father wanted to protect him and ensured he did not see a woman. A severe drought struck the kingdom, and the King was advised by sages that entry of a celibate sage into the kingdom would bring torrential rains. King sent beautiful girls into the forest, who met him when his father was away. Rishya shringa followed them like a kitten since he never saw a woman before. When he entered the kingdom, there were heavy rains. Later he married the princess.

S

Sachin - Sachin Tendulkar is a cricket legend, scored a hundred centuries.

Sambarala Rambabu - A Telugu hit movie of 1970, hero lives under the staircase, and that house has many portions and many families.

Sixer - A cricket term, when a batsman hits the ball over the boundary line, he gets six runs.

Saree - A garment consisting of a length of cotton or silk (five to six meters long) draped elaborately around the body, a traditional dress of Indian women.

Sardar - A Sikh, often used as a title or address.

Sant Kabir - A famous 15th-century Hindi poet.

ST - Stern Thruster - Propeller fitted in aft gives momentum to the ship.

Saraswati - Hindu Goddess of knowledge, wisdom, art, music, and learning.

T

Telugu -a language spoken by people of two south Indian states, Andhra Pradesh and Telangana. Telugu speaking people are also called 'Telugus.'

Tirupati - A town in south India, famous for Lord Venkateswara's temple, world's richest temple.

Telegraph - In ships, engine order telegraph is a communication device for Navigation Bridge to ask engineers to give desired speed.

Tansen - Prominent figure of Hindustani Classical music of the 16th century.

U

UMS - Unmanned Machinery Spaces. In modern ships, Engine rooms are unmanned at night. Any alarm would buzz in duty engineer's cabin, and he would attend.

Upma - A south Indian breakfast dish.

V

Veena - One of the oldest Indian musical instruments.

Vinoba Bhave - An Indian advocate of non-violence and human rights of the 20th century and started *Bhoodaan* (Land gift) movement.

Vratam - Pious observances such as fasting, worship.

Vinayaka chavithi - A ten-day Hindu festival celebrated to honor the elephant-headed Lord Ganesha's birthday. A movie by that name was released.

Vayanam - A procedure of married women exchanging fruits, and other items after completion of certain religious protocols.

Vibhuti - Ash applied to the forehead.

W

Wild Bunch - A 1969 movie starring William Holden, Robert Ryan.

X

Y

Yorker - Cricket term, a ball bowled so that it pitches immediately under the bat.

Z

Zamindar - A landowner, on who leases his land to tenant farmers.

2/E - Second Engineer.

3/E - Third Engineer.

4/E - Fourth Engineer.

5/E - Fifth Engineer.

Printed in the United States
By Bookmasters